# Come Out of Her, My People
# Persecution Begins
## by C. W. Steinle

Come Out of Her, My People: Persecution Begins
by C. W. Steinle
Copyright 2013 by C. W. Steinle
ISBN: 978-1-304-23098-0

All rights reserved. No part of this book shall be reproduced, stored in a retrieval system, or transmitted by any means – electronic, mechanical, photocopying, recording, or otherwise – without written permission from the publisher.

Unless otherwise noted, Scripture quotations in this book are taken from the New King James Version. Copyright © 1982 by Thomas Nelson, Inc. Used by permission. All rights reserved.

# Table of Contents

## Persecution Begins

| | |
|---|---|
| Introduction to Persecution Begins | 5 |
| Is Fallen, Is Fallen – The North American Church | 17 |
| Abominations that Lead to Desolation | 29 |
| Pre-Trib Rapture History | 39 |
| Pre-Trib's Faulty Proof-Texts | 49 |
| What About the Jews? | 65 |
| The Last Enemy of Christ | 67 |

## Come Out of Her My People: Fourth Edition

| | |
|---|---|
| Preface to Fourth Edition | 93 |
| Introduction to Fourth Edition | 97 |
| Chapter 1: Two Millennia of Interpretations | 101 |
| Chapter 2: Babylon the Great | 117 |
| Chapter 3: The Outline of the Age (Rev. Six) | 121 |
| Chapter 4: The Heavenly Kingdom Completed | 135 |
| Chapter 5: The Seventh Seal and the Seven Trumpets | 139 |
| Chapter 6: The Secrets of the Separate Scroll | 145 |
| Chapter 7: The Beasts of Power and Deception | 155 |
| Chapter 8: Approaching the Time of God's Wrath | 175 |
| Chapter 9: The Wrath of God | 181 |
| Chapter 10: Mystery Babylon | 187 |
| Appendix: The Book of Revelation 1 - 5; 9 - 21 | 193 |

# Come Out of Her My People: Persecution Begins

## Introduction

When *Come Out of Her My People* was first written in late 2005, few people were willing to consider that the United States of America could really be the Great Harlot of Revelation. With all that has happened in the last eight years, thousands of people are asking the question, "How could any nation fit the definition of Babylon better than the United States of America?" And still thousands more have actually begun to refer to America as Babylon. Warming up to the notion that America just might be a wicked nation is similar to the process of discovering ones own personal need for salvation. A sinner must finally come to that, "Could it be me?" moment. "Could *I* be the sinner that Jesus died on the cross to save?" "Aren't I basically a *good* person like Mom said?" "Could there be a dark corner in *my* soul?" And finally, "Could I be self-deceived and corrupt at my very core?"

This kind of questioning opens the door to humility, whereby the lost soul begins to consider that God might be right when the Bible states, *"There is none righteous, no, not one; There is none who understands; There is none who seeks after God. They have all turned aside; They have together become unprofitable; There is none who does good, no, not one."*-Romans 3:10-12 Americans must also come to a similar, "Could it be us?" moment. The hardest heart to reach is that of a soul whose self-assessment has placed them on a pedestal; above reproach. But that is exactly what the daughter of Babylon said; *"I sit as queen."*

*"And you have said in your heart,*
*'I am, and there is no one else besides me.'*
*11 Therefore evil shall come upon you;*
*You shall not know from where it arises.*
*And trouble shall fall upon you;*
*You will not be able to put it off.*
*And desolation shall come upon you suddenly,*
*Which you shall not know."*-Isaiah 47:10b-11

If America is not the Great Harlot of Revelation, her judgment might fall at any moment. But if America is the Great Harlot, she must establish a reputation for persecuting the saints prior to her destruction. Because I

## Come Out of Her My People: Persecution Begins

am convinced that America is the Great Harlot, I also believe that persecution will begin soon. The scandalous Internal Revenue Service policy of targeting religious institutions, the acceptance of abnormal sexual behavior, and the Obama-"care" mandate to force Christians to violate their consciences regarding birth control, all cause me to anticipate persecution sooner than later.

Just this week as I was writing this introduction, three foreboding episodes revealed the hearts of the ungodly. As atheists dedicated a monument at the Bradford County Florida courthouse, Eric Hovind stood atop the pedestal thanking the atheists for creating a platform from which to proclaim Christ. The atheists called out several times, "Bring out the lions!" and, "Where are the Romans when you need them?" Within hours of this event, a gathering of pro-life proponents in Texas were heckled by pro-choice antagonists chanting, "Hail Satan." Violence is already in the hearts of ungodly Americans. Later in this same week, two Christians were beaten for witnessing at a Gay rally.

I have made a long journey from serving the Lord in my local church to becoming a watchman of America's demise. While returning from Israel in 1998, I began to consider, from an international viewpoint, what America looks like to the rest of the world. During that visit to Israel I had been spat upon multiple times as I walked through the Muslim Quarter. And even little children would stand at my feet and clap their hands at me in disgust. (This is a Middle Eastern gesture accompanied by a contorted jeering expression of the face.) As my plane sat on the tarmac at the Tel Aviv airport I thought about what I, as an American, represented to the rest of the world. How does the world view America?

Decadent, immoral, liberal, controlling, meddling in foreign affairs, rejecting and mocking Biblical Christianity, despising the laws of God (lawlessness), polluting the rest of the world through media, trade, and banking "requirements." An eerie feeling came over me as I realized that America no longer had an international reputation as a bastion of righteousness. In fact, just the opposite view had existed for decades. Since the early 1960's, Americans were forced to take an introspective look at themselves because of a thought provoking movie titled, "The Ugly American." This movie examined the civility of U.S. travelers through the eyes of the Asian culture.

# Introduction

Americans began to ask themselves, "Just how civilized are we compared to the rest of the world?"

On the day of 9/11 these reflections on America all came together. Even though I thought, at that time, the Great Harlot of Revelation would not exist until I had been raptured; it was difficult to imagine how a nation could fit the harlot's description more perfectly than the United States of America. Her citizens live in comparative luxury, making other nations rich through her trading (China for example). She is portrayed as an importer rather that an exporter. She is the world's policeman, and *"Who can make war with the beast?"* America was unknown at the writing of Revelation, qualifying her identity as a mystery (a *"musterion"*; something that has not yet been revealed). And in the Biblical context, just as Israel forsook God, America has become an adulterous nation.

Whether the mark of the beast has been incorporated at the time of Babylon's destruction is up for debate and is discussed in detail hereafter. But two of the best guesses for what this mark might be were given by Irenaeus in the second century. As a second generation student of St. John, Irenaeus' proposal deserves credibility. He gives one interpretation of 666 as a redundancy of the numeral six. He proposes that six represents the 6,000 years of the kingdom of man. According to ancient Jewish tradition there would be 2,000 years of "Wilderness", 2,000 years of the "Days of Elijah", and then 2,000 years of the "Days of Messiah." At the end of that time, a millennial reign of God upon the earth would finish out the time line of this age. This legend probably prompted the question to Jesus about Elijah coming before the Christ. Irenaeus' other suggestion was that the number 666 was a numeric equivalent for the name of the False Prophet.

If one or both of these two theories happens to be incorrect, then perhaps the *"number of man"* is simply the numbering of mankind. This would explain why King David got in so much hot water over numbering the fighting men of Israel. What if a unique "World Tracking Number" is assigned to everyone on the planet so that they can all be tracked by computers? Instead of names being given based on people's God-given personalities, people would merely be issued a numeric identity by a man-made government. Personal identification using a name may actually become prohibited so that no one person

## Come Out of Her My People: Persecution Begins

could ever rise up to gain popularity. This sounds like a wicked enough scheme to me; but how would we ever see this coming?

The only prophecy regarding the Great Harlot that must certainly occur before her destruction is the shedding of blood of the saints all over the world. *"And in her was found the blood of prophets and saints, and of all who were slain on the earth."-Revelation 18:24* The way Christians are mocked in media foretells the full-scale physical persecution that will soon erupt. The same social forces are coming against the American Church that resulted in the near annihilation of the Russian Orthodox Church. In less than 30 years, Russian and the Eastern European nations saw at least 50 million Christians and 90% of the Christian churches destroyed. And it was not the Muslims who took their lives, but the atheist communists.

Persecution came suddenly to Eastern Europe and Russia after the Darwinian socialists came to power. Marxism and its offshoots are violently opposed to Christ. (If the reader is not aware of the demonic roots of socialism and communism please stop reading here and purchase *"Marx & Satan"* by Richard Wurmbrand – founder of Voice of the Martyrs. It is short, easy to read, and is required reading for the days ahead.) No matter how civilized the opponents of Christianity appear to be, the same society which has celebrated the downfall of holy matrimony and glorified homosexuality will not, at the same time, tolerate Biblical Christianity. *"Yes, and all who desire to live godly in Christ Jesus will suffer persecution."- 2nd Timothy 3:12*

A growing number of people are at last wondering, "Could it be us?" Could America be the Great Harlot? After eight years, I still believe that *Come Out of Her My People* is the most realistic interpretation of Revelation for people who expect the tribulation to begin during this generation. I firmly believe there is enough proof in this book to show that the One-Third Judgments of Revelation could well be describing the destruction of the United States. But first a notorious level of persecution must become manifest. This could take several more generations to come to its fullness. Or it could happen overnight like it did in Germany, Russia, Romania, and North Korea. Even if the reader is convinced of a pre-tribulation rapture of the Church, this persecution will still occur in advance of that event. My reason for this statement is explained later in this book. But let me take a moment to suggest the following.

# Introduction

If the Great Tribulation were to begin during the present generation, the Great Harlot must exist today. It would take at least decades for a single nation to gain the reputations which are listed in Revelation:

1. Trading Capital - Chief Importer
2. Living in Luxury
3. Top Military Force
4. Unfaithful to God
5. Unknown when Revelation was Written
6. A Gathering Place of the Wicked
7. Spreading her Filth throughout the World

The second reason why the Great Harlot must exist at the onset of the tribulation is the fact that the golden age of commerce described in Revelation Seventeen and Eighteen could not possibly develop within centuries of the One-Third Trumpet Judgments. The destruction of one-third of the people, places, and things on the earth would be far more traumatic than the world wars or mini ice ages of times past. Chapters Eight and Nine of Revelation describe the greatest catastrophe since Noah's flood. So once again, we must either assume that Mystery Babylon:

- Exists before the beginning of Revelation, and is merely memorialized in chapters 14, 17, and 18; or else

- The Book of Revelation covers a period of hundreds, or even thousands of years.

If you believe in a literal interpretation of Revelation, you *must* choose one of these two options. Next; if you believe the prophecies of Revelation will be fulfilled in a seven year period, then you can only assume that the Great Harlot exists at the onset of Revelation; and, that she must first establish her reputation as a persecutor of the saints in order to fulfill all of the Revelation prophecies. So if the reader believes that the events of Revelation will begin soon, then he or she should consider that persecution is just as likely to begin sooner than later. Certainly nothing in Scripture would indicate that persecution would be held back from the present generation. And especially as we see the day approaching.

# Come Out of Her My People: Persecution Begins

The question I am asked most often - once a person is ready to face the difficult time ahead is: "When do I need to flee?" I always give the same answer. "Look at Revelation 18:4. What do you see there?"

*"And I heard another voice from heaven saying, "Come out of her, my people, lest you share in her sins, and lest you receive of her plagues."*

What people are really asking is, "How long can I stay and enjoy the luxuries of America and avoid the hassles of relocating?" "How long before the plagues begin?" But what is the first reason given for coming out of Babylon? *"Lest you share in her sins."*

How long did Lot live in Sodom? Long enough that a group of angels had to be sent to get him out just before it was destroyed. But how should Lot have responded? Shouldn't Lot have distanced himself from that region where sin had overtaken the culture? James tells us, *"Pure and undefiled religion before God and the Father is this: to visit orphans and widows in their trouble, and to keep oneself unspotted from the world."-James 1:27*

So, how are you doing at keeping yourself unspotted? How would you say the American Church is doing at remaining unspotted? Are you able to avoid the television programs, movies, and radio programs that mock God and endorse all manner of evil? How's your walk with the Lord going? Are you becoming stronger and stronger in your battle against personal sin? The first and foremost reason to flee from Babylon is that you might not share in her sins. So the main question you must ask yourself is, "How long can I stay here and still remain unspotted?" Maybe we've already stayed too long!

Now we can go on to consider how long it might be before Babylon will experience plagues. As has been previously stated, and as you will learn when you read *Come Out of Her My People*, the only prophecy left unfulfilled is the persecution of God's people. The mark that everyone is waiting for will probably come long after horrific martyrdom is in full swing. This conclusion is based on Revelation 14:8-10a which indicates that Babylon is merely a test case for the use of the mark. Listen to God's words to the nations, which are spoken after Babylon is fallen, to those who survive her destruction.

*"And another angel followed, saying, "Babylon is fallen, is fallen, that great city, because she has made all nations drink of the wine of the wrath of her fornication." Then a third angel followed them, saying with a loud voice, "If anyone worships the*

# Introduction

*beast and his image, and receives his mark on his forehead or on his hand, he himself shall also drink of the wine of the wrath of God, which is poured out full strength into the cup of His indignation."*

The key words in understanding the timing of the mark in respect to Babylon and the rest of the world are: *"is fallen"* and *"shall also."* Babylon's fall takes place before the wrath of God represented by the bowls later in Chapter 14. Babylon *is* fallen. The warning of verse 10 above takes a simple "if – then" form. *"If anyone worships the beast and his image, and receives his mark on his forehead or on his hand, he himself shall also drink of the wine of the wrath of God."* This point is most significant because those who dwell in Mystery Babylon should not be waiting for the mark, but should be looking for the persecution. The mark might even be seen as an acceptable identifier at first. It may not be until after Babylon's destruction, after hearing the stern warning of Revelation 14:10, that a clear distinction is made regarding the damnation of the mark.

So if the U. S. A. is the Great Harlot, the blood of the saints will be shed around the world before she is judged. How close are we to physical persecution? To answer that question we need to look at how the majority of the population views Christianity. How are the rights of God's people being affected? Are the Ten Commandments being posted in our courts, or are they being removed? Are we hearing the name of Jesus more and more in public prayer, or rarely? Are Christians receiving more respect as they are portrayed in media, or are they being mocked?

To predict how long it might be until Christians are treated violently, just look at how quickly the attitude of the public is changing. At least the last two generations of American students have been trained in public schools (and by television) to mock God. At the same time these upcoming generations have embraced Satanism, spiritualism, and Darwinism. (Isn't it amazing that you will find skulls and crossbones stickers on the same bumpers beside Darwin stickers or crystals hanging from the rearview mirror?) Apparently these "higher powers" evolved? Romans 1:22 says, *"Professing to be wise, they became fools."* They are willingly ignorant. Or, as Kent Hovind has said, They have become *'Dumb on purpose.*

# Come Out of Her My People: Persecution Begins

It should be obvious to any informed Christian that the popular public attitude toward Christianity has soured. Humanism, atheism, Darwinism, Islam, and all manner of foreign gods, which *"neither you, nor your fathers have known,"* are now being honored and defended, in the media, our schools, and in our courtrooms.

Most pastors would agree that we have already entered the beginning of the Last Days according to Paul's definition. *"But know this, that in the last days perilous times will come: For men will be lovers of themselves, lovers of money, boasters, proud, blasphemers, disobedient to parents, unthankful, unholy, unloving, unforgiving, slanderers, without self-control, brutal, despisers of good, traitors, headstrong, haughty, lovers of pleasure rather than lovers of God, having a form of godliness but denying its power."-2nd Timothy 3:1-5* The worldly people of the last days will not only be selfish, ungodly and lawless, they will also be without self-control, brutal – violent. The next chapter takes a closer look at our prospective persecutors; those who are about to make war with the saints.

God has called me to be a herald of that voice from heaven saying, *"Come out of her, my people, lest you share in her sins, and lest you receive of her plagues. For her sins have reached to heaven, and God has remembered her iniquities."* When *"Come Out of Her My People"* was first written, I believed that the actual time of its fulfillment would be after my lifetime. I thought it would take at least a few more generations until the sins of America came to their fullness. I knew that she must first persecute the saints in order to fully identify her as the Great Harlot. But my focus was on the hour of her demise. Now, as persecution is on our doorsteps, I realize that the warning of the coming persecution is just as important as the warning that she will ultimately be destroyed. The warning is twofold - sins and plagues.

The time for warning about the coming persecution of Christians has arrived. I will leave it up to the reader to follow the news. I recommend following the end-times events on Trunews.com, and reading John Price's books which portray likely scenarios of the coming judgment: *The End of America* and *The Warning*. My calling is to teach the Word; and particularly, the words of Revelation.

Now I face a great challenge when presenting my interpretation of Revelation. The challenge has been getting the Church to heed the words of the prophecies of Revelation.

# Introduction

The Book of Revelation has been rejected by the Eastern Churches, spiritualized by the Roman Catholic Church, and made irrelevant by most Protestant Churches. By 'irrelevant' I am not referring to the Letters to the Churches, but to the manner by which the prophetic chapters have been sealed up until a later date - as someone else's problem. Once again, even if the reader is banking on the rapture, nothing in the Book of Revelation says that it all takes place in seven years. Your pastor will have to teach you that, because it is not stated in the Bible.

The author has an extreme adversity to extra-Biblical teachings. And especially the nonsense born out of the Nineteenth Century. Whether it was so-called scientific Christianity, dispensational theology, or restored Christianity spoken by angels; it makes no difference to me. I'll just take my Bible - thank you very much. The Bible, the Holy Spirit, and me; that works just fine for me. And I highly recommend it.

So I have no interest in convincing the reader that I have anything noteworthy to say. We'll let the Bible do the talking. And we'll cut through pre-painted pictures that have become modern day legend and get right down to what the Bible says; and, what the Bible does not say. I have no authority to speak the words, "Come out of her, my people." My hope and prayer is that the ears of the American Church would be opened to hear the voice of the One who calls from heaven. *"And I heard another voice from heaven saying, 'Come out of her, my people, lest you share in her sins, and lest you receive of her plagues. For her sins have reached to heaven, and God has remembered her iniquities.'"*

Now I am certain that the only One who can open the ears of the Church is the Lord Jesus Christ who *"opens and no one shuts, and shuts and no one opens."* The power that is able to stir the Church to action comes from God alone. It is God's Word that is *"living and powerful"* to quicken the body of Christ. *"How then shall they call on Him in whom they have not believed? And how shall they believe in Him of whom they have not heard? And how shall they hear without a preacher?"*-Romans 10:14,15 In the present case; "How shall they hear if they believe that the prophecies of Revelation do not apply to the Church?" This book takes two approaches in overcoming this obstacle. One approach is to present the history of end-times interpretation which exposes the motives and novelty of the popular "Left Behind" doctrine.

# Come Out of Her My People: Persecution Begins

And the second approach is to prove, once and for all, the meaning of certain verses which have been redefined by the Futurists.

I promise not to waste the reader's time. Every verse which I will present in these opening chapters is translated using the most trusted references. The reader will have no doubt that they have heard the exact meanings of the words in the Bible. If the reader still chooses to embrace an interpretation that is contrary to the obvious meaning, that is between God and themselves. But I will have presented the reader with the meanings of the original manuscripts accurately and fairly.

I am absolutely certain that if the reader is willing to trust the original manuscripts of the New Testament, and if the reader is willing to believe the work of the most trusted Greek scholars, then he or she will understand why *"the words of the prophecies"* of the Book of Revelation were written for this very hour. I realize that the reader has a great trust invested in their own church pastor and others who may disagree with my opinions. So I would also challenge pastors to notify me if they can find a single word of the Bible which is wrongly interpreted in this book and its references.

I am so concerned that the reader would understand the meanings of Biblical words, that most of the key words in this book have been linked directly to broadly accepted lexical sources. (These links can be entered by hand for readers who are reading the printed version). This has been done to eliminate any suspicion that I have interpreted a word with bias in order to be persuasive. As Paul has written:

*"And my speech and my preaching were not with persuasive words of human wisdom, but in demonstration of the Spirit and of power, that your faith should not be in the wisdom of men but in the power of God."-1st Corinthians 2:4,5*

You may be thinking, "If I need to know anything important, my pastor will let me know." I can assure you as a pastor myself that honor is due and appreciated by those who must give an account. I can also assure you that it is extremely difficult for a pastor to change his theological position. Pastors are expected to continue in the bent of their seminary and of their denomination. Because a change of stance can result in their termination, little or no effort is made to do further research in a disputed area of theology. Sadly, therefore, you may be in the position of asking your pastor to read this book after you

# Introduction

have read it yourself - and have seen for yourself what the Bible actually says, and does not say.

As I point out in *"Come Out of Her My People,"* God has used words to communicate with us. A word has a certain meaning.

The meaning of a word can flex a little based on its context. But God has written His word so that it can be understood. Words are not wildcards. A word cannot mean whatever somebody wants it to mean, otherwise words would be useless. For instance, a word doesn't also mean the opposite of that word. Greek words are even more specific than English words. Therefore, it is more difficult for people to misinterpret the Greek. This is why Tyndale and the King James translators used the Greek as their source texts. So the key word studies in this book will rely on the original Greek as the authority for the meaning of words.

Let me also assure the reader that I regularly review the major Greek texts used in the most popular Bibles. This includes the *Textus Receptus*, the *Majority Text*, and the *Alexandrian Texts*, including the earliest texts of the second and third centuries. Contrary to what you may have been told, these texts agree to the letter in most passages. And the slight variations do not affect any doctrines of the Christian faith, major or minor. But to appease those readers who might be "King James only," most Greek references have been taken from the *Textus Receptus*.

The reader will be thrilled when they discover that the meanings of some Greek words agree with their prior understanding. But they will most likely feel uneasy when the meanings do not support their previous conceptions. Such is the nature of truth. The author can fully identify with such discomfort after coming out of the cult religion of my youth; and then finding out years later that the origin of the pre-tribulation rapture theory was quite new and lacking in Biblical support. Both of these awakenings were uncomfortable for me, and took years to leave behind. The author can fully identify with the reader who is shocked to find that their prior stance was incorrect.

So buckle up; rough roads ahead.

## Is Fallen, Is Fallen – The North American Church

Is it any surprise that the unbelieving world objects to the thought of there being only one true God? They believe that Christians are being arrogant and intolerant even to insinuate that they have found the real God. Whether or not an individual believes in any god at all makes little difference to their sense of fairness. But the fact of the matter is, it is not difficult at all to prove by overwhelming evidence that the God of the Bible is the only true God. In the absence of any other real God, all that God has to do in order to prove Himself is to show up. And so He has.

When God showed up on Mount Carmel the people who had been persuaded to worship the false god, Baal, immediately conceded, "The Lord, He is God." And when John the Baptist's disciples came to Jesus asking for proof that He was the long awaited for Messiah, Jesus told them merely to go back and tell John all of the miracles which He had performed. So what is the ultimate evidence that the Bible's God is the one true God? His testimony.

Some religions may claim that their god is the creator. And all religions may claim that their god is worthy to be worshipped. But the God of the Bible not only claims to be the Creator, He has proven beyond all doubt that He is the Effecter. What other religion's God has a voluminous book (the Bible) recording how He has affected the real world by miraculously delivering His people, by hearing and answering prayer, by telling in advance what He would do in the future, and by raising His Son from the dead?

Now add to the Bible the personal testimonies of one single believer. Count the many ways that God has proven Himself as Effecter in that one life by answering prayers and delivering him through the perils of life. And finally, multiply his testimony by ten thousand - times tens-of-thousands. This, my dear reader, is the testimony of the ONE TRUE GOD!

# Come Out of Her My People: Persecution Begins

*"You are My witnesses," says the* LORD,
*"And My servant whom I have chosen,*
*That you may know and believe Me,*
*And understand that I am He.*
*Before Me there was no God formed,*
*Nor shall there be after Me.*
*I, even I, am the* LORD,
*And besides Me there is no savior.*
*I have declared and saved,*
*I have proclaimed,*
*And there was no foreign god among you;*
*Therefore you are My witnesses,"*
*Says the* LORD, *"that I am God.*
*Indeed before the day was, I am He;*
*And there is no one who can deliver out of My hand;*
*I work, and who will reverse it?"-Isaiah 43:10-13*

So where is the testimony of the gods of all the other religions? Where is the evidence that they can *do* anything? The atheist's only solution to this void of evidence is to propose that all religion is nothing more than man's desire for superstition. The followers of false gods have no real grounds to object to their proposal. But the Lord God Almighty has fully revealed Himself, and overwhelmingly proven Himself. Those who reject Him worship a false god, themselves, or the Devil. But let the reader be sure, there is only one true God. And while there is light, let us boast in the Lord.

Jesus has overcome the world! But Daniel describes a dire future before Jesus appears again in the clouds. God allows the defeat described below just prior to Christ's return. Some may say that the saints referred to here are Jews. I would merely point out two obvious facts: 1) that God allows these (His) people to be persecuted almost to extinction; and, 2) that this persecution occurs before the time of His wrath.

*"He shall speak pompous words against the Most High,*
*Shall persecute the saints of the Most High,*
*And shall intend to change times and law.*
*Then the saints shall be given into his hand*
*For a time and times and half a time."-Daniel 7:25*

# Is Fallen, Is Fallen - The North American Church

In Daniel Chapter Twelve, Daniel is told that the end will come *"when the power of the holy people has been completely shattered."*- Daniel 12:7 Because Christians stand up for God as the one and only Creator and Savior, they are detestable to all non-Christians. This polarization is inevitable. Convictions are more compelling than attitudes. A bad attitude might motivate someone to violence; but convictions drive men to the battlefields.

Like Israel's mother, Rebecca, America has two nations warring within her. This war is a spiritual battle, but it is war nonetheless. Those who believe America is a Christian nation are pitted against those who insist that it is not; and some would say that it never was. The disseminators of revised history have been successful in causing people to doubt that America was founded as a Christian nation. But they cannot deny the voices of her founders and leaders:

George Washington said: *"It is the duty of all nations to acknowledge the providence of Almighty God, to obey His will, to be grateful for His benefits, and humbly to implore His protection and favor."*

-- And from Washington's Farwell Address:

*"It is impossible to govern the world without God and the Bible. Of all the dispositions and habits that lead to political prosperity, our religion and morality are the indispensable supporters. Let us with caution indulge the supposition that morality can be maintained without religion. Reason and experience both forbid us to expect that our national morality can prevail in exclusion of religious principle."*

Benjamin Franklin declared: *"Here is my Creed. I believe in one God, the Creator of the Universe. That He governs it by His Providence. That He ought to be worshipped."*

John Adams' stated: *"The Declaration of Independence laid the cornerstone of human government upon the first precepts of Christianity."*

John Jay, our first Supreme Court Justice, advised: *"Providence has given to our people the choice of their rulers, and it is the duty as well as the privilege and interest of our Christian Nation to select and prefer Christians for their rulers."*

Abraham Lincoln cautioned: *"The only assurance of our nation's safety is to lay our foundation in morality and religion."*

## Come Out of Her My People: Persecution Begins

Woodrow Wilson boldly declared: *"America was born a Christian nation - America was born to exemplify that devotion to the elements of righteousness which are derived from the revelations of Holy Scripture."*

Calvin Coolidge expressed these concerns: *"The foundations of our society and our government rest so much on the teachings of the Bible that it would be difficult to support them if faith in these teachings would cease to be practically universal in our country."*

Christians are frustrated that ungodliness has overtaken the United States so quickly. The forces of darkness have swept in so quickly that the godly citizens of the land feel like the nation has been hijacked. But this battle between light and dark is easy to understand if we look at it from a spiritual perspective.

The real opposing forces in America are not the Democrats and the Republicans, the conservatives and the liberals, or the elite and the ninety-nine percenters. The battle is between those who fear the Lord and those who do not. As we quoted above, the founders of the nation sought to be independent from England, but were pleased to be dependent on God. Christians who have been delivered from sin rejoice in God's law and view freedom as a blessing from God. The New America has been taken captive by sin and will endorse any government that promises them the right to keep sinning. As Jesus said, *"Whoever sins is a slave to sin."*

Christians stand amazed that anyone would be willing to give up their privacy - and their freedom - without resistance. The New America is willing to forsake every other freedom for the freedom to sin. And a sinner who has been ensnared by sin will do anything, and give up anything, to continue to feed their lusts. The New American majority desires to be independent from God, even if it means the loss of personal and national independence.

How do we get the nation turned back to righteousness? Over the last decade Christians have been looking for help from their government representatives to stop America's slide into immorality. Christians don't understand why the government doesn't do something to protect the rights of the godly. Can't our judges distinguish between the clean and the unclean, the holy and the unholy?

# Is Fallen, Is Fallen - The North American Church

In 1947 President Harry Truman assured Pope Pius XII in a letter: *"This is a Christian Nation. More than a half century ago that declaration was written into the decrees of the highest court in this land. It is not without significance that the valiant pioneers who left Europe to establish settlements here, at the very beginning of their colonial enterprises, declared their faith in the Christian religion and made ample provision for its practice and for its support."*

So why isn't the government helping the Church, instead of standing by, as the Church flails and lashes out like a wounded animal? Where is that "ample provision for its practice and support?" The ungodly and the media hover over the Church like a bunch of vultures ready to pick the carcass clean.

Despite what the atheist community wants people to believe, the founders of this country where overwhelming Christian. At the time of the revolution, nine out of the thirteen colonies were taxing their citizens to support their Christian churches. When the First Amendment was ratified in 1791, there was an immediate problem. The amendment stated the government would not "establish" religion. But nine of the states had already established the Christian Church as their state religion. So they invented something called disestablishment. Disestablishment allowed the states which had been sponsoring Christian Churches to phase out the taxpayers' support of these churches. Connecticut didn't disestablish until 1818. New Hampshire disestablished the following year in 1819. But Massachusetts didn't disestablish until 1833.

These little known facts prove just how profoundly rooted in Christianity America was at her beginning. But our noble Christian heritage is being ignored by our history books and by our leaders. How is it possible that the government cannot "establish religion," and yet government officials can instruct us that we are "not a Christian nation?" Is it legal for a government official to "establish" our religious preference - or non-preference? Obviously not, according to the First Amendment.

The government, corporate America, and the media have now trodden past the mandate for disestablishment and are blatantly bent toward the full scale disenfranchisement of religion. The rise of the unsaved and the decline of Christianity have both been encouraged by the media

# Come Out of Her My People: Persecution Begins

and by an educational system programmed to bring ungodliness and temptation into every home. It was once naively assumed that sexual imagery was being presented for the purpose of selling more products. But now it has become obvious that sinister masterminds were using Balaam's tactic of sexual defilement to undermine the nation's morals and to disqualify the people from taking a stand for righteousness.

How many in the Church were successful at avoiding promiscuity during the seventies? Now, just like hopeless drug addicts, the sinners who have been ensnared by sin will do anything, and give up anything, to continue to feed their lusts. Satan's tactics for sidelining God's people were clearly laid out in 2nd Peter 2:18-20:

*"For when they speak great swelling words of emptiness, they allure through the lusts of the flesh, through lewdness, the ones who have actually escaped from those who live in error. [19] While they promise them liberty, they themselves are slaves of corruption; for by whom a person is overcome, by him also he is brought into bondage. [20] For if, after they have escaped the pollutions of the world through the knowledge of the Lord and Savior Jesus Christ, they are again entangled in them and overcome, the latter end is worse for them than the beginning."*

The people with the big money behind the multimedia machine have formulated their evil scheme right out of the Christian's own playbook. It appears that the real leaders of the nation have purposefully driven the proud and the brave to the demoralizing gates of socialism by legitimizing man's depravity. Intoxicated by lawlessness, the ungodly now placidly submit to any authority; as long as they are promised their 'right' to sin. And how can parents who have been desensitized to sin object when their elementary aged children are taught that sexual deviation is perfectly right and natural?

But Christ, on the other hand, stands ready to deliver the sinner from his bondage. And the Church, by God's grace, will continue to reach out to the lost with the good news of salvation. The freedom to exercise religion is also part of the First Amendment. But it is naive to believe that that the evil forces which have turned the nation against Christianity will allow their destructive plans to fail. It is realistic to assume that the government will do whatever it takes to stop any future national revivals. Salvation is directly opposed to their goal of captivity.

Christians must continue to preach the gospel. Great national evangelical campaigns are underway; and there is no doubt that many souls will be saved. But any substantial disturbance to the atheists' agenda will be put down quickly, even forcibly. Their campaign of captivity has come too far for them to accept anything less that the complete overthrow of Christianity in America. This time the Satanists and the government will join forces and persecute the Church just like the Communists did in the eastern hemisphere. And this time the United Nations will be ready to assist the government in dealing with the Christian enemies of the new post-Christian regime.

Sound like conspiracy theory? If only it were. How can this be happening? Christians are shocked and frustrated that the forces of darkness were able to overtake the country so quickly. They are angry that their nation has been hijacked. Their attitude varies little from that of the founding fathers.

*"Liberty must at all hazards be supported. We have a right to it, derived from our Maker. But if we had not, our fathers have earned and bought it for us, at the expense of their ease, their estates, their pleasure, and their blood." - John Adams in Dissertation on the Canon and Feudal Law, 1765*

But there was never any hope for a Christian Democracy. It is nearly an oxymoron. Jesus was telling the truth when He said, *"Enter by the narrow gate; for wide is the gate and broad is the way that leads to destruction, and there are many who go in by it. Because narrow is the gate and difficult is the way which leads to life, and there are few who find it."-Matthew 7:13,14* The lost will always outnumber the redeemed. God's chosen people will never be more than a remnant until the Lord returns. A Christian democracy could only be short-lived due to the fallen state of mankind's heart. The faith of the American people would have failed several times already in the last 200 years if it had not been for the great revivals which served periodically to turn the majority of the nation back to God.

Persecution will hereafter spread throughout the world. The reader should be thoroughly convinced by reading *"Come Out of Her My People"* that the beasts of Revelation are nations as defined by the book of Daniel. *"The fourth beast shall be a fourth kingdom on earth."- Daniel 7:24a* An image of a nation is most likely a model of that nation's form of government. How else could an image be made of a nation?

# Come Out of Her My People: Persecution Begins

The same evil forces that are leading the American Church to the slaughter are even now spreading their humanistic ideals of lawlessness throughout the world.

The final world "religion" will be some strange and unlikely freak. The fourth beast will be a weird admixture of other nations. This beast may be part democratic, part Islamic, and part socialistic. Or it might be communistic and Satanic, combined with some form of cult-religion. But whatever its form, America will be its predecessor. America will be the test tube for this final amalgamation. The final beast will be an image taken from the melting pot of the world. America is the head, not the tail. The "image" will very shortly be incorporated into the final one-world government. Once the one-world government comes against the Church, the dreaded words of Revelation 14:13 will become effective; *"Blessed are the dead who die in the Lord from now on."*

What nations or world powers were ever *"given a voice"* like the inescapable siren of mass-communications? America has used her multi-media voice to broadcast *"the filthiness of her fornications"* throughout the world. Is there even a remnant of saints who are willing or able to stop their ears to the blasphemous deluge that pours continuously from her mouth? Is it any surprise that the world listens to her voice? And is there any doubt that Satan himself stands behind the megaphone?

Now the reader is probably thinking, "These things will never happen to me." Because we are so self-centered by nature, it is difficult for us to believe the cold realities of history. More people have been killed in wars in the last 200 years that in all of the rest of history combined. Is mankind becoming more civilized? At least 200 million Christians and Jews have been martyred during that same period of time. It might be good for the skeptical reader to review a couple of online resources about persecution:

http://en.wikipedia.org/wiki/Persecution_of_Christians#Early_Modern_period_.281500_to_1815.29

http://www.persecution.com/

If you are American or British, your great-grandparents may have either been slaves or slave owners. Your grandparents probably either fought or were killed in war. Why is it so hard for us to believe that these things really happened? Why does the human mind quarantine these realities into a secluded corner of the brain under a category called "unthinkable?" Be assured; the evil day is at hand.

A murderous spirit has already overtaken the United States and much of the world. As I present the proof for what I have just stated, please be assured that if you have sinned in this area and believed in the Lamb of God for forgiveness, you are indeed forgiven. And if you have sinned in this area in ignorance, the Lord Jesus stands ready to forgive and to heal. The sin that I am referring to is the abortion of the unborn.

A major contributing factor to the abortion rate has been the effect of humanism and Darwinism that is taught in the schools. Students are not taught about the varying stages of a baby as it grows in the womb; when the color of the child's eyes are determined, when the child's nerves are developed enough to feel pain, etc. Instead they are taught that a "developing embryo," not an "unborn baby," looks like a tadpole. Teachers explain this is perfectly natural since we are all just complicated "accidents" from evolutionary processes. So it's only expected that all life forms in their beginning stages would look similar to tadpoles. This line of reasoning leads a person to believe that aborting a baby in the womb is essentially no different than destroying a laboratory experiment in a Petri dish.

The humanists do not classify this *choice* as "the taking of a life." In which case, please consider the maternal affection described by the ancient Hebrew word for compassion. "*Rachum*" is the word commonly used in the Old Testament to mean compassion. This word's origin stems from a similar Hebrew word - "*Rechem*", which means "womb." During the siege of Jerusalem by the Babylonians, the people reached the point of starvation. Jeremiah used this word for compassion to magnify the people's desperation. *"The hands of the compassionate women have cooked their own children; They became food for them in the destruction of the daughter of my people."*-Lamentations 4:10

This Hebrew word for compassion was based upon the natural affection that a mother would feel as she caressed her stomach during pregnancy. The point that Jeremiah is making is that the very same women, who had once cherished the children within their wombs, were now forced by the madness of starvation to kill and eat them.

# Come Out of Her My People: Persecution Begins

This example is given by Jeremiah as the most grievous violation of conscience conceivable in order to point out the severity of Jerusalem's punishment. Where is this compassion in the 21st Century?

America's conscience has been slowly seared to the point where many of her women have switched off this natural compassion. Today, situations of desperation are seldom the reason for aborting one's baby. Pregnancy is merely seen as untimely, unplanned, or inconvenient. Why is there no love lost, no *compassion*, as babies are removed and discarded? Can you imagine what Jeremiah's reaction would be today? The Biblical standards of family, sexual purity, and the worship of our Creator have all been rejected. The fear of the Lord, which is the gatekeeper of the Christian conscience, has been trampled under the feet of today's heartless society.

The Christian Church now walks among a people who cannot distinguish good from evil. There is nothing holding them back from expressing their hostility toward Christians. Anger toward Christ's Church already fills their hearts, but the notion of tolerance has kept them at bay - Until now. Now their anger is beginning to spill through the cracks in the dike. Their violence has overcome their own ability to resist it. Once the persecution of Christians has been set in motion, there is nothing to stop it. The same society who freely terminates the lives of their own children will have no qualms about exterminating the Church.

Look at the religious leaders who opposed Jesus. They believed in God. And yet Jesus knew they had murder in their hearts. When Jesus confronted them about the wickedness within them, they said He was crazy or demon possessed.

*"I know that you are Abraham's descendants, but you seek to kill Me, because My word has no place in you. I speak what I have seen with My Father, and you do what you have seen with your father." They answered and said to Him, "Abraham is our father." Jesus said to them, "If you were Abraham's children, you would do the works of Abraham. But now you seek to kill Me, a Man who has told you the truth which I heard from God. Abraham did not do this. You do the deeds of your father."- John 8:37-41*

These children of Abraham were not worshipping the Devil, and yet they did eventually have Jesus crucified. Just imagine what people who openly worship Satan are capable of!

# Is Fallen, Is Fallen - The North American Church

The American Church slumbers beside an explosive tinderbox. The ungodly majority is smoldering with hatred. America is only moments away from bursting into a violent inferno. Just as in Sodom, the wicked of the land will consume or destroy everything lovely and fair. So the message of *"Come Out of Her My People"* is given once more - before the persecution begins.

Please consider how persecution might affect you and your family. Each Christian must be obedient to the Lord's calling. Each individual must decide whether to shake the dust off of their feet and move to a safer environment; or to offer the bodies of themselves and their families as a sacrificial witness to Christ. There is no right answer for everyone. But it is time to stop pretending. It's time to prepare.

# Come Out of Her My People: Persecution Begins

## Abominations that Lead to Desolation

*"They threw dust on their heads and cried out, weeping and wailing, and saying, 'Alas, alas, that great city, in which all who had ships on the sea became rich by her wealth! For in one hour she is <u>made desolate</u>.'" - Revelation 18:19*

When students of Bible prophecy think of an abomination that leads to desolation, what usually comes to mind? The abomination that leads to desolation spoken of in Daniel's visions. There are three references in Daniel to such abominations. But it is the first citation in Daniel which broadens the discussion beyond that single abomination which will ultimately be set up in the Temple. Daniel 9:27 reads:

*"And on the wing of abominations shall be one who makes desolate, even until the consummation, which is determined, is poured out on the desolate."*

In this chapter we are going to look at three particular sins that are called abominations, and which lead to desolation. These sins are: infanticide, the worship of foreign gods, and homosexuality. But before any further discussion, it needs to be emphasized that none of these sins are the unforgivable sin.

Jesus came to take away the sins of the world. That includes your sins and mine. Paul's words to the Corinthians in Chapter Six accomplish the dual purpose of declaring the sinfulness of various behaviors, and yet reassuring those who have fled to Christ for refuge that they have been forgiven and cleansed by the blood of Christ.

*"Do you not know that the unrighteous will not inherit the kingdom of God? Do not be deceived. Neither fornicators, nor idolaters, nor adulterers, nor homosexuals, nor sodomites, nor thieves, nor covetous, nor drunkards, nor revilers, nor extortioners will inherit the kingdom of God. And such were some of you. But you were washed, but you were sanctified, but you were justified in the name of the Lord Jesus and by the Spirit of our God."-1st Corinthians 6:9-11*

### Infanticide

The Bible clearly links the sins of Manasseh to the desolation of Judah. *"And the LORD sent against him raiding bands of Chaldeans, bands of Syrians, bands of Moabites, and bands of the people of Ammon; He sent them against Judah to destroy it, according to the word of the LORD which He had spoken by His servants the prophets. ³ Surely at the commandment of the LORD this came upon Judah, <u>to remove them</u> from His sight <u>because of the sins of Manasseh</u>, according to all that he had done, ⁴ and also because of <u>the innocent blood</u> that he had shed; for he had filled Jerusalem <u>with innocent blood</u>, which the LORD would not pardon."-2ⁿᵈ Kings 24:1-4 (emphasis added)*

Not only did Manasseh kill his own newborn son, he also encouraged his countrymen to engage in this practice. This was the "innocent blood" that brought desolation to Judah. The Hinnom Valley, on the south side of Jerusalem, was the central location in Judah where parents would put their children to death. The Hebrew words for "Valley of Hinnom" are "Ge Hinnom." We are familiar with the Greek translation of this place as "*Gehenna.*" Gehenna was the city dump. Because this place was so vile from the continuous burning of foul rubbish, and from the wickedness perpetrated there, Gehenna became synonymous with hell itself. And it certainly was for the babies who were burned to death there in the arms of red-hot iron cradles.

The practice of infanticide was never approved by God. Jeremiah 19 speaks of God's distain for this sin: *". . . and have filled this place with the blood of the innocents they have also built the high places of Baal, to burn their sons with fire for burnt offerings to Baal, <u>which I did not command or speak, nor did it come into My mind.</u>" (emphasis added)* Infanticide was brought into Israel primarily by the worshipers of Baal and Molech. It was the blood of innocent children that filled Jerusalem which caused God to drive the Jews out from their land. God Himself determined to make Judah desolate.

# Abominations that Lead to Desolation

## Idolatry – Worshipping Foreign Gods

*"Has a nation changed its gods,*
*Which are not gods?*
*But My people have changed their Glory*
*For what does not profit.*
*¹² Be astonished, O heavens, at this,*
*And be horribly afraid;*
*Be very desolate," says the* LORD.*"-Jeremiah 2:11*

Along with the sin of infanticide, Manasseh also led Judah into another sin leading to desolation; namely, the worship of foreign gods. The Lord God stated in the commandments: *"You shall have no other gods before Me. You shall not make for yourself a carved image—any likeness of anything that is in heaven above, or that is in the earth beneath, or that is in the water under the earth; you shall not bow down to them nor serve them."-Exodus 20:4-5a*

Moses warned the Children of Israel before they entered the Promised Land, and Joshua and Solomon repeated the warning - that God would drive the people out from their inheritance if they forsook the God who had called them out of Egypt. But Israel was not faithful to keep themselves separate from the nations around them. Soon they began to worship the gods of the surrounding nations. King Manasseh accommodated the people's demand for places to worship each of these foreign gods.

2nd Kings 21 gives a detailed account of Manasseh's sins.

*"¹Manasseh was twelve years old when he became king, and he reigned fifty-five years in Jerusalem. His mother's name was Hephzibah. ²And he did evil in the sight of the* LORD*, according to <u>the abominations of the nations</u> whom the* LORD *had cast out before the children of Israel. ³ For he rebuilt the high places which Hezekiah his father had destroyed; he raised up altars for Baal, and made a wooden image, as Ahab king of Israel had done; and he worshiped all the host of heaven and served them. ⁴ He also built altars in the house of the* LORD*, of which the* LORD *had said, "In Jerusalem I will put My name." ⁵ And he built altars for all the host of heaven in the two courts of the house of the* LORD*.*

## Come Out of Her My People: Persecution Begins

⁶ Also <u>he made his son pass through the fire</u>, practiced soothsaying, used witchcraft, and consulted spiritists and mediums. He did much evil in the sight of the LORD, to provoke Him to anger. ⁷ He even set a carved image of Asherah that he had made, in the house of which the LORD had said to David and to Solomon his son, "In this house and in Jerusalem, which I have chosen out of all the tribes of Israel, I will put My name forever; ⁸ and I will not make the feet of Israel wander anymore from the land which I gave their fathers—only if they are careful to do according to all that I have commanded them, and according to all the law that My servant Moses commanded them." ⁹ But they paid no attention, and Manasseh seduced them to do more evil than the nations whom the LORD had destroyed before the children of Israel.

¹⁰ And the LORD spoke by His servants the prophets, saying, ¹¹ "Because Manasseh king of Judah has done <u>these abominations</u> (he has acted more wickedly than all the Amorites who were before him, and has also made Judah sin with his idols), ¹² therefore thus says the LORD God of Israel: 'Behold, I am bringing such calamity upon Jerusalem and Judah, that whoever hears of it, both his ears will tingle. ¹³ And I will stretch over Jerusalem the measuring line of Samaria and the plummet of the house of Ahab; I will wipe Jerusalem as one wipes a dish, wiping it and turning it upside down. ¹⁴ So I will forsake the remnant of My inheritance and deliver them into the hand of their enemies; and they shall become victims of plunder to all their enemies, ¹⁵ because they have done evil in My sight, and have provoked Me to anger since the day their fathers came out of Egypt, even to this day.'"

¹⁶ Moreover <u>Manasseh shed very much innocent blood</u>, till he had filled Jerusalem from one end to another, besides his sin by which he made Judah sin, in doing evil in the sight of the LORD. — (emphasis added)

## Homosexuality

Homosexuality is another abomination that will justify America's desolation. No one could read through the Bible and conclude that the practice of homosexuality is not a sin. It is called "an abomination" in the Mosaic law. Sodom was destroyed for its sodomy. The tribe of Benjamin faced extinction because of this sin. And it is found among specifically mentioned sins in the New Testament. But for a society which has been overtaken by the sins of fornication and adultery, the sin of homosexuality has come to be tolerated. Now some states have even sanctioned the practice of tempting little school-age children with this sin under the guise of diversification education. Even the Church itself has become unwilling to admit that the Bible speaks out against homosexuality.

We hear the statement more and more, "Well the Bible doesn't really say that homosexuality is wrong." This is a lie. The fact that this lie is so pervasive can only lead to the conclusion that people aren't reading their Bibles. We are about to study a section of scripture which speaks out so vehemently against this sin that the reader might be shocked by the severity of God's condemnation. Homosexuality is not the only sin which is exposed by Romans Chapter One. Homosexuality is, however, the most explicitly described in Romans Chapter One, Verses 24 through 28.

Before we examine those verses we need to understand their context. What we find in the following verses is that God's wrath is revealed by the gospel; and that He utterly condemns every form of ungodliness. But in order to honor man's God-given free will, God allows people who reject Him to commit the destructive sins that they desire. This, however, doesn't mean that God's attitude toward those sins has changed. The Bible also says that, *"The heavens declare the glory of God; and the firmament shows His handiwork."-Psalms 19:1* God says He has made His creation in such a way that He cannot be denied – that He can only be ignored. The consequence for ignoring the Creator, who is also the Sustainer, is to be given over to corruption; the opposite of being sustained. We have the choice to be sustained, or to be corrupted.

*[18] For the wrath of God is revealed from heaven against all ungodliness and unrighteousness of men, who suppress the truth in unrighteousness, [19] because what may be known of God is manifest in them, for God has shown it to them. [20] For since*

the creation of the world His invisible attributes are clearly seen, being understood by the things that are made, even His eternal power and Godhead, so that they are without excuse, [21] because, although they knew God, they did not glorify Him as God, nor were thankful, but became futile in their thoughts, and their foolish hearts were darkened. [22] Professing to be wise, they became fools, [23] and changed the glory of the incorruptible God into an image made like corruptible man—and birds and four-footed animals and creeping things.

Three times in the next verses, God uses the term "given over." God is going to let them have it! Because they're worshipping corruptible man, God is going to "give them over" to corrupt their own bodies among themselves. *"Among themselves"* distinguishes this behavior from an act of sin that is carried out alone. This could be the first reference to the sin of homosexuality. And then, because they exchanged the truth for a lie, God "gives them over" to self-destruction. And thirdly, because they don't want to think about God, He "gives them over" to a debased mind. So let's read verses 24 through 28; and then we will look at the Greek words from the original manuscripts in order to understand precisely what is being said.

*"[24] Therefore God also gave them up to uncleanness, in the lusts of their hearts, to dishonor their bodies among themselves, [25] who exchanged the truth of God for the lie, and worshiped and served the creature rather than the Creator, who is blessed forever. Amen. [26] For this reason God gave them up to vile passions. For even their women exchanged the natural use for what is against nature. [27] Likewise also the men, leaving the natural use of the woman, burned in their lust for one another, men with men committing what is shameful, and receiving in themselves the penalty of their error which was due. [28] And even as they did not like to retain God in their knowledge, God gave them over to a debased mind, to do those things which are not fitting; [29] being filled with all unrighteousness, sexual immorality, wickedness, covetousness, maliciousness; full of envy, murder, strife, deceit, evil-mindedness; they are whisperers, [30] backbiters, haters of God, violent, proud, boasters, inventors of evil things, disobedient to parents, [31] undiscerning, untrustworthy, unloving, unforgiving, unmerciful; [32] who, knowing the righteous judgment of God, that those who practice such things are deserving of death, not only do the same but also approve of those who practice them."*

Verses 29 through 32 are included so that we might recognize that all of these things are evidence that people are not worshiping Creator God as they should. They're not serving Him. They're not acknowledging Him. They're not thinking about Him, or glorifying Him in their lives.

# Abominations that Lead to Desolation

The opening verses of Chapter Two drives home the fact that no one is pleasing God perfectly by their desires, their thoughts, or their behavior. Without the redeeming work of Jesus we would all be disapproved by God. But praise be to God's grace by which He has made us accepted in His Beloved Son!

Now let's go back to verse 24 and observe how strongly God condemns the sin of homosexuality. If you are reading the electronic version, you may click on the Greek words and go directly to Strong's Online.

*"Therefore God also gave them up to uncleanness (*ἀκαθαρσίαν (akatharsian) uncleanness*)."* *Katharas* means clean, or pure. So, *"a-katharas"* means not clean or pure, indicating filth or defilement. So, God gave them up to be dirty and defiled. In the Old Testament, anyone defiled was disqualified to serve before God in the tabernacle, and later in the Temple.

*"in the lusts (*ἐπιθυμίαις (epithymiais) desires*) of their hearts."* *Epithumia* is a strong desire – in this case in a bad sense. So it means an irregular or inordinate desire.

*"to dishonor (*ἀτιμάζεσθαι (atimazesthai) to be dishonored*) their bodies"* *Atomotzo* is another Greek word that uses an alpha prefix to express the antonym of the word. Here the root word is *timao*: to honor or give honor. Timothy means God honorer, from *timao* and Theo. *(A)- tomotzo* means; to dishonor, to treat with indignity, or to abuse.

*"among themselves"* I think it's interesting that it adds *"among themselves"* because it points to an inward or private focus, a selfish aspect. *"Among themselves"* gives the impression of a separate group which exists apart from the whole of humanity. They have gone off by themselves and they interact only among their own kind – those who have rejected God.

*"who exchanged the truth of God for the lie (*ψεύδει (pseudei) falsehood*), and worshiped and served the creature rather than the Creator, who is blessed forever. Amen."* The word for *"lie"* is *pseude*. *Pseudei* is translated "falsehood." Everyone believes in something. They can either believe the truth of God, or they can believe in something else. But here we are talking about *the* truth of God vs. *the* falsehood. The Father of all truths, vs. the father of all lies. The context of the prior verses indicates that *the* truth is the fact that God IS – as God has given His name as "I Am," or "I Exist." The lie would then be that God is not – the denial of God's existence or the willful ignorance of God.

## Come Out of Her My People: Persecution Begins

*"For this reason God gave them up to vile (ἀτιμίας (atimias) of dishonor) passions (πάθη (pathē) passions)"* The word for passions is *pathe*. It is the root from which we get the English word "pathology" - the study of disease. Notice how derogatorily it is used in Colossian 3:5, *"Therefore put to death your members which are on the earth: fornication, uncleanness, passion (πάθος (pathos) passion), evil desire, and covetousness, which is idolatry."* Greek scholar Spiros Zodiates describes *"pathe"* as a diseased condition of the soul, from which the outwardly expressed defilements spring forth. They emanate from this diseased condition. But in Romans 1:26, *pathe* is further modified by the word *atimias*. We learned above that *timao* means; to honor. Therefore *a-timias* means "degrading." So the compound rendered in English as *"vile passion"* is properly interpreted as "degrading unhealthy desires." The *pathe atimias* describes a diseased lust which dishonors those that indulge in it. It is a self-destructive mechanism which degrades the perpetrator just as the homosexual has chosen to degrade God.

*"For even their women exchanged the natural (φυσικήν (physikēn) natural) use for what is against (παρα (para) against) nature(φύσιν (physin) nature) . Likewise also the men, leaving the natural use of the woman"*

This is the most explicit description of homosexuality found in the Bible. Some people have said that the Bible doesn't say anything about homosexuality. It may not use the English word, but what would they call men burning with lust for other men? The Greek in this passage is self -explanatory. Homosexuality is *para fusen;* "against nature." It is paranormal. It is not instinctive. Isn't it peculiar that the same society which is so concerned about nature would embrace an activity that is contrary to nature?

*"burned (ἐξεκαύθησαν (exekauthēsan) were inflamed) in their lust (ὀρέξει (orexei) desire) for one another"* Here the word for *lust* is not *epithumia* . This time Paul uses a form of *orexis*. This word comes from *orego*. It means to reach for, or to grab.

*"Men with men committing what is shameful (ασχημοσύνην (aschēmosynēn) shame )"* *Askemeneo* is a very unusual word. It is used in the Greek Septuagint in Leviticus 18:16. The verse reads, *"Thou shalt not uncover the nakedness (askemeneo) of thy brother's wife."* Here it literally means "to inappropriately expose someone's private parts."

## Abominations that Lead to Desolation

The word is translated here in Romans, politely in English, as "shameful." God says that men being inflamed by other men is shameful.

*and receiving in themselves the penalty* (ἀντιμισθίαν (antimisthian) recompense)  A *misthos* is a reward. An *anti-misthos* is just the opposite of a reward. It is a retribution. There's a penalty attached to this shameful behavior.

"*Of their error (*πλάνης (planēs) error  Note that this is not *pseude*, which was used above for "falsehood." *Plane* is where we get the English word "planet." It means to wander out of the way. So this "*error*" is a delusion, a deviation, or wrong opinion.

"*which was due (*ἔδει (edei) did it behove) (ἀπολαμβάνοντες (apolambanontes) receiving )"  *Edei* is used to tell us that the penalty is just, certain, and appropriate for the offense. And just as men received other men, they will also receive the penalty.

"*And even as they did not like to retain God in their knowledge, God gave them over to a debased mind* (ἀδόκιμον (adokimon) a depraved)"  The root word for depraved is *dokomon* meaning "approved." It is akin to *dokome*, which is Greek for "character". *A-dokimon* describes disapproved character. This could easily be a reference to men whose character has already been damaged as a result of the just reward which they have already received.

"*to do those things which are not fitting* (καθήκοντα (kathēkonta) fitting)" *Katheko* means "proper" or "right." *Kathekonta* means "wrong" or "improper."

So let's summarize this section of Romans, which purportedly doesn't say anything against homosexuality.  God's Word lists fourteen derogatory terms for the practice of homosexuality. They are: unclean, lustful, dishonoring, self-focused, based on a falsehood, degrading, from a self-destructive disease of the soul, against nature, a craving, shameful, deserves a penalty, the result of wandering off, degrading, and, not fitting (wrong). So in this little area we see this behavior thoroughly exposed and explicitly described as sin. Never let it be said that the Bible doesn't speak out against homosexuality.

## Come Out of Her My People: Persecution Begins

God speaks out very strongly against it. In fact, because it is the most explicitly described sin among the many sins listed in Romans Chapter One, homosexuality is the most obvious indicator that someone has stopped worshiping God as they should; that their heart has turned away from God, that they're not serving God, and that they don't want to think about God. No matter what they might say, this text tells us that in their hearts they do not even believe in the existence of God.

So why would a homosexual be appointed to model Christ to the Church? This is counter-productive to building up the body of Christ, to say the least. How could Christ be glorified by something shameful? It's like promoting a card-carrying coward to the office of five-star general. This makes a mockery of the precious body of Christ. Simple logic would mandate that we not honor a behavior that is the most indicative of someone who is not honoring God. Nor may we approve of those who practice such things.

The approval of sin *is* a sin.

## Pre-Trib Rapture History

Prior to presenting the historical origins of Futurism and John Darby's Dispensationalism, please consider the attitude of one of Darby's contemporaries, Charles Spurgeon. C.H. Spurgeon's thoughts regarding the end-times are represented below by his grandson and minister, Tommie Spurgeon.

### Charles Spurgeon and End-time Prophecy

"Charles Spurgeon believed that the Baptist faith was exactly the same as the early Church under the Apostles and he taught that. Yet today if he was applying for a job as a pastor in a Baptist church and he told them how he believed about the Rapture and the Resurrection he would be rejected. His scriptural understanding and messages are praised by many and they often place him at the top of the list for their spiritual leadership. But there are things in Prophecy that he taught that the Baptist would reject as heresy. One of the reasons many do not know what CH Spurgeon taught on Prophecy was the fact that he never preached in direct messages such as a sermon on the rapture or end times. But we know what he believed by what he included in his messages of salvation and enlightenment because he often included his belief in prophecy in the message itself rather than it being the main topic of his sermon.

What most believers do not know is that Charles Spurgeon believed that the Rapture and Resurrection would happen at the same time following the Great Tribulation. That the judgement seat of Christ would happen and Satan would be bond for a thousand years He also believed that Jesus would then literally set up his kingdom on earth and rule for a thousand years. He believed that a second resurrection would occur after the thousand-year reign for the unrighteous dead. This would be followed by the great white throne judgement of God and then there would be a new heaven and a new earth.

# Come Out of Her My People: Persecution Begins

During Spurgeon's day there was another preacher that people today believe was a knowledgeable man on prophecy. His name was John Darby. It is amazing to me that the Baptist organization would accept his teachings over Charles Spurgeon. Charles did not care for the teachings of Darby and if he were alive today would be preaching in direct opposition to him. He did it back then and he would continue to do it today. What I am referring to is the belief that the Rapture and Resurrection would occur before the tribulation. How could anyone believe that Darby had a greater understanding than what CH Spurgeon did? Spurgeon was not ignorant when it came to prophetic teachings and took them just as serious as his teachings on grace because he wanted his listeners to know the truth. However his main focus was on the cross of Christ and Salvation because he felt that it was more important than prophecy, however he did include prophecy teachings in his preaching and teaching. He did not reject end-time prophecy or think that it was wrong to be enlightened by it."

An article at www.spurgeon.org/mainpage.html had the following to say:

- Charles Haddon Spurgeon, Pastor of the Metropolitan Tabernacle and contemporary of Darby published criticism of Darby and Brethrenism. His main criticism was that Darby and the Plymouth Brethren rejected the vicarious purpose of Christ's obedience as well as imputed righteousness. He viewed these of such importance and so central to the gospel that it led him to this statement about the rest of their belief. "With the deadly heresies entertained and taught by the Plymouth Brethren, in relation to some of the most momentous of all the doctrines of the gospel, and to which I have adverted at some length, I feel assured that my readers will not be surprised at any other views, however unscriptural and pernicious they may be, which the Darbyites have embraced and zealously seek to propagate"

"Another thing that Charles Spurgeon rejected about John Darby was his teachings on dispensationalism. This belief teaches that the Jews are under a different covenant than the one we have to day and do not need to be saved through the preaching of the Gospel the same as the Gentiles. He believed that when Jesus came back he would rule over them in Jerusalem but they would be saved by their own covenant with him. At that time dispensationalism taught that Israel would **not** go back to the land of Palestine until Jesus returned at Armageddon. Charles Spurgeon disagreed with their teaching and said that he believed that the Jews would return to the land of Palestine before Jesus came back. He was right and John Darby was wrong. Charles also taught that the Jews had to be saved through the Gospel of Jesus Christ and that many would be born-again before Jesus came back. Clarence Larkin came along after Darby and improved upon his theory of dispensationalism by including that 144,000 Jews would be saved during the tribulation but the rest would not accept Jesus until he comes back. Charles Spurgeon would have rejected this as well.

This issue may not seem to be important to some but it is very important to me and those that are trying to reach the Jews with the Gospel of Jesus Christ. What I would like to point out is that most churches believe John Darby and Clarence Larkin over Charles Spurgeon. Charles Spurgeon in our day couldn't be licensed or perform any duties in any church such as Baptist, Assembly of God, Church of God, Methodist, etc because he didn't believe that the Rapture would occur before the Tribulation. There were many more great men of God in his day and before that did not accept that and wouldn't accept it to this very day. Why does it matter? There are over 13million Jews in the world today that need to hear the Gospel of Jesus Christ. The modern day teaching of pretribulation rapture and the teachings on dispensationalism prevent a very large number of Christians from even praying that the Jews will be saved. It is interesting to note that many evangelicals are supportive to Israel because they want to be blessed by doing so, but they are only interested in blessing Israel in material ways, not spiritual. Their salvation is very important and Satan has thrown up a smoke screen to keep Christians from seeking God for Israel's salvation. The Scriptures teach us that it is our responsibility to reach Israel with the Gospel of Jesus Christ.

## Come Out of Her My People: Persecution Begins

The churches in America are so dug into dispensation teachings that they would not allow Spurgeon or any other great man of God to pastor or preach in any of their churches. I am amazed at that. In fact many churches will run off members that do not agree with it or peer-pressure a person until they are afraid of not being accepted unless they do. We do not realize how anti-Semitic this is.

John Hagee will tell you that to preach the Gospel to the Jews is a waste of time. Yet if you were to tell people such as Jews for Jesus or other Jews that have been born again you would soon realize how ridiculous this is. Their souls are as important as any Gentile and we should realize it. It took me a long time to realize why people like John Hagee and others could be so hard when it comes to the Jews and salvation? Now I realize that they are defending what they were taught in Bible College being taught dispensation teachings. They don't want to lose their license. By the way John Hagee does have a great concern when it comes to protecting the lives of the Jews and I appreciate what he is doing with defending Israel. But it is very important that while we protect the sinner that we provide the Gospel for their souls as well and not teach against it. The teaching of pre-tribulation Rapture leaves the Jews out of the Rapture because most will be saved during the Tribulation period itself and the Bible is clear on this. But they will have to receive the Gospel from us, the Gentiles. There are only two Resurrections in Scripture; one when Jesus comes back and the other at the end of the millenium for the unrighteous dead. The Rapture and Resurrection occur at the same time in the same moment. If we miss the Rapture there will be no eternal life because we won't be changed. To leave the Jews out of this and to say that God prefers us over them is anti-Semitic and a sin.

The reason that I am telling the Church about all of these things is not to be critical of others but to open the eyes of Church to do what God has called us to do. It is try to get others to pray for the salvation of Israel whether their pastors do or not. If the pastor wants to pray for the salvation of Israel that is more than great but if he opposes it we need to do what we know is right in our hearts and not worry about it. I would like to encourage everyone especially Baptist to search their hearts and ask themselves whether they believe John Darby or CH Spurgeon when it comes to Biblical truth. God Bless You."

Your Brother in Christ,
Tommie Spurgeon
http://www.americaisraelprophecy.com/founder.html

## Pre-Trib Rapture History

Although the four views Revelation are contained in *"Come Out of Her My People,"* the following summary is given as a concise account to help start the process of broadening the reader's perspective. This introduction may stir the reader to study Church History. If we do not understand the past, we may not understand the future. And we certainly won't understand how we got to be where we are now. I would recommend Bruce Shelley's summary as a starting point. And then tackle Philip Schaff's collection in order to know who shaped the Church's past, and why they made their choices.

The birth pangs of tribulation that the world is beginning to witness will quickly accelerate from occasional groanings into full-fledged contractions. These tribulations should drive more and more people to research end-time prophecies. The last few decades have spawned increasing numbers of end-time prophecy web sites, books, and movies. The internet has changed the common person's access to knowledge.

In previous generations people were trapped in a fairly small learning environment, primarily within their own generation unless they had an extensive library nearby. In former days knowledge was acquired through the medium of printed material. The situation is different today. As people are doing research on the internet, they are finding out what people believed 100 years ago in just a few seconds. They're finding out what people believed 1,000 years ago. And they are able to compare and digest this information in an attempt to make sense of it all. In fact, the reader would be wise to research the information presented below for themselves as they read this brief summary of eschatological history.

When we look at Revelation, we see that over the last two thousand years people have held four distinct opinions on how to interpretation John's prophecies. The least popular view is called Preterism. Preterism makes a lot of sense if you believe that most of the prophecies in Revelation have already happened. Most people do not believe that to be the case so this view will not be discussed in detail in this summary. It assumes that John wrote Revelation before the fall of Jerusalem and that all, or most, of Revelation was fulfilled by 70 AD when Jerusalem was sacked by the Romans. The Preterits' View would have been the most applicable and intuitive to the first century Church if Revelation had

## Come Out of Her My People: Persecution Begins

been written before Jerusalem's fall. The vast majority of scholars believe that Revelation was written after Jerusalem's fall, making Preterism the least applicable interpretation to everyone living after the first century. Because Revelation obviously takes us to the very end of the age, it is assumed by most that its prophecies must be fulfilled in the future. Preterism excludes too many of the prophecies from future fulfillment to seem applicable to the last days. Information about Preterism is readily available on the internet.

Early church fathers trying to interpret *"time, times, and half a time"* in Revelation Chapter 12 and Daniel Chapters 7 and 12 had differing viewpoints. If "time" equals one year, then "times" equals two years, and "half a time" would then equal half of a year. Many believed that Revelation referenced a seven-year period, divided into two 3½ year increments. Justin Martyr, who lived from 100 to 163 AD, interpreted 3½ years as 350 years. Irenaeus, an early church leader who lived from 115 to 202 AD, believed there would be 6,000 years of man's reign - with 3½ literal years at the end of man's kingdom. Irenaeus saw a final thousand years as the kingdom of God on the earth as the restored Sabbath rest. But literal interpretations of Revelation soon yielded to a new method of Biblical interpretation known as idealism, or spiritualization.

The Spiritual View developed between 200 and 400 AD and was accepted until the reformation, roughly 1550 to 1650. So for approximately 1,200 years people held the Spiritual View. Here's how this method of interpretation developed. Greek philosophers begin to realize that the worship of the gods was illogical. Plato started breaking life down into good and evil, between the spiritual realm and the material realm. Soon a man named Philo determined that the Jewish faith could be explained by using Plato's philosophy. When Greek Christians studied their Bibles they began to incorporate these philosophical "mechanics" to reveal the spiritual principles behind the story line.

Clement of Alexandria, who lived from 150 to 215 AD, started a Christian school and began to teach from the Platonic point of view. He had a student, Origen, who began to write commentaries on the Bible using the principles of Philosophy.

# Pre-Trib Rapture History

Here is an example from Origen's commentary on Luke 10:30-37. His philosophical meanings from Jesus' parable of the Good Samaritan miss the entire point of Jesus' teaching and reach for the "higher" spiritual meaning. Here are Origins conclusions.

The traveler in the Good Samaritan is Adam. Jerusalem, which is where the traveler was going, is Paradise. Jericho is the world. The robbers are hostile demons. The priest is the law. The Levite is the prophets. The Good Samaritan is Christ. The traveler's wounds are disobedience. The donkey is the Lord's body. The inn is the church. And the two denari that he paid to the innkeeper were the Father and the Son. The innkeeper is the bishop.

You get the idea. This is spiritualizing the Scriptures. *(Like the 24 elders in Revelation is really the Church.)* The Platonists felt like the obvious meaning was too earthly. The higher spiritual meaning became the focus of the Church. The obvious meanings where considered mundane and of little value compared to the "mysteries" from God. The church came up with a rule that only the bishops were spiritual enough to receive the correct meanings to these mysteries. It is obvious that if anybody and everybody began to interpret the Bible, they couldn't possibly all end up with the same meanings. What if some people thought the innkeeper was a priest? Or that the two denari were just a couple coins? All of Christendom would fall into confusion.

So these spiritualized interpretations of the Bible became the "mysteries" within the church. Now you understand one of the main reasons the Catholic Church didn't want the people to be able to interpret the Bible for themselves. The safe thing to do was to keep the Bible in a foreign language and have the bishops tell everybody what it really meant. This went on for about 1,200 years! The Book of Revelation was spiritualized along with the rest of the Bible. Revelation was seen as a general battle between good and evil, filled with rich symbolisms. This era brought us paintings of beasts and dragons and weird looking creatures. Now let's move on to the next popular method of interpreting Revelation.

The Historical view came about with the Reformation. You could call it the Reformation View. When Wycliffe and Tyndale began to translate the Bible they understood the clear meanings when they read

## Come Out of Her My People: Persecution Begins

it in the original language. They were so personally moved that they determined to share it with everyone. So they began to translate the Bible into the common language so everyone could read it for themselves. When people read Revelation, they saw an entity shedding the blood of the saints. They looked at the time that the Roman Catholic Church had been ruling over the Church, and saw that it had been about 1,260 years. They saw that the description of the antichrist spoken of in Revelation looked strikingly similar to the papacy. They actually believed they were living out the 12th and 13th chapters of Revelation.

Following are some quotes from Protestant Reformers. Martin Luther said, *"We here are of the conviction that the papacy is the seat of the true and real antichrist."* John Calvin, *"To some we seem slanderous and petulant, but we call the Roman pontiff 'antichrist'. Seeing then, it is certain that the Roman pontiff has impugnitily transferred to himself the most peculiar properties of God and Christ. There cannot be a doubt that he is the leader and standard bearer of an impious and abominable kingdom."* These quotes certainly portray their beliefs at that time.

The Historical View was carried through the 1700's by Matthew Henry. His commentary is available online. John Wesley came along in the 1800's with this quote referencing the Pope. *"He is in an emphatic sense the man of sin. He increases all manner of sin above measure. He is, too, properly styled the son of perdition as he has caused the death of numberless multitudes both of his opposers and followers, exalted himself above all that is called God, is worshipped, claiming the highest power, claiming the prerogatives that belong to God alone."*

The idea that the papacy was the antichrist really fueled the Reformation. This is why so many people were willing to die for their beliefs. They believed Revelation should be interpreted literally. They thought they had identified the key players mentioned in the Book. They had no idea that someone would come along later and say that Revelation hadn't really started yet. The Historical interpretation continued for about 350 years, from 1550 until about 1950. This was the third of the Revelation interpretation viewpoints. I encourage people to do their own search on this topic. Go to Biblestudytools.com and read these Reformation commentaries for yourselves.

# Pre-Trib Rapture History

The fourth viewpoint, held from about 1900 or 1950 until today is called Futurism. Futurism, like Preterism, places most of the prophecies of Revelation outside of the lifetime of its present day readers. Just as Preterism pushes their application into the past, Futurism pushes the fulfillment of Revelations prophecy beyond their current application to the Church. Here is a brief explanation of how the Futuristic View was invented, and how it came into the Churches of North America.

Go to your favorite internet search provider and type in these three words: Francisco, Ribera, Futurism. You will find a number of resources which credit Ribera as the Father of Futurism. In 1590, Francisco Ribera published a commentary as part of the counter-reformation in an attempt to stop the Reformation. He came up with a theory that interpreted everything after chapter three of Revelation as future prophecy. He is called, "The Father of Futurism." He said that at some future time, a future church would arise with a different papacy. This would mean that the antichrist couldn't be their current church or the current papacy. This attempt to discredit the Reformer's accusations that the papacy was the antichrist eventually helped bring the Reformation to an end. It worked! A number of Protestants picked up on the Futuristic viewpoint. It came into England through the Archbishop of Canterbury. Then it got picked up by Edward Irving (1792-1843).

Now we come to John Nelson Darby, who lived from 1800 to 1881. He was extremely influential in the Futurist Movement. The reader should search for: "John Nelson Darby Rapture." There was a growing anti-Protestant climate in England. In 1830, he came up with what's called "Dispensationalism." This is a theory that God does different things with different groups of people at different times. Darby used Ribera's break point between Revelation chapters three and four and did something that Ribera never did. Ribera had merely insisted that the Church of Revelation would be a different Church than the Reformers were battling. But Darby used Ribera's break between chapters to take the church away altogether.

People researching Futurism should also look up "Margaret McDonald," in the same era, around 1830, in Great Britain. What is intriguing to me about this is the fact that when you look up these articles on "the rapture," "John Nelson Darby," and "Margaret

47

McDonald," what you will finds is a controversy over which one of them really discovered the "pre-tribulation rapture." The reason this seems so strange to me is because the argument itself shows that it was not a popular idea prior to 1830. Yes, it should be acknowledged that the thought of a pre-trib rapture was entertained briefly by two or three theologians prior to Darby. But the idea was always dropped like a hot rock. As can be seen in the Reformers' writings, and by the Geneva Bible, the pre-nineteenth century church believed in the eminence of the tribulation *and* the eminence of Christ's return. As much as a paradox as this would seem, many denominations maintain both the notions of predestination and of free will; and they would consider this "rightly dividing the Word of God."

In Daniel chapter 12, Daniel is told, *"But you, Daniel, shut up the words and seal the book until the time of the end."* And again he says, *"Go your way, Daniel, for the words are closed up and sealed until the time of the end."* So Daniel was told to seal up his prophecies concerning the end. However, John was instructed by God very clearly in chapter 20, *"Do not seal the words of the prophecy of this book."*

But that's exactly what Ribera did in 1590 by stating that none of these prophecies would happen until the far distant future - at the end of time.

## Come Out of Her My People: Persecution Begins

# Pre-Trib's Faulty Proof-Texts

The two main sections of Scripture quoted by defenders of the pre-tribulation rapture are Revelation 3:10 and the latter verses of 1st Thessalonians Chapter Four. We'll look at the Revelation verse first. Revelation 3:7-13 is Jesus' letter to the Philadelphian Church. The pre-trib teachers claim that God is promising, in these verses, to take the Church out of the world just before the Great Tribulation. The verse of particular interest is verse ten.

*"Because you have kept My command to persevere, I also will keep you from the hour of trial which shall come upon the whole world, to test those who dwell on the earth."-Revelation 3:10*

The argument made by modern Futurists is that *"kept from"* actually means *"taken out of."* The conclusion is that the Philadelphians, or a similar type of the Philadelphian Church, will be taken out of the world before the *"hour of trial."* The best way to test this theory is to examine the original Greek; and then to ask the question, "Has St. John used this same Greek word in his other writings?"

λαβεῖν (labein) *take* This is the word "to take." (If reading the digital version click on the word to go directly to Strong's for examples of usage.) Many forms of this word are used throughout John's writings and its many forms mean: to take, to receive, to hold on.

τηρήσω (tērēsō) *will keep* This is the future tense of "to keep." *Tereso* is the word John has used in the verse above. In fact, he has used it twice in this one verse. This word implies the maintenance of, safety, or care. The changes in prefixes and suffixes below only indicate tense and usage in the Greek. Now look again at Revelation 3:10.

*"Because you have kept (ἐτήρησάς) My command to persevere, I also will keep (τηρήσω) you from the hour of trial which shall come upon the whole world, to test those who dwell on the earth."*

You see that John is using the same word in both instances. The epsilon prefix on the first mention of *kept* merely puts it in the past tense, indicating that the Philadelphia Church had already *kept* His command to persevere. What kind of Bible scholar would interpret the same word to mean two different things when they are used in the same verse? Should the verse be interpreted, "Because you have *taken out* My command?" Of course not! Keep means keep, and it does not mean "taken out."

Understanding what the text says (and does not say) should be enough to put this argument to rest. But now let's look at how John has used this word for 'kept' in his gospel. In the seventeenth chapter of John we find Jesus' prayer to the Father. Here John uses this word for safekeeping; profoundly contrasting the idea of being 'lifted out of trouble' with the promise of being 'kept safe through trials.'

*"I do not pray that You should take them out of the world, but that You should keep* τηρήσης (tērēsēs) *them from the evil one."-John 17:15*

Obviously "keeping" the Apostles from the evil one did not mean taking them out of the evil one. Keeping the Apostles from the evil one must have meant that they would not be overcome by the evil one; that they would be kept safe from the evil one.

Now in the same way, Jesus speaks to the Church of Philadelphia. He promises to keep (persevere) them in the midst of their trial, just as they had kept His command to persevere. Jesus is merely reciprocating their obedience with the promise to keep them in return. He is not submitting the dissimilar promise of taking them out of harm's way. This is a simple apples-to-apples reward for the Philadelphians' own perseverance.

If further proof of Revelation 3:10's failure to support the pre-tribulation theory is needed, we only have to consider the order in which these "types" of churches appear in Revelation; and how they are expected to emerge over history - by those who choose to extrapolate the seven church types into the future. The Laodicean Church is the type expected to exist at the time of the end, not the Philadelphian type. If the Philadelphians were intended to be the recipients of "take out," they should at least be home when the doorbell rings. Why didn't Jesus give the Laodicean Church an opportunity to escape the hour of trial if they were the type of church that would exist in the last days? Trying to force Revelation 3:10 to point to the rapture is a miserable failure on all accounts.

Now let's take a look at the second pre-tribulation rapture proof text; 1st Thessalonians Chapter Four, verses 13 through 18. This is the most descriptive account of the rapture found anywhere in the Bible. This detailed description rests within the context of Paul's words of comfort to the bereaved members of the Thessalonian Church.

*"13 But I do not want you to be ignorant, brethren, concerning those who have fallen asleep, lest you sorrow as others who have no hope. 14 For if we believe that Jesus died and rose again, even so God will bring with Him those who sleep in Jesus." 15 For this we say to you by the word of the Lord, that we who are alive and remain until the coming of the Lord will by no means precede those who are asleep. 16 For the Lord Himself will descend from heaven with a shout, with the voice of an archangel, and with the trumpet of God. And the dead in Christ will rise first. 17 Then we who are alive and remain shall be caught up together with them in the clouds to meet the Lord in the air. And thus we shall always be with the Lord. 18 Therefore comfort one another with these words."*

In accordance with basic Bible interpretation guidelines, the very first step in determining the meaning of this passage is to establish its single main theme. In other words, if these verses were to be bound as a stand-alone book, what would it be called? What was Paul's motive in conveying these thoughts?

The first and last verses are focused on giving comfort to those who have lost their loved ones. The first verse also implies that the bereaved would be less grieved and more hopeful if they were more informed about the things that Paul is about to share with them. Paul doesn't want those who have lost their loved ones to think that those who have died are going to miss out on anything that those still living will experience; and particularly, that the dead would be deprived of participating in the Lord's return. But the overall objective of comfort through education calls for a title along the lines of: "Paul's Words of Comfort to the Bereaved."

The next step in the interpretation process is to observe the words themselves. As in our examination of Revelation 3:10 above, the Greek is the most reliable source of the original meaning of these words.

Verse 14, *"For if we believe that Jesus died and rose again, even so God will bring with Him those who sleep in Jesus."*

# Come Out of Her My People: Persecution Begins

This verse takes the form of an "if – then" statement. "If" we believe that Jesus died and rose again; then (even so), or (and thus) – *"God will bring with Him those who sleep in Jesus."* The conditional statement is that one believes in the death and resurrection of Jesus. If we believe in the death and resurrection of Jesus, *even so* we must also believe what Jesus has promised to His followers that *"because I live, you will live also."* John 5:25 says, *"Most assuredly, I say to you, the hour is coming, and now is, when the dead will hear the voice of the Son of God; and those who hear will live."* The dead are going to hear the voice of Jesus and rise. 1st Thessalonians 4:14 ties these two resurrections together. We believe in the death and resurrection of Jesus; and *even so*, we believe that God is going to raise those who have fallen asleep.

Verse 15, *"For this we say to you by the word of the Lord, that we who are alive and remain until the coming of the Lord will by no means precede those who are asleep."*

Verse 14 is presented with the full confidence of an oath; *"by the word of the Lord."* Paul is furthermore crediting the Lord Himself as the source for the sequencing of these events. According to Paul and the Lord; it's the resurrection of the dead first, and the rapture of the living second. (See *"The Last Enemy of Christ"* contained within this book for an in depth study of the timing of end-times events.) *"By no means"* is formed by two Greek words, two words for "not." It might say, "They will 'not, not' precede those who are asleep." In the Greek it has the meaning, "It absolutely won't happen. No way, no how." This term stated in the Greek's most emphatic negative expression is that the living will not precede those who have died.

And how long will the Thessalonians remain alive until the dead are raised and the living are raptured? *"Until the coming of the Lord."* Notice that it does not say, "Until a calling from the Lord," God's Word says, *"the coming of the Lord."* This distinction will be amplified further in the next verse.

Verse 16, *"For the Lord Himself will descend from heaven with a shout, with the voice of an archangel, and with the trumpet of God. And the dead in Christ will rise first."*

This verse contains so many important elements that we must examine its individual phrases to properly appreciate its ramifications. The first phrase identifies three different arguments which would persuade the Thessalonians that Paul is describing the second coming of Christ.

*"For the Lord Himself"*

On occasion the Greek language will insert a pronoun in addition to the noun being referenced in order to magnify the importance its subject. Here the Greek (αὖτός (autos) *he*) reiterates the identity of the one being referred to. There is also another Greek word in the original texts, including the Textus Receptus, upon which the King James Bible is based. The Greek word ὅτι (hoti) *that* appears before "Himself." In a true word-for-word translation the verse would read, "For that He Lord." The Online Interlinear translation of this verse captures the true meaning of this phrase as, "For that same Lord." Another good translation would be, *"For that self-same Lord."* By using these words, anyone familiar with the Book of Acts would tend to associate them with *"that same Jesus"* from Luke's record of the ascension in Acts 1:9-11.

*"Now when He had spoken these things, while they watched, He was taken up, and a cloud received Him out of their sight. ¹⁰ And while they looked steadfastly toward heaven as He went up, behold, two men stood by them in white apparel, ¹¹ who also said, "Men of Galilee, why do you stand gazing up into heaven? This same Jesus, who was taken up from you into heaven, will so come in like manner as you saw Him go into heaven."*

Because Paul has just mentioned "the coming of the Lord," it would appear that Paul is deliberately calling to mind the mental image of the Lord's bodily return. Although this may not provide conclusive evidence that this "coming" is the bodily second coming of Christ; please consider the next two phrases as further supporting evidence.

*"Will descend"*

The Lord – that same Lord will descend (καταβήσεται (katabēsetai) *will descend*). This exact word is used in Romans 10:7 asking the question, *"Who will descend into the abyss?"* Καταβάς (katabas) *having descended* is the past tense of this word. Please click on this word (in the ebook) or look it up to observe its usage. It is usually translated "come down" as in the Gospel of John where Jesus referred to Himself as the one who *"comes down from heaven,"* and *"the bread that came down from heaven."* Paul first referred to this event as *"the coming of the Lord"* in verse 15. Now verse 16 furthers his description. Jesus is *"coming"* and He's *"coming down – descending."*

*"From heaven"*

Here the operative word is *"from."* This is a common word in the Greek pronounced "apa." The point in examining this word is to differentiate what this preposition is not saying. It does not mean "in," or "near," or "around." The Greek has other words that mean those things. ἀπ' (ap') *from*, which omits the final alpha because it precedes a word beginning with a vowel, conveys a separation between two positions. Just like its use in English, "from" generally implies departure. An object was there, and now is here; the object came *from* its former position.

This study seems mundane except that it is necessary in order to express the precision of the original Greek text. *"From heaven"* means that Jesus has distanced Himself *from* heaven. He was in heaven, and now he has separated Himself *from* heaven. He's not merely coming *in* heaven, or descending *in* heaven. He's going to descend *from* heaven. He's not going to get up from His throne and walk a few steps - and call to the church. No. He is, once again, going to depart from His place in heaven and *descend*.

*"For the Lord Himself will descend from heaven."* What Paul has written means that the same Jesus who has ascended will also *come down from* heaven – *"in like manner as you saw Him go into heaven." "In like manner"* means that the same processes will reoccur; except that they will occur in a reverse manner. When Jesus was taken up *to* heaven he ascended *from* the earth. When Jesus returns *from* heaven, he will *descend* to earth. When Jesus ascended into heaven he disappeared from sight. When Jesus descends He will reappear; and this is the blessed hope. *"Looking for the blessed hope and glorious appearing of our great God and Savior Jesus Christ."*-Titus 2:13

Let's put this all together now. From verse 15: *"the coming of the Lord."* From verse 16: *"the self-same Lord,"* *"will come down,"* *"from heaven."* These four terms all verify that the Lord is "coming." He's coming; He will come down; He's departing from heaven. If we respect the meaning of these four phrases, we cannot contradict their meaning and say, "But He's not coming," or "He's not *really* coming," or "He's not *really* leaving heaven." If we do that, then words would have no constant meaning, and the Holy Bible would be rendered useless and utterly meaningless.

Hopefully, a teacher of God's Word who has been teaching that these words don't really mean what they say would be honest enough to confess that they have chosen to override the common meaning of the words. And if they insist on teaching something which is contrary to the clear writings of the ancient texts, they should at least inform their hearers that they are presenting their own opinion. But if not, *"We shall all appear before the judgment seat of Christ."*

*"With a shout, with the voice of an archangel, and with the trumpet of God."* The Bible describes a truly *glorious appearing* at Christ's return that every eye will witness. This celebration, once again, lends itself to the conclusion that Paul is describing the bodily return of Jesus.

*"And the dead in Christ will rise first."* Once Paul has painted this mental picture of Christ's descent, he returns to his original focus; the comfort provided by the knowledge that the resurrection of the dead will precede the rapture of the living.

Verse 17, *"Then we who are alive and remain will be caught up together with them to meet the Lord in the air. And thus we will always be with the Lord. Therefore, comfort one another with these words."*

Paul begins with the word *"then"* inferring for the third time the priority of the resurrection. *"Then"* When? After the dead have risen. He continues to bring this chronology to the forefront. Then, and only then, will the living be raptured. Why is Paul driving this point home with such repetition? May I suggest three reasons why the resurrection of dead could provide so great a comfort to those left among the living.

## Come Out of Her My People: Persecution Begins

First let me offer the most obvious reason. The very fanfare which Paul has just described will be the grandest entry in history. The bereaved would be grieved to think that they would be privileged to see this glorious appearing, while at the same time contemplating that their deceased would miss experiencing this event with *their* own senses. They would surely desire to share the exhilaration of His appearing with their beloved.

The second likely reason for finding comfort in the resurrection of the dead is similar. That is; the hope of Job.

*"25 For I know that my Redeemer lives,
And He shall stand at last on the earth;
26 And after my skin is destroyed, this I know,
That in my flesh I shall see God,
27 Whom I shall see for myself,
And my eyes shall behold, and not another.
How my heart yearns within me!"-Job 19:25-27*

This is the comfort that Paul is getting across; "Don't worry. The dead are going to burst forth from their graves. They're going to be standing beside you; and they're going to share in the privilege of seeing the Lord descending with their own eyes - just like you. They're not going to miss out on a thing." This is the comfort that's being given. "And then you will continue to share the moment together."

A third reason for comfort is simply the joy of sharing in Christian fellowship. Paul was holding out the promise to the Thessalonians that their loved ones would be caught up *together* in the clouds to meet the Lord in the air. *Koinonia* is the comfort! Paul was painting the picture of the dead being raised and standing at their side. So as to say, "You will be able to behold the Lord's appearing together." And then the resurrected saints and the living saints will rise to meet the Lord in the air – together again, forever more. *"And thus we shall always be with the Lord."*

*"To meet the Lord in the air"*

To further support the resolve that Jesus is coming and not merely planning a fly-by, we need only study the word *"meet."*

ἀπάντησιν (apantēsin) *meet* This exact word is used three times in the New Testament; Matthew 25:6, Acts 28:15, and here in 1st Thessalonians. In every instance it is used to describe a greeting party, not a departure. Let's look at its usage in Matthew because of the striking similarity between Paul's usage and its usage by our Lord Jesus.

*"Then the kingdom of heaven shall be likened to ten virgins who took their lamps and went out to meet the bridegroom. ² Now five of them were wise, and five were foolish. ³ Those who were foolish took their lamps and took no oil with them, ⁴ but the wise took oil in their vessels with their lamps. ⁵ But while the bridegroom was delayed, they all slumbered and slept. ⁶ And at midnight a cry was heard: 'Behold, the bridegroom is coming; go out to meet him!' ⁷ Then all those virgins arose and trimmed their lamps. ⁸ And the foolish said to the wise, 'Give us some of your oil, for our lamps are going out.' ⁹ But the wise answered, saying, 'No, lest there should not be enough for us and you; but go rather to those who sell, and buy for yourselves.' ¹⁰ And while they went to buy, the bridegroom came, and those who were ready went in with him to the wedding; and the door was shut. ¹¹ Afterward the other virgins came also, saying, 'Lord, Lord, open to us!' ¹² But he answered and said, 'Assuredly, I say to you, I do not know you.' ¹³ Watch therefore, for you know neither the day nor the hour in which the Son of Man is coming."*-Matthew 25:1-13 emphasis added

Paul told the Thessalonians in verse 15 that his statements concerning these end-times events were *"by the word of the Lord,"* so it is reasonable to assume that Paul was recalling these very words of Jesus from Matthew's gospel as he addressed the concerns of the Thessalonians. And because the Greek in which these words were originally circulated among the churches is so precise, we can also reasonably assume that Paul would have handled these words consistently because they were *"the word of the Lord."*

So in verses 1 and 6 of Matthew Chapter 25, were the ten virgins going out to be taken away by the Lord? Or were they going out meet Him with the intention of escorting Him back to the bride?

The answer is obvious. Their lanterns were lighted specifically for the purpose of leading Him back to where they had come from. Once again this word for *"meet"* is clarified in Acts 28:15:

*"And from there, when the brethren heard about us, they came <u>to meet</u> us as far as Appii Forum and Three Inns. When Paul saw them, he thanked God and took courage."* emphasis added

These believers from Italy were not going out to meet Paul with any thought of returning with him to Malta. Their meeting was nothing more that a greeting. *Apantesin* is also used several times in the Greek Septuagint version of the Old Testament. The reader who is thorough enough to investigate these Old Testament passages will only find further proof that *apantesin* is a meeting and not a one-way departure.

Consider a simple example. If someone is coming from heaven, (or they're coming from Chicago, or they're flying in from Europe,) we would go to the air (or the airport) to meet them. That wouldn't mean that we were going back with them. There is nothing in the passage that says Jesus is doing a yo-yo thing where He's descending, and then He's going to bob back up with those who have gone to meet him.

This is a greeting party. We're going to meet the Lord in the air. The meeting is the purpose. The "catching up" will be like a father lifting his children up when they run to meet him after an absence. The father is not going to jump back in his car and drive the kids back to his workplace. The father has *"come" "from"* work. He came home for a purpose.

Jesus is descending. Paul has given a sufficient description of His descent as the bodily second coming of Christ. Nothing here says that He's returning back up into heaven at the time of this meeting. Furthermore there is no indication whatever that Jesus will be deviating from His earthbound course of direction. It is the greeting party which will turn and accompany the Lord back to the earth.

*"Therefore, comfort one another with these words."*

It's all about comforting the bereaved. It starts out with that. It wraps up with that. These verses are all about God's counsel to the living regarding their dead. They're going to burst forth from their graves. They're not going to miss out on anything. So you don't have to sorrow as those who have no hope. Isn't it interesting that verse 17 (the part about the rapture) is ripped out and presented in books and movies without the context of the comfort, or a depiction of the resurrection of the dead? The movies depict the saints as though they were ascending straight into heaven. No voices. No trumpets. No appearing. No descending. And no coming. And certainly no thought about the resurrection of the dead. Is that how an honest filmmaker would portray 1st Thessalonians Four? Is that any way to treat the very Word of God?

The authors and screenwriters *have* studied these verses. They know *exactly* what their doing. But they don't want the audience to think about the fact that the resurrection of the dead occurs first - even though that's pointed out in this text three times. Three times! This concealment is most certainly made because the Bible places the resurrection of the dead at the end of the age, after the Great Tribulation. People who are trying to force the idea of the pre-tribulation rapture of the church either can't use this verse (which is the only verse in the Bible that actually refers to this meeting in the air as the rapture); or, they must strip it of its context and only portray the rapture scene by itself. Because if they present the rapture verse in its context, it becomes obvious that it is *not* a pre-tribulation rapture at all. It's a rapture *after* the resurrection of the dead.

Some people just don't want to teach it the way it's written in the Bible, so they extract what fits their purpose and assume that you will never study it on your own. When examining doctrine, we have to hold it up against the standard of the Word of God. Does it agree with what God's Word says, or is it contrary to what God's Word says? If we don't go by the Bible, then what are we going to go by? Because if you're just going to pull out a phrase from five or six verses and plant it somewhere by itself, you can make the Bible say anything you want. But we don't want to do that, do we? Don't we want to cling to what the Bible actually says - no matter who's trying to write a good book, or make a good movie?

## Fractured Analogies from the Past

Although the most pre-trib teachers insist that they have interpreted the Book of Revelation literally, they still hold on to remnants from Christian Platonism. (Remember that the Platonists turned the entire Bible into a series of analogies.) Even today, the Catholics still don't believe that Jesus will literally return before the millennium.

But in the midst of the pre-tribbers' literal interpretation, suddenly they will throw in an analogy as a hangover from the Middle Ages. To make matters worse, they don't complete these analogies. I call these fractured analogies. A parable may have a main theme surrounded by incidental details. But an analogy should be able to find a meaning for each of its components, or else the unidentified elements would serve no purpose, and would therefore be without spiritual meaning.

One of my favorite fractured analogies is the pre-trib interpretation of the 24 elders in Revelation. The pre-tribbers expect the Church to be in heaven after the Letters to the Churches. They point to the fact that from Chapter Four through Chapter Nineteen, the 24 elders are found stationed in heaven. Therefore, since the Church is supposed to be in heaven, the 24 elders are really the Church. But we find that there are three groups gathered around in the throne room; the 24 elders, the four living creatures, and the angels. So when the pre-trib proponents claim that the 24 elders are really the Church, I ask the question, "Then who are the four living creatures, and the angels?" Quite obviously, the four living creatures are none other than *the four living creatures*. And likewise, the angels - are angels. The point being; you can't just pick out one character and make that character into an analogy, while ignoring the rest of the characters in the scene. It doesn't work that way.

Another more famous fractured analogy occurs when the rider of the white apocalyptic horse is tagged with the task of bearing the Antichrist. Nothing whatsoever is said about the Antichrist in Chapter Six of Revelation. The first seventeen verses of the chapter are presented below. Although these verses are covered in more detail later in this book, it is needful to review them now in order to show the folly of pinning the Antichrist to the white horse.

*"Now I saw when the Lamb opened one of the seals; and I heard one of the four living creatures saying with a voice like thunder, "Come and see." ² And I looked, and behold, a white horse. He who sat on it had a bow; and a crown was given to him, and he went out conquering and to conquer.*

*³ When He opened the second seal, I heard the second living creature saying, "Come and see." ⁴ Another horse, fiery red, went out. And it was granted to the one who sat on it to take peace from the earth, and that people should kill one another; and there was given to him a great sword.*

*⁵ When He opened the third seal, I heard the third living creature say, "Come and see." So I looked, and behold, a black horse, and he who sat on it had a pair of scales in his hand. ⁶ And I heard a voice in the midst of the four living creatures saying, "A quart of wheat for a denarius, and three quarts of barley for a denarius; and do not harm the oil and the wine."*

*⁷ When He opened the fourth seal, I heard the voice of the fourth living creature saying, "Come and see." ⁸ So I looked, and behold, a pale horse. And the name of him who sat on it was Death, and Hades followed with him. And power was given to them over a fourth of the earth, to kill with sword, with hunger, with death, and by the beasts of the earth.*

*⁹ When He opened the fifth seal, I saw under the altar the souls of those who had been slain for the word of God and for the testimony which they held. ¹⁰ And they cried with a loud voice, saying, "How long, O Lord, holy and true, until You judge and avenge our blood on those who dwell on the earth?" ¹¹ Then a white robe was given to each of them; and it was said to them that they should rest a little while longer, until both the number of their fellow servants and their brethren, who would be killed as they were, was completed.*

*¹² I looked when He opened the sixth seal, and behold, there was a great earthquake; and the sun became black as sackcloth of hair, and the moon became like blood. ¹³ And the stars of heaven fell to the earth, as a fig tree drops its late figs when it is shaken by a mighty wind. ¹⁴ Then the sky receded as a scroll when it is rolled up, and every mountain and island was moved out of its place. ¹⁵ And the kings of the earth, the great men, the rich men, the commanders, the mighty men, every slave and every free man, hid themselves in the caves and in the rocks of the mountains, ¹⁶ and said to the mountains and rocks, "Fall on us and hide us from the face of Him who sits on the throne and from the wrath of the Lamb! ¹⁷ For the great day of His wrath has come, and who is able to stand?"*

## Come Out of Her My People: Persecution Begins

In order to interpret these seals and horses and riders correctly, we have to find some common element among them. These seals could represent different states of existence based upon the observation that some have died and are beneath the altar and some are experiencing catastrophic disasters. But most Bible scholars agree that they represent a series of conditions, or events. The Futurist would place these events after the rapture. And others, myself included, have seen these events beginning to unfold after the seven Revelation Churches had been conquered by the Muslims. The assumption that these seals represent segments of time is further enforced by the use of the word "when" at the beginning of each descriptive passage. These seals are the focus of the chapter, "The Outline of the Age," presented later in the fourth edition of *Come Out of Her My People*.

But putting a famous character on the white horse demands that the identities of the other riders also be established. If the rider of the white horse is the Antichrist, then who is the rider of the black horse holding the scales? And what about the fact that some of the seals don't even have horses, much less riders? Putting the Antichrist on the white horse is another example of a fractured analogy; where one member is spiritually interpreted, and the rest are left unidentified. If the rider of the white horse is the only rider with a name, the Lone Ranger may be a more appropriate name for him. Using haphazard and splintered symbolisms is a very poor method of Bible interpretation, to say the least.

The texts examined above in this chapter are not the only glaring deficiencies of Futurism. I would also recommend that the reader look at each occurrence of the phrase "*after these things*," especially as John uses the phrase in the book of Revelation. Chapter Seven of Revelation opens with the words "*After these things*." The wrath of God has just come upon the earth at the end of Chapter Six. Does that mean that the Bible has no more to say about the wrath of God?

Look at what has just taken place before these words are used in Revelation 7:9. The 144,000 have just been sealed. Does that mean that the Jews are not to be found in Revelation "*after these things?*" But the pre-tribulation rapture teachers would tell you that "*after these things*" means the Church as just been raptured at the beginning of Chapter Four. Is this the way for serious Bible scholars to interpret the Scriptures? If God wanted you to know that the Church had been raptured at the beginning of Chapter Four, wouldn't He use *words easy to understand?* Wouldn't the Lord who said, "Let the little children come to Me," speak in plain enough language that a child could understand it?

God *has* spoken plainly. And He has placed the rapture *after* the resurrection of the dead.

# Come Out of Her My People: Persecution Begins

## What About the Jews?

I'm pretty sure that I'm part Jewish. I have a little bit of that complexion, nose and some names on the maternal side of my family that would cause me to believe that I am part Jewish. I love the land of Israel. I am very pro-Israel. I have visited, toured, and taught there. I've been all over the land of Israel, from Mt. Hermon down to the Wilderness of Zin, and all points in between. I just absolutely love the place and its people.

People who teach the pre-tribulation rapture theory use John Nelson Darby's "Dispensationalism" to divide the Bible into verses that deal with the Jews and verses that deal with the church. They would say that you are not really honoring the Jews unless you give them some time at the end, after the church is gone, for God to fulfill His promises to them.

First of all, Paul says, "There is no longer Jew or Greek." Is that true? Paul writes in Ephesians 2 that they have both been reconciled through the cross; and that God has taken the Christians and the Jews and made "one new man" out of the two. Paul also says, *"Not all who call themselves Israel are really Israel, but there is a remnant of Jews who are elected by grace that are the true Israel of God."*

Romans 11:7 says that, *"Israel has not obtained what it seeks, but the elect have obtained it."* So the Jews who believe in Jesus have become part of the church; and the Gentiles who believe in Jesus have been grafted in and have become part of true Israel. Believing Jews and Gentiles have become one new man. I would say, *"What God has joined together, let not man separate."* When you try to separate what God has joined together, you are going to end up with a big mess.

Let's discuss the pre-tribulation rapture plan for the Jews. What is the special time that they say God has reserved for the Jews? It's the most horrendous time that has ever come upon the planet; the seven years that the pre-tribbers expect to be spared from because God would not allow His Church to go through it.

## Come Out of Her My People: Persecution Begins

Here's how the pre-tribulation rapture proponents see God's blessing to Israel. After serving as slaves in Egypt, being taken captive by Assyrians, slaughtered by the Greeks, oppressed and driven out by the Romans, suffering persecution all over the world, going through Hitler's holocaust, and even now, having to fight for their tiny piece of promised land; after all this, that God is going to bless them in the end by subjecting them to the most horrific seven years in the history of the world. That's how God is going to bless His people? What a slap in the face! Is this the time of blessing that God has reserved for His special people?

Then, after this terrible time, that God wouldn't let the church touch with a ten-foot pole, the Church comes back for a thousand years of earthly bliss.

Well how about if the thousand year millennium was the time that God fulfills His promises to the Jews? Wouldn't that make a whole lot more sense than giving them seven years of hell on earth as their big blessing?

When the dispensationalists separate the Jewish people from the Church, the Jews, like usual, end up with the short end of the stick. One of the verses the pre-tribbers use is in Romans Chapter Eleven. It says that when the time of the Gentiles is fulfilled, that Israel will be saved. *Israel* will be delivered; not the church, *the Jews*. But the pre-tribbers teach that when the time of the Gentiles is fulfilled, the Church will be saved; that the Church will be delivered out of tribulation. And the poor Jews will get left behind to get beat up one more time.

If you're going to try and break it out and separate it, here's the way that fits a whole lot better. What if the time of the Gentiles includes everything up until the Millennium; and then all Israel is saved? Going through the tribulation is not my idea of being saved. How could it possibly honor the Jews to say that the Church would be rescued; while the Jews get left behind to go through the tribulation? This type of thinking is nothing less than bigotry. But they say, "If you're not pre-trib, then you're trying to keep God's promises to the Jews from being fulfilled." I believe in God's promises; and that they will be fulfilled. It's the pre-tribbers dispensational matrix that I have a problem with. So stop already with trying to do the Jews a favor by giving them the tribulation! They don't want it any more than the church does!

# The Last Enemy of Christ
# Paul's Chronology of Christ's Return

[Original Published in 2011 by C.W. Stienle]

*"Repent therefore and be converted, that your sins may be blotted out, so that times of refreshing may come from the presence of the Lord, and that He may send Jesus Christ, who was preached to you before, whom heaven must receive until the times of restoration of all things, which God has spoken by the mouth of all His holy prophets since the world began."-Acts 3:19-21*

According to Peter's words above, Jesus has been received into heaven *"until the times of restoration of all things."* *"Until"* indicates that there is a definite period of time assigned to Christ's station in heaven. There will come a time when Jesus will arise from the Father's right hand and descend, just as he ascended. The event that will trigger Christ's return is given as *"the times of restoration of all things."*

Paul makes this same observation by quoting the first verse of Psalm 110. *"The Lord said to my Lord, 'Sit at My right hand, till I make Your enemies Your footstool.'"* Once all of Christ's enemies have been made His footstool, Christ will be released for His second coming. The logical conclusion is that the time of restoration and the time when Jesus' enemies have been subdued are either one and the same event, or very closely related.

The fact that Christ's attendance at the right hand of the Father has a finite duration, and a condition upon which his retention in heaven depends, has caused me to examine this subject in greater detail. The results of my studies are documented in this booklet.

This time is also a period which God has predicted *"by the mouth of all His holy prophets since the world began."* Could Revelation 10:5-7 be referring to this same future event?

- *"The angel whom I saw standing on the sea and on the land raised up his hand to heaven and swore by Him who lives forever and ever, who created heaven and the things that are in it, the earth and the things that are in it, and the sea and the things that are in it, that there should be delay no longer, but in the days of the* *sounding of the seventh angel, when he is about to sound, the mystery of God would be finished, <u>as He declared to His servants the prophets</u>."* emphasis added

*The Last Enemy of Christ* is included in this edition of *Come Out of Her My People* as an aid in understanding the underlying basis for Paul's statements in the Thessalonian letters.

## Introduction to The Last Enemy of Christ

The best introduction to this booklet is *The Last Enemy of Christ* video: http://youtu.be/lY9enX0knwM By his own estimation, Paul was a Pharisee of Pharisees. The Pharisees were experts both in the law and in the spiritual aspects of theology. God had also gifted Paul with the ability to understand the mysteries of the Spirit, and the ability to correctly interpret Old Testament prophecies. So when the churches were uncertain about end-time events, Paul was able to address their concerns by recounting the precise sequence in which the End would unfold.

These end-time references found in Paul's Epistles appear to have been based on a technical understanding which Paul consistently applied as he rehearsed various end-times events. Furthermore, certain Old Testament verses appear to form a framework from which Paul's technical knowledge of eschatology was derived.

The aim of this booklet is to identify these underlying scriptures, and to suggest a hypothetical framework capable of supporting the specific statements which Paul includes in his epistles. The opening chapters of this booklet will review verses containing possible foundations for Paul's understanding of the End. After discussing potentially key components, the Letters to the Thessalonians will be used to test the validity of our findings.

The Twelfth Chapter of Daniel yields most of the facts necessary to build a suitable framework. Many of the other premises are found in First Corinthians Fifteen. After a brief discussion on *The Resurrection of the Dead*, the key concepts used to create the framework will be established as Daniel Twelve and the Corinthians excerpt are expounded in a commentary fashion.

May the reader be open-minded as various events and their timing are suggested, knowing that there will be a reward for such patience when the proposed framework is put to the test in the latter chapters of this booklet.

# Chapter One - The Resurrection of the Dead

*"But perceiving that one group were Sadducees and the other Pharisees, Paul began crying out in the Council, "Brethren, I am a Pharisee, a son of Pharisees; I am on trial for the hope and resurrection of the dead!" As he said this, there occurred a dissension between the Pharisees and Sadducees, and the assembly was divided. For the Sadducees say that there is no resurrection, nor an angel, nor a spirit, but the Pharisees acknowledge them all."-Acts 23:6-8*

On more than one occasion Paul defended himself against the accusations of the Jewish authorities by stating his hope in the resurrection of the dead. Obviously, these Jewish leaders were not engaged in a debate concerning the resurrection of Jesus since both groups denied the claims of Christ. Nevertheless, both parties were passionately divided over a different resurrection - the *resurrection of the dead*.

The *resurrection of the dead* is clearly predicted in the books of the Prophets. The Pharisees embraced the prophetic books; whereas the Sadducees clung to the writings of Moses (which Jesus demonstrated also contain references to eternal life.)

This resurrection at the end of the age represents the culmination of all other prophecies concerning the age of man. Thus, Paul often referred to the resurrection of the dead as the object of the Pharisee's hope.

*"But this I admit to you, that according to the Way which they call a sect I do serve the God of our fathers, believing everything that is in accordance with the Law and that is written in the Prophets; having a hope in God, which these men cherish themselves, that there shall certainly be a resurrection of both the righteous and the wicked."-Acts 24:14,15*

## Chapter Two - The Delineation of Daniel

Paul's eschatological time line appears to be based primarily on Daniel Chapter Twelve. Each verse in the chapter is expounded upon briefly below, even though not every verse is essential to the establishment of Paul's chronology. The reader may be familiar with other valid interpretations, but please be patient to see how these assumptions come together to support the upcoming conclusions.

### *Daniel 12 (NASV)*

*"Now at that time Michael, the great prince who stands guard over the sons of your people, will arise. And there will be a time of distress such as never occurred since there was a nation until that time; and at that time your people, everyone who is found written in the book, will be rescued. Many of those who sleep in the dust of the ground will awake, these to everlasting life, but the others to disgrace and everlasting contempt. Those who have insight will shine brightly like the brightness of the expanse of heaven, and those who lead the many to righteousness, like the stars forever and ever. But as for you, Daniel, conceal these words and seal up the book until the end of time; many will go back and forth, and knowledge will increase."*

*Then I, Daniel, looked and behold, two others were standing, one on this bank of the river and the other on that bank of the river. And one said to the man dressed in linen, who was above the waters of the river, "How long will it be until the end of these wonders?" I heard the man dressed in linen, who was above the waters of the river, as he raised his right hand and his left toward heaven, and swore by Him who lives forever that it would be for a time, times, and half a time; and as soon as they finish shattering the power of the holy people, all these events will be completed. As for me, I heard but could not understand; so I said, "My lord, what will be the outcome of these events?" He said, "Go your way, Daniel, for these words are concealed and sealed up until the end time. Many will be purged, purified and refined, but the wicked will act wickedly; and none of the wicked will understand, but those who have insight will understand. From the time that the regular sacrifice is abolished and the abomination of desolation is set up, there will be 1,290 days. How blessed is he who keeps waiting and attains to the 1,335 days! But as for you, go your way to the end; then you will enter into rest and rise again for your allotted portion at the end of the age."*

## Come Out of Her My People: Persecution Begins

*[1]Now at that time Michael, the great prince who stands guard over the sons of your people, will arise and there will be a time of distress such as never occurred since there was a nation until that time;*

Looking to scripture as the best interpreter of scripture, the following verses from Daniel Chapter Ten, and one verse from Revelation, give insight into this mystery of the spiritual realm. Daniel is told by Gabriel that the heavenly force which tipped the balance toward victory over Satan was Michael the Archangel.

*"But the prince of the kingdom of Persia withstood me twenty-one days; and behold, Michael, one of the chief princes, came to help me, for I had been left alone there with the kings of Persia." - Daniel 10:13*

*"No one upholds me against these, except Michael your prince." - Daniel 10:21b*

The following section from Revelation shows how Michael *"arising"* will bring about the *"time of distress"*:

*"And war broke out in heaven: Michael and his angels fought with the dragon; and the dragon and his angels fought, but they did not prevail, nor was a place found for them in heaven any longer. So the great dragon was cast out, that serpent of old, called the Devil and Satan, who deceives the whole world; he was cast to the earth, and his angels were cast out with him. Then I heard a loud voice saying in heaven, "Now salvation, and strength, and the kingdom of our God, and the power of His Christ have come, for the accuser of our brethren, who accused them before our God day and night, has been cast down. And they overcame him by the blood of the Lamb and by the word of their testimony, and they did not love their lives to the death. Therefore rejoice, O heavens, and you who dwell in them! Woe to the inhabitants of the earth and the sea! For the devil has come down to you, having great wrath, because he knows that he has a short time." - Revelation 12:7-12*

### and at that time

Verse One of Daniel Twelve began with *"Now at that time."* Daniel reiterates, *"and at that time"* - still at this same time of the end - the next three events will occur: the deliverance of those written in the book, the resurrection to judgment, and the reward of the insightful and the pastoral. These events are not necessarily given in their chronological order; rather, they are said to be included in the same future period of time.

*your people, everyone who is found written in the book, will be rescued.*

Peter gave assurance that *"the Lord knows how to rescue the godly from temptation, and to keep the unrighteous under punishment for the day of judgment."-2nd Peter 2:9*

Many have added words to the Book of Revelation by inserting their opinions where the scriptures are silent. There are, however, two clearly stated passages in Revelation which actually describe the rescue of the godly. The first is Revelation Chapter Nine, at the sounding of the fifth trumpet.

*"Then out of the smoke came locusts upon the earth, and power was given them, as the scorpions of the earth have power. They were told not to hurt the grass of the earth, nor any green thing, nor any tree, but only the men who do not have the seal of God on their foreheads."-Revelation 9:3,4*

But the phrase from Revelation with the most similar language to Daniel's prophecy is found in Revelation Chapter Twenty in what is known as "The Great White Throne Judgment."

*"Then I saw a great white throne and Him who sat upon it, from whose presence earth and heaven fled away, and no place was found for them. And I saw the dead, the great and the small, standing before the throne, and books were opened; and another book was opened, which is the book of life; and the dead were judged from the things which were written in the books, according to their deeds. And the sea gave up the dead which were in it, and death and Hades gave up the dead which were in them; and they were judged, every one of them according to their deeds. Then death and Hades were thrown into the lake of fire. This is the second death, the lake of fire. And if anyone's name was not found written in the book of life, he was thrown into the lake of fire."-Revelation 20:11-15*

**2 Many of those who sleep in the dust of the ground will awake, these to everlasting life, but the others to disgrace and everlasting contempt.**

Daniel 12:2 is a clear declaration of the *resurrection of the dead*. And these people who are raised will be immediately divided into two groups. Both groups will enter an everlasting estate; one to life, and the other to disgrace and contempt. The New Testament passages restating this coming judgment are too numerous to quote in this brief treatise. A

## Come Out of Her My People: Persecution Begins

representative listing would include: many of Jesus' parables, His Olivet-Discourse-discussion of the goats and sheep, numerous examples from the Epistles, the grape harvest of Revelation Fourteen, and the white throne judgment above.

***3 Those who have insight will shine brightly like the brightness of the expanse of heaven, and those who lead the many to righteousness, like the stars forever and ever.***

Verse Three appears to be the foundation for Paul's Bema Seat Judgment of the Just. Here is a reward for two virtuous activities. The first, for those who have *insight*; who understand and know God's truths, who have vision beyond the superficial, who have grasped the mysteries of God as Paul did, and who have diligently sought after God.

The second righteous behavior that will find special reward is that of evangelism, instructing, discipling, and counseling. This is the others-oriented response to the personal pursuit of God, previously referred to as *insight*. This is putting shoes to the feet of the Gospel message. . . the fulfillment of the Great Commission.

When Paul states in Romans 14 and 2$^{nd}$ Corinthians 5, *"We will all"* stand at Christ's bema (place of judgment); he is speaking to the audience of the Church. "We" are the justified believers in Christ. This Bema is a separate judgment for those who have passed into life by virtue of their names being found in the Lamb's book of life. *"Truly, truly, I say to you, he who hears My word, and believes Him who sent Me, has eternal life, and does not come into judgment, but has passed out of death into life."-John 5:24* Jesus is saying that the believer has already passed into life - that first everlasting state; as opposed to the second estate of disgrace and contempt *(Daniel 12:2 above)*.

***4 But as for you, Daniel, conceal these words and seal up the book until the end of time; many will go back and forth,***

Daniel is told that these prophetic words will not be fulfilled until the time of the end. By telling Daniel *"many will go back and forth,"* the messenger is likely conveying the length of time by which the end would be delayed.

Daniel knew from Jeremiah's prophecy that the Jews would not return to the Holy Land until a 70 year term of captivity had been completed. At that time many would *"go back"* to Israel. But Daniel was being instructed that the end would be postponed beyond that first *aliyah* (Heb. *return to Israel*). *Going back and forth* may have been a prophecy of further Diasporas. A second exile occurred when the Jews were exiled by the Romans at the beginning of the second century. As a result of the Zionist Movement and the sympathies drawn by the Holocaust of World War II, the Jews have once again *gone back* to the Promised Land.

### *and knowledge will increase.*

Through further prophecy, including the prophecies of Paul, a more precise knowledge of these end-time events would be given in God's own good time. Even in the last book of the Bible, the phrase *"let the reader understand"* is given to accommodate the ever-increasing knowledge of the End which God continues to impart to mankind.

***5 Then I, Daniel, looked and behold, two others were standing, one on this bank of the river and the other on that bank of the river. 6 And one said to the man dressed in linen, who was above the waters of the river, "How long will it be until the end of these wonders?"***

Initially, Daniel is not given the knowledge of when these events will begin. Instead he is told when they will end.

***7 I heard the man dressed in linen, who was above the waters of the river, as he raised his right hand and his left toward heaven, and swore by Him who lives forever that it would be for a time, times, and half a time;***

Once again, Daniel is not told when these things will happen, but now he is informed of their duration - how long it *"would be."* Now the duration of these end-time events is stated as three and one-half times. This span of time continued to be honored by the earliest Church Fathers. Irenaeus, a second generation bishop in the line of St. John, mentions this three-and-one-half times period in his writings.

## Come Out of Her My People: Persecution Begins

*"But when this Antichrist shall have devastated all things in this world, he will reign for three years and six months, and sit in the temple at Jerusalem; and then the Lord will come from heaven in the clouds, in the glory of the Father, sending this man and those who follow him into the lake of fire; but bringing in for the righteous the times of the kingdom, that is, the rest, the hallowed seventh day; and restoring to Abraham the promised inheritance, in which kingdom the Lord declared, that "many coming from the east and from the west should sit down with Abraham, Isaac, and Jacob." (Against Heresies, book V, Chapter 30, Section 4)*

**and as soon as they finish shattering the power of the holy people, all these events will be completed.**

Here is given the condition under which all these events will transpire. Jesus asked the haunting question, *"Nevertheless, when the Son of Man comes, will He really find faith on the earth?"* Sadly, these words from Daniel would indicate that the "falling away" must take place before these end times events can be fulfilled.

**⁸ As for me, I heard but could not understand; so I said, "My lord, what will be the outcome of these events?" ⁹ He said, "Go your way, Daniel, for these words are concealed and sealed up until the end time. ¹⁰ Many will be purged, purified and refined, but the wicked will act wickedly; and none of the wicked will understand, but those who have insight will understand. ¹¹ From the time that the regular sacrifice is abolished and the abomination of desolation is set up, there will be 1,290 days.**

Daniel was left yearning for more information. Because knowledge of these events had not yet increased, he did not have available the body of further information that has been added for us since his death. A recap of the duration of the end-times is given, and one last piece of the puzzle is imparted to honor this man beloved by God. Daniel is told that an abominable object would be set up in the Temple, similar to the abominations of Manasseh; which even though repented of later, brought about the desolation - the very captivity that had swept Daniel from his homeland.

# The Last Enemy of Christ

*12 How blessed is he who keeps waiting and attains to the 1,335 days!*

This waiting period of 45 days remains a mystery.

*13 But as for you, go your way to the end; then you will enter into rest and rise again for your allotted portion at the end of the age.*

Daniel is assured of his participation in the *resurrection of the dead*. This is the final feature of this prophecy of the End. Could this be one of the reasons why Paul was so insistent that *"the last enemy to be overcome is death?"*

## Chapter Three - The Last Enemy

Chapter Fifteen of Paul's First Epistle to the Corinthians contains the Bible's lengthiest discussion of Christ's resurrection. But this chapter is not limited to the subject of Christ's resurrection. Paul skillfully transitions into a rare look at his technical understanding of the *resurrection of the dead*. As in the study of Daniel Chapter Twelve, the scriptural selection is quoted in full, and then dissected verse-by-verse below.

### 1ˢᵗ *Corinthians 15:20-28 (NASV)*

*"But now Christ has been raised from the dead, the first fruits of those who are asleep. For since by a man came death, by a man also came the resurrection of the dead. For as in Adam all die, so also in Christ all will be made alive. But each in his own order: Christ the first fruits, after that those who are Christ's at His coming, then comes the end, when He hands over the kingdom to the God and Father, when He has abolished all rule and all authority and power. For He must reign until He has put all His enemies under His feet. The last enemy that will be abolished is death. For He has put all things in subjection under His feet. But when He says, "All things are put in subjection," it is evident that He is excepted who put all things in subjection to Him. When all things are subjected to Him, then the Son Himself also will be subjected to the One who subjected all things to Him, so that God may be all in all."*

**²⁰ But now Christ has been raised from the dead, the first fruits of those who are asleep.**

Paul begins his change of focus from Jesus' resurrection to the *resurrection of the dead* by making a distinction between the two. This is necessary from a technical standpoint in order to prove that Christ's resurrection did not fully satisfy what Paul is about to designate - *"the last enemy"* - death. Even though Christ has risen, the last enemy (death) has still not been defeated with regard to *"those who are asleep."* Thus, the need from Paul's Pharisaical sense of precision to make the distinction that this last enemy remained undefeated even after Christ's resurrection. Verses 20 through 23 are devoted to meticulously segregating these two resurrections. The distinction is initially made by calling Christ's resurrection the *"first fruits"* and classifying it separately from the resurrection of the rest of the dead - *"those who are asleep."*

**21** *For since by a man came death, by a man also came the resurrection of the dead.*

Paul points out that Christ has been given the power and honor of being the initiator of the *resurrection of the dead*. Jesus said, *"Because I live, you shall live also."* Jesus also declared in John Chapter Five; *"Most assuredly, I say to you, the hour is coming, and now is, when the dead will hear the voice of the Son of God; and those who hear will live. For as the Father has life in Himself, so He has granted the Son to have life in Himself and has given Him authority to execute judgment also, because He is the Son of Man. Do not marvel at this; for the hour is coming in which all who are in the graves will hear His voice and come forth—those who have done good, to the resurrection of life, and those who have done evil, to the resurrection of condemnation."-John 5:25-29*

**22** *For as in Adam all die, so also in Christ all will be made alive.*

The development of Paul's thought on this subject is found in Romans 5:23-29. *"Therefore, just as through one man sin entered the world, and death through sin, and thus death spread to all men, because all sinned— (For until the law sin was in the world, but sin is not imputed when there is no law. Nevertheless death reigned from Adam to Moses, even over those who had not sinned according to the likeness of the transgression of Adam, who is a type of Him who was to come. But the free gift is not like the offense. For if by the one man's offense many died, much more the grace of God and the gift by the grace of the one Man, Jesus Christ, abounded to many. And the gift is not like that which came through the one who sinned. For the judgment which came from one offense resulted in condemnation, but the free gift which came from many offenses resulted in justification. For if by the one man's offense death reigned through the one, much more those who receive abundance of grace and of the gift of righteousness will reign in life through the One, Jesus Christ.) Therefore, as through one man's offense judgment came to all men, resulting in condemnation, even so through one Man's righteous act the free gift came to all men, resulting in justification of life. For as by one man's disobedience many were made sinners, so also by one Man's obedience many will be made righteous."*

**23** *But each in his own order: Christ the first fruits, after that those who are Christ's at His coming,*

Paul adds further distinction by placing these two resurrections in sequence; "first" - and then "after." Notice Paul's use of the term *"first fruits"* rather than referring to the "first resurrection" and "second resurrection." Paul is careful not to call Christ's resurrection the first resurrection because, technically, the first resurrection *is* the *resurrection of the dead.* The second resurrection is inferred by Revelation 20:5 as a final judgment which will come after Christ's millennial reign.

**²⁴ *then comes the end, when He hands over the kingdom to the God and Father, when He has abolished all rule and all authority and power.***

Jesus' reign at the Father's right hand in heaven has a duration; it is not indefinite. There will come a Day when Christ will arise and return to the earth to physically reign over the kingdoms of the earth (albeit in His glorified body). *"This Jesus, who has been taken up from you into heaven, will come in just the same way as you have watched Him go into heaven."-Acts 2:11b* Twice in Revelation we hear similar declarations:

*"We give You thanks, O Lord God, the Almighty, who are and who were, because You have taken Your great power and have begun to reign."-Revelation 11:17*

*"Now the salvation, and the power, and the kingdom of our God and the authority of His Christ have come."-Revelation 12:10*

**²⁵ *For He must reign until He has put all His enemies under His feet.***

Jesus' reign at the Father's right hand has a condition. He must reign from heaven *"until..."* Something must be accomplished before Jesus' reign in heaven is brought to its completion - Christ's enemies must be subdued.

Paul is referring here to the first verse of Psalm 110. *"The LORD said to my Lord, "Sit at My right hand, till I make Your enemies Your footstool."* Paul couples the aspects of the duration and condition of Christ's heavenly reign with the following statement about Christ's last enemy.

**²⁶ *The last enemy that will be abolished is death.***

This determination, that death will be Christ's last enemy, is a kingpin in Paul's chronological framework. There are, however, no scriptural references which directly state the fact of death's subordination to all other enemies. There are several verses that do express the fact that death will be permanently eradicated.

*"He will swallow up death forever, and the Lord GOD will wipe away tears from all faces; the rebuke of His people He will take away from all the earth; for the LORD has spoken."-Isaiah 25:8*

*"I will ransom them from the power of the grave; I will redeem them from death. O Death, I will be your plagues! O Grave, I will be your destruction! Pity is hidden from My eyes."-Hosea 13:14*

The death which Paul is referring to here is that state of death which is holding the dead in their graves. The *resurrection of the dead* will be accomplished when the power of death is defeated. Jesus will have mastered death when, at his command, the dead hear His voice and rise to life. At this time the enemy of death will become the footstool of Christ. After the millennial reign, when every soul is emptied from Hades, Hades will have no more purpose. At that time death will no longer occur. But Christ's technical victory over death will have already been won at the *resurrection of the dead*.

**27 For He has put all things in subjection under His feet.**

Jesus declared after His own resurrection, *"All authority has been given to Me in heaven and on earth."-Matthew 28:18*

**But when He says, "All things are put in subjection," it is evident that He is excepted who put all things in subjection to Him. 28 When all things are subjected to Him, then the Son Himself also will be subjected to the One who subjected all things to Him, so that God may be all in all.**

The Son will leave heaven to spend a second season as Christ upon the earth while the Father continues to reign in heaven. To interpret these last verses in a manner that would deem the Son of God to be less than God-the-Son would be contrary to the entire body of doctrine contained in the rest of scripture; and would expressly contradict the truth that *"Jesus is the same yesterday, today, and forever."*

# Come Out of Her My People: Persecution Begins

## Chapter Four - Comforting the Thessalonians

### 1ˢᵗ Thessalonians 4:13-18

*"But we do not want you to be uninformed, brethren, about those who are asleep, so that you will not grieve as do the rest who have no hope. For if we believe that Jesus died and rose again, even so God will bring with Him those who have fallen asleep in Jesus. For this we say to you by the word of the Lord, that we who are alive and remain until the coming of the Lord, will not precede those who have fallen asleep. For the Lord Himself will descend from heaven with a shout, with the voice of the archangel and with the trumpet of God, and the dead in Christ will rise first. Then we who are alive and remain will be caught up together with them in the clouds to meet the Lord in the air, and so we shall always be with the Lord. Therefore comfort one another with these words."*

**¹³ But we do not want you to be uninformed, brethren, about those who are asleep, so that you will not grieve as do the rest who have no hope.**

Paul desires to share more information with the Thessalonians about those believers who had already died. Paul's goal is to restore to them the proper hope - the hope that is reserved for the believer in Christ. Jesus assured His followers: *"This is the will of the Father who sent Me, that of all He has given Me I should lose nothing, but should raise it up at the last day. And this is the will of Him who sent Me, that everyone who sees the Son and believes in Him may have everlasting life; and I will raise him up at the last day."*-John 6:39-30

The Gentiles of Macedonia were not likely to be familiar with the Old Testament scriptures, yet concerning the resurrection of the dead their ignorance placed them in danger of despair over their departed loved ones. Paul is not so concerned here with listing the Biblical references underlying the facts he is about to restate. Instead, he presents a summary based on his own extensive knowledge, trusting that his counsel would be received as truth.

**¹⁴ For if we believe that Jesus died and rose again, even so God will bring with Him those who have fallen asleep in Jesus.**

Jesus said, *"Because I live, you will live also."* Just as God brought Jesus up from the grave, even so God will bring up those believers who have died before Christ's return.

*15 For this we say to you by the word of the Lord, that we who are alive and remain until the coming of the Lord, will not precede those who have fallen asleep. 16 For the Lord Himself will descend from heaven with a shout, with the voice of the archangel and with the trumpet of God, and the dead in Christ will rise first.*

Paul is certain that the resurrection of the dead will occur prior to the gathering of the living to be with the Lord. Paul is drawing on his technical understanding to insist that Christ's victory over death, recognized by the *resurrection of the dead*, must precede Christ's departure from the right hand of the Father.

The presentation of this sequence would have planted a glorious impression in the minds of those who had been preoccupied with remorse. Now they might anticipate seeing their predecessors bursting forth from their graves before all would rise together to meet the Lord. Now they could be certain that a premature death would not prevent the deceased from being eye witnesses of the Lord's glorious return. Now those who had gone before would be on par in every respect with those who were still alive at Christ's second coming.

*17 Then we who are alive and remain will be caught up together with them in the clouds to meet the Lord in the air, and so we shall always be with the Lord.*

*Then* - when Christ's enemies have been made His footstool - the Lord will begin His descent from the Father's side, and the living will rise along with those just released from their tombs.

*18 Therefore comfort one another with these words.*

What a joyous prospect! To know that those who have died prior to Christ's return will not be deprived of any good thing. And not only that, but they will actually be given priority in the day of our Lord's return.

# Chapter Five - Cautioning the Thessalonians

### 2nd Thessalonians 2:1-12

*"Now we request you, brethren, with regard to the coming of our Lord Jesus Christ and our gathering together to Him, that you not be quickly shaken from your composure or be disturbed either by a spirit or a message or a letter as if from us, to the effect that the day of the Lord has come. Let no one in any way deceive you, for it will not come unless the apostasy comes first, and the man of lawlessness is revealed, the son of destruction, who opposes and exalts himself above every so-called god or object of worship, so that he takes his seat in the temple of God, displaying himself as being God. Do you not remember that while I was still with you, I was telling you these things? And you know what restrains him now, so that in his time he will be revealed. For the mystery of lawlessness is already at work; only he who now restrains will do so until he is taken out of the way. Then that lawless one will be revealed whom the Lord will slay with the breath of His mouth and bring to an end by the appearance of His coming; that is, the one whose coming is in accord with the activity of Satan, with all power and signs and false wonders, and with all the deception of wickedness for those who perish, because they did not receive the love of the truth so as to be saved. For this reason God will send upon them a deluding influence so that they will believe what is false, in order that they all may be judged who did not believe the truth, but took pleasure in wickedness."*

Before beginning this commentary, it is needful to note that the author's focus continues to be on Paul's eschatological framework and not on the various views concerning the rapture, in vogue or out. The commentary will examine the text itself, relying on a literal interpretation.

**¹ Now we request you, brethren, with regard to the coming of our Lord Jesus Christ and our gathering together to Him,**

The text does read, *"the* coming;" not another coming, nor a later second coming. Verse one also addresses *"our gathering,"* not *theirs*. Furthermore, the letter is written to the Church. This particular Church is located in a Roman (Gentile) city of Northern Greece. These observations should reasonably beckon the assumption that Paul is once again discussing the same coming of Christ, and the same gathering in the clouds, that were the subject of the previous chapter.

# Come Out of Her My People: Persecution Begins

If the reader is otherwise inclined - please at least be willing to test the framework one last time.

*² that you not be quickly shaken from your composure or be disturbed either by a spirit or a message or a letter as if from us, to the effect that the day of the Lord has come.*

The commencement of *the day of the Lord* is in question. Could Paul have been mistaken in his previous communications? Had the Lord returned without the anticipated *resurrection of the dead* and the gathering together?

*³ Let no one in any way deceive you, for it will not come unless the apostasy comes first,*

Paul lists the first of two prerequisites to the time of the Lord's return (which is also the time of *the resurrection of the dead*). Recall the last phrase of Daniel 12:7; *"And as soon as they finish shattering the power of the holy people, all these events will be completed."* Daniel will participate in the *resurrection of the dead* and Daniel was told expressly that the holy people would be rendered powerless before he would awaken to receive his reward.

*and the man of lawlessness is revealed, the son of destruction, ⁴ who opposes and exalts himself above every so-called god or object of worship, so that he takes his seat in the temple of God, displaying himself as being God.*

The second stipulation is also supported by Daniel Twelve. The abominable object appears to be the *man of lawlessness* himself.

*Do you not remember that while I was still with you, I was telling you these things?*

It is quite likely that Paul had imparted some of his insights from the book of Daniel while he was still with them. It is possible that Paul also communicated some of the observations he had shared with the Corinthians, which were mentioned in the third chapter of this booklet.

*⁶ And you know what restrains him now, so that in his time he will be revealed.*

What restrains? What situation or predicament? In the original Greek text, the word for *restrains* is *"Kataxon,"* from the Greek word *"echo"* - to hold. Not surprisingly, this word also appears in the book of Daniel. *"No one upholds me against these, except Michael your prince."* (Daniel 10:21b) The Greek Old Testament (Septuagint) of Paul's day read, *"There is no one holding with me. . ."* The root of the Greek word used here is *"echo"* - to hold.

*⁷ For the mystery of lawlessness is already at work; only he who now restrains will do so until he is taken out of the way. ⁸ Then that lawless one will be revealed whom the Lord will slay with the breath of His mouth and bring to an end by the appearance of His coming;*

Here we must entertain the possibility that Michael the Archangel is involved somehow in this restraining. As we studied Daniel Twelve and Revelation we saw how Michael wrestled Satan out of heaven. (*Hold* is still an important wrestling term today.) If it were necessary in Paul's theology for Jesus' victory over His enemies to be accomplished prior to His return, and if Paul, like St. John, understood that Satan's fall would result in the earthly manifestation of the son of perdition; then it would be logical to expect the appearance of this man of sin before Christ's return. And this is exactly what Paul has stipulated.

It would appear that the son of perdition could not fully be revealed (although the mystery of lawlessness had already commenced) until Satan, Michael's angelic nemesis, was thrown down from heaven. This evil one will not be fully manifested on earth until he is fully ejected from heaven.

In Paul's chronology, the last of Jesus' enemies (death) would be overcome as the dead were raised at His coming. Since death is the last enemy to be overcome before Christ returns, the next-to-the-last enemy (that is Satan) would need to be overcome prior to this last enemy. This places Satan's ejection from heaven (and the simultaneous revelation of the lawless one) just before the dead are raised. And so

## Come Out of Her My People: Persecution Begins

Paul states, *"For it will not come unless the apostasy comes first, and the man of lawlessness is revealed."*

*[9] that is, the one whose coming is in accord with the activity of Satan, with all power and signs and false wonders, [10] and with all the deception of wickedness for those who perish, because they did not receive the love of the truth so as to be saved. [11] For this reason God will send upon them a deluding influence so that they will believe what is false, [12] in order that they all may be judged who did not believe the truth, but took pleasure in wickedness.*

The Protestant Reformers died torturous deaths because of their conviction that the pope was the man of perdition. They had their reasons to believe they were right. Today the earthshaking signs of the *"beginning of sorrows,"* the rise of Satanism, and the humanists' rejection of truth, altogether point to the time of the end. Surely the Lord will come for us soon.

# St. Paul's Chronology of Christ's Return

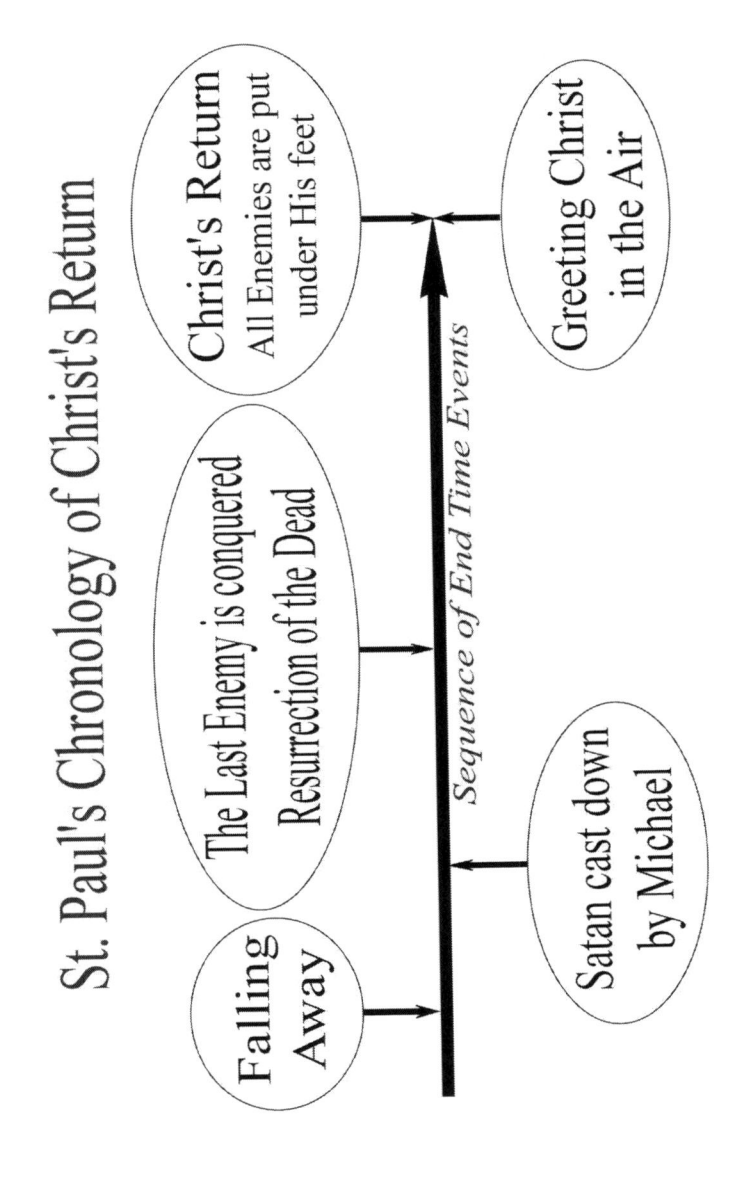

- **Christ's Return** — All Enemies are put under His feet
- **Greeting Christ in the Air**
- **The Last Enemy is conquered** — Resurrection of the Dead
- **Satan cast down by Michael**
- **Falling Away**

*Sequence of End Time Events*

# Chapter Six - Honoring Christ's Heavenly Reign

### Stephen's vision

As Stephen was being stoned by the Christ rejecting Jews, he was given a vision of Jesus. *"But being full of the Holy Spirit, he gazed intently into heaven and saw the glory of God, and Jesus standing at the right hand of God; and he said, "Behold, I see the heavens opened up and the Son of Man standing at the right hand of God."-Acts 7:55-56* This vision was not a hallucination, but a precious glimpse of Christ's true position in glory.

As Christians seek the face of God, may they look beyond Calvary's offering and consider the risen Lord at the right hand of power. *"Looking unto Jesus, the author and finisher of our faith, who for the joy that was set before Him endured the cross, despising the shame, <u>and has sat down at the right hand of the throne of God</u>."-Hebrews 12:2 (emphasis added)*

Jesus told the unbelieving Jews that they "did not know where Jesus was from or where He was going." But Jesus told His disciples, *"I came forth from the Father and have come into the world. Again, I leave the world and go to the Father."-John 16:28* This understanding, that Jesus is at the right hand of power, is an empowering concept. The flowing river of the Spirit, Who anoints us with power, proceeds from above. Comprehending where we are to direct our prayers gives clarity and focus to our spiritual vision.

Our key verse from Psalm 110 is presented below - followed by our marching orders while Christ remains at the Father's right hand.

### *Psalm 110:1*

[1] *"The LORD says to my Lord:*
*"Sit at My right hand*
*Until I make Your enemies a footstool for Your feet."*
[2] *The LORD will stretch forth Your strong scepter from Zion, saying,*
*"Rule in the midst of Your enemies."*
[3] *Your people will volunteer freely in the day of Your power;*
*In holy array, from the womb of the dawn,*

# The Last Enemy of Christ

*Your youth are to You as the dew."*

In verse one we see that it is God Who is making Christ's enemies His footstool. Verse two states that God's power would proceed from Zion. This is precisely why the disciples were instructed to wait in Jerusalem for the promise of the Father. In fact, the disciples were in an upper room located on David's hill - known as Mount Zion - when the power of God was poured out in the Person of the Holy Spirit. The indwelling Spirit is ruling in the midst of God's people today, while we wait for Jesus to take up his throne upon the earth.

Verse three tells us that we are in the Lord's Army. But what kind of volunteers should we be?
We are supposed be actively involved in Christ's victory over His enemies. There are too many Christians who are bunkered down crying "Get me out of here!" Their itching ears long for teachers who will encourage them in their inactivity. Listen to Jesus warning in Luke 12:42-48:

*"And the Lord said, 'Who then is that faithful and wise steward, whom his master will make ruler over his household, to give them their portion of food in due season? Blessed is that servant whom his master will find so doing when he comes. Truly, I say to you that he will make him ruler over all that he has. But if that servant says in his heart, 'My master is delaying his coming,' and begins to beat the male and female servants, and to eat and drink and be drunk, the master of that servant will come on a day when he is not looking for him, and at an hour when he is not aware, and will cut him in two and appoint him his portion with the unbelievers. And that servant who knew his master's will, and did not prepare himself or do according to his will, shall be beaten with many stripes. But he who did not know, yet committed things deserving of stripes, shall be beaten with few. For everyone to whom much is given, from him much will be required; and to whom much has been committed, of him they will ask the more."*

Jesus said it was to our advantage that He went away and sent the Holy Spirit to be the power of God in our midst. Brothers and Sisters, let us take a more active and serious role in our service to Christ during His stay in heaven. He will not be there indefinitely. May God use you and me, as we are filled with the Holy Spirit, to help make His enemies His footstool.

He is coming soon!

# Come Out of Her My People: Persecution Begins

# Come Out of Her My People: Fourth Edition
# Preface

Before Jesus returns, a great city will rule over the kings of the earth. She will live in luxury and be a world trading center. Motivated by hatred, all other nations will form an alliance bent on destroying the Great Harlot.

*"And I heard another voice from heaven saying. 'Come out of her, My people lest you share in her sins, and lest you receive of her plagues.'"-Revelation 18:4*

When the dreadful day of September 11, 2001 came, I was dropping one of our children off at school. I had only driven a few blocks on my way back to the house when the Christian radio station I was listening to broke away from its musical format to make a special announcement. Now due to the fact that Phoenix, Arizona, is protected from hurricanes, tornadoes and major earthquakes, our announcements are not often truly "special." But this time, I could tell by the announcer's voice that he was genuinely troubled about something concerning the World Trade Center Towers. Then one of those overly unemotional statesmen read a scripted news report; he said a plane had run into one of the Twin Towers. I began to picture a little single-engine private plane bouncing off of the side of a concrete and steel building and then tumbling onto the streets below. My brief fantasy was interrupted by a discussion between several network broadcasters talking about the commercial airliner, and speculating over the number of passengers potentially onboard. While trying to adjust the scale of my previous misconception, I caught the announcer commenting that the crash may not have been an accident. Although I rarely watch television, I began racing home to turn on the morning news.

Arriving at the house, I turned on the television and called Gwen, my wife, to come downstairs. I gave her a summary of the news I had heard on the radio, and we watched the live action on the television together. Bystanders were describing the size and type of the commercial jet which had pierced the first tower. The news desk team interrupted the audio portion of the broadcast to report that another low flying airliner was barreling toward the downtown vicinity; a district eminently to be designated, "Ground Zero." As the news cameras were panning the hole in the first tower, gushing black smoke rolled upward from the upper stories like an upside down waterfall. The second plane sprang from behind a building on the right of our screen. A moment later, it ripped into the second tower like it was made of paper and popsicle-sticks. We gazed; expecting the airliner, or at least its fuselage, to emerge from the other side of the building. But the ignoble engineers had planned the speed of these vessels with deadly precision. Their steel-melting incendiary was injected into the vulnerable centers of the doomed buildings. My wife and I watched with heartbreaking horror as the first tower's top began to give way. Each of the highest floors collapsed and paused. I thought the remaining floors might hold fast. It was like watching in slow motion, as the building began imploding. The floors started giving way with ever increasing speed, until the lower stories just disintegrated under the weight and velocity of the free falling top of the Tower. We never considered that the second tower could copy this crushing cascade of concrete and smoke. Within minutes, both of these landmarks had fallen, and thousands of innocent lives were cut short.

At that moment, Revelation Chapters 17 and 18 came to mind, and the phrase *"is fallen, is fallen"* echoed in my head. I ran upstairs to get my Bible and came back down to find more of our family standing in front of the television. Turning in my Bible to these verses, I read aloud:

*"The kings of the earth who committed fornication and lived luxuriously with her will weep and lament for her, when they see the smoke of her burning, standing at a distance for fear of her torment, saying, 'Alas, alas, that great city Babylon, that mighty city! For in one hour your judgment has come.' And the merchants of the earth will weep and mourn over her, for no one buys their merchandise anymore."-Revelation 18:9-11*

*"For in one hour such great riches came to nothing.' Every shipmaster, all who travel by ship, sailors, and as many as trade on the sea, stood at a distance and cried out when they saw the smoke of her burning, saying, 'What is like this great city?'"-Revelation 18:17-18*

I felt that these verses were being fulfilled before our eyes. Over the next months, I was compelled to take up a regular study of the Book of Revelation. One morning the command, *"Come out of her, my people, lest you share in her sins, and lest you receive of her plagues"-Revelation 18:4*, jumped off the page, as if God were speaking to me personally. I realized that to the extent that I was convinced of the identity of Babylon the Great, I was also responsible for obedience to God's command to *"Come out."*

God gave me a strong confirmation that I should pursue the writing of this book. My wife and I were making a connecting flight at Chicago O'Hare when a young man asked us if we were Christians. We had just prayed over our meal and he was sitting at the table beside ours. We affirmed our faith and he proceeded to share that he was on his way to Israel to study Hebrew. I felt inclined to offer my thoughts on Revelation. After I had gotten into the meat of my opinion, he interrupted and said it sounded like I had been reading *"Let My People Go"* by Tom Hess. He was amazed when I told him that I was unfamiliar with that work. I was encouraged by the way God had arranged this "random" meeting. And it turned out that Hess had addressed the Jews need to *"Come out"* in the same way that God was compelling me to warn Christians. I have reviewed the Book of Revelation several hundred times during these intervening years; and I am pleased to share my observations so the reader might decide how to respond to this command.

Several years have now passed since the first printing of this book. I have continued my research on the subjects covered herein; both in my regular reading through the Word, and other readings and travels. My wife and I made another trip to the Holy Land, as well as our third Footsteps of Paul tour. Last summer we spent a week in Egypt and then traveled along the way of the Exodus, though Jordan and up to Mount Nebo, where Moses overlooked the Promised Land. On our last tour of Israel I was privileged to teach from the South steps of the Temple, and at the top of the Tel at Megiddo overlooking Armageddon (the hills of the Valley of Megiddo, and site of the End Times "War to end all wars."

I have also had time to study the history of the interpretation of the book of Revelation. I was surprised to learn that several hundred full-length commentaries on Revelation had been written by the end of the Second Century. Few of these are intact, but references to those commentaries, found in other ancient documents, shed light on the Early Churches' understanding of John's prophecies. Some of those commentators were known to have conversed with St. John's personal friends. I highly recommend Steve Gregg's work on the four views of Revelation. See for yourself how others have interpreted the last book of the Bible.

This Fourth Edition differs from the previous editions by making a distinction between Daniel's week of the covenant and the last 19 chapters of Revelation. Further research has led to the conclusion that Revelation was sealed during the 16th Century, contrary to the angel's instruction; *"Do not seal the words of the prophecy of this book, for the time is at hand."* How then can the intricate details of Futurism stand upon such a plainly forbidden premise?

*This book is dedicated to my blessed Savior, the Lord Jesus Christ, and my wife, Gwendolyn, who is the perfect helpmeet given to me by the grace of God.*

*Jeremiah, the prophet, dearly loved Israel, as he warned God's people that they would be scattered. Like Jeremiah, I also love and pray for my country, the United States of America. I pray that God's grace and mercy would continue to guide and protect her. And I pray for a revival among Jesus' people, resulting in the conversion of the majority of our citizens to saving faith in our Lord and Savior, Jesus Christ.*

## Introduction to Fourth Edition

The original disciples of Jesus expected His return at any moment and referred to their era as "the last days." When James, the brother of Jesus, wrote his letter to the first generation church, he said; *"You also be patient. Establish your hearts, for the coming of the Lord is at hand."-James 5:8* It is evident, from the frequent inclusion of such verses in the New Testament, that God intends for every generation to be expectant of Christ's return. It is consistent with God's Word for every generation to live in the presence of wars, and rumors of war, and other conditions prophesied in the Old and New Testaments that would cause them to genuinely expect the end.

Some of the conclusions and interpretation of Scripture in this book, regarding the *"time of the end"-Daniel 12:4*, hereafter referred to as "End Times," will challenge the reader's prior understanding. These challenges, however, do not involve foundational Christian doctrine, such as the doctrine of salvation, or the doctrine of the substitution and vicarious sacrifice of Christ Jesus for our sins. It is the prayer of the author that the reader will develop stronger faith and a greater motivation to follow God's plan, however His plan ultimately unfolds.

When Christ came, treading outside the guidelines established by the religious rulers of His day, those rulers were slow to yield, or completely unyielding. When the reality of Christ's life ran contrary to their preconceived ideas, they concluded that He couldn't be the Messiah. The Jews were expecting a "supernatural" appearance of their King at Christ's first coming. They were looking for the sky to open, and the Lord to appear in all His glory. This is, in fact, the expectation of Christians for Christ's <u>second</u> coming. In the same way, time has allowed a great deal of speculation about the yet unfulfilled prophecies and symbolisms predicted in God's Word. What will it actually "look like?" As time unfolds, the details of reality must supersede man's best drawn assumptions, or else we risk missing the moment, as did the scoffers in Jesus' day. As Jesus said to them, *"You know how to discern the face of the sky, but you cannot discern the signs of the times."-Matthew 16:3*

# Come Out of Her My People: Persecution Begins

The timely and correct interpretation of the command to *"Come out of her, my people"* in Revelation 18:4 becomes more significant as we consider its context. We will see when we study Chapter 18 that this warning comes after an initial attack, but just before the total destruction of the Great Harlot. The spirit of the prophets of our day proclaims, "The time of the end of the age is at hand." The increase of natural disasters and the reestablishment of the nation of Israel substantiate these End Time prophesies. Jesus said in Matthew 24:34, *"Assuredly, I say to you, this generation will by no means pass away till all these things take place."* If the generation that experiences the *"beginnings of sorrows"* spoken of in Matthew 24:8 will live to see the End Times, then it becomes necessary to consider the people and nations of our time to determine if, and how, they are spoken of in the Biblical account of the End Times.

Paul writes in 1st Thessalonians 4 verses 1 through 6; *"But concerning the times and the seasons, brethren, you have no need that I should write to you. For you yourselves know perfectly that the day of the Lord so comes as a thief in the night. For when they say, 'Peace and safety!' Then sudden destruction comes upon them, as labor pains upon a pregnant woman. And they shall not escape. But you, brethren, are not in darkness, so that this Day should overtake you as a thief. You are all sons of light and sons of the day. We are not of the night nor of darkness. 6 Therefore let us not sleep, as others do, but let us watch and be sober."*

First, Paul describes the state of the unbeliever; *"when they say 'peace and safety'. . .sudden destruction.. . .comes as a thief in the night."* They will not see the signs of the times, nor understand that the end is near. On the other hand, the Christian who is walking in the light will see the Day of the Lord's coming just as clearly as he would see someone climbing through his window in broad daylight. The outcomes of that Day will also be contrary for the lost and the saved. The people who have rejected Christ's rescue will experience God's wrath, which has been waiting for Adam's unrepentant children. Those who have made a sincere profession of personal faith in Jesus' sacrifice for their sins will escape and share in Christ's inheritance; new life, a new heaven, and a new earth.

So what sort of signs of the times should those who "walk in the day" be able to see as the Day approaches? Some highly visible characters are identified in John's prophecies. One of these characters is a nation that rules over all the other nations, and is such a mighty world power that the other nations proclaim, *"Who is like the beast? Who is able to make war with him?"-Revelation 13:4* (If the reader is not used to picturing the *"beast"* as a nation, please hold your objection for a few chapters.) At the present time only one nation is strong enough to be the world's policeman. The Great Harlot, and/or Babylon the Great, is also clearly spoken of as the trading capital of the world. Because it would typically take decades, if not centuries, for a nation to establish such a global reputation, we must consider the United States of America in one, or both, of these roles; if indeed, we are living out the final generation. If the reader believes in the popular Futuristic approach to interpreting the book of Revelation, then the global stage must be "pre-set" for an action packed seven-year blitz. (Futurism reserves the events occurring after Chapter Three of Revelation for a period of time yet to come.) But even if one holds the Historical viewpoint concerning End Times prophecy, the historical timeline of Biblical fulfillment also places us near the end of the age. (These views are discussed in the next chapter.)

Another, and perhaps the most significant, similarity between the Great Harlot and the United States is how perfectly she exemplifies *"the Mother of all Harlots."* What is the source of legalized fetal abortion? Where have premarital sex and the homosexual lifestyle been legitimized and promoted? What is the world's source of pornographic images? Not to mention the Biblical definition of spiritual adultery; turning away from the Holy One of Israel. *"The inhabitants of the earth were made drunk with the wine of her fornications."-Revelation 17:2b* Has any nation ever been so successful at spreading her filth throughout the earth? Could a future nation possibly match the breadth and depth of moral depravity that this great country has poured out upon the globe? Hard act to follow! Dare I suggest; impossible. What more could be indulged in? How could a nation be more influential?

So how could the identity of Babylon the Great be relevant to us today? Well, if you're not a believer in salvation by faith in Jesus, then the 'destruction of a part of the planet near you' should be extremely relevant! And if you are a believer, and specifically a believer in the pre-Tribulation rapture of the church, shouldn't you at least be informed enough to warn others? Babylon's importance is also elevated when we learn that the book of Revelation hasn't always been tied to Daniel's *"last week."* Chapters 4-18 weren't equated with

Daniel's seven-year covenant week until Francisco Ribera's theory was published in 1590. His motive: to defend the Pope against the Protestants' assumption that he was the false prophet of Revelation. Ribera effectively sealed the last 19 chapters of Revelation until the time of the end.

But God told John expressly not to seal Revelation; *"And he said to me, 'Do not seal the words of the prophecy of this book, for the time is at hand.'"*-Revelation 22:10 Daniel's "sealed week" is referenced within John's prophecy. What is the conclusion? God has made a distinction between Daniel's week of the covenant and the book of Revelation. One was to be sealed and the other was not to be sealed. They cannot, therefore, be speaking of identical events. Revelation includes Daniel's week but is broadly greater in scope than Daniel's final week.

The reader may also be unaware that the proposal of a pre-second-coming rapture wasn't suggested or taught in any church prior to the 1800's. (See http://www.comeoutofhermypeople.com or the link in Chapter 4 of the e-book.)

Because this book deals primarily with the identity and chronology of Babylon the Great, and because many books have been written about the letters to the Seven Churches, our focus will be on Chapters 6 through 18 of Revelation. This book is not intended to be a complete commentary on the chapters covered. In fact, the author's dilemma was whether to include only those verses germane to Mystery Babylon, or to discuss every verse in true commentary form. It is in respect of St. John's warning and the author's fear of the Lord that each verse is included. *"And if anyone takes away from the words of the book of this prophecy, God shall take away his part from the Book of Life, from the holy city, and from the things which are written in this book."*-Revelation 22:19 So the verses are included even though the commentary is sketchy and "thin" in places where the Spirit hasn't prompted the author to expound. There are many full commentaries of Revelation, and perhaps one of them should be the reader's first study before digesting the focused discussion in this book. The chapters of Revelation before and after those examined in the body of this book are included in the appendix, in obedience to John's warning. Please read the entire Book of Revelation. See the Appendix for Chapters 1-5 and 19-22.

## Chapter 1: Two Millennia of Interpretations

From the writing of Revelation until today, four distinct interpretations of Revelation have been promoted and accepted by the majority of believing Christians. By name, the four ways to understand John's prophetic book are: Preterist, Spiritual, Historical, and Futurist. The charts at the end of this chapter show the life and time in which these views were predominantly held. If you are a Christian, you are most likely totally convinced of the veracity of the interpretation which you have been taught. But please appreciate the fact that although the Church has endured a variety of interpretations, heaven has been increased in every generation by those who have repented and believed in our Lord Jesus Christ. This means that heaven is full of saints who spent all of their time on earth believing something different about Revelation than is popularly held today; and, we will all spend eternity loving one another.

*The Holy Bible makes this promise: "All Scripture is given by inspiration of God, and is profitable for doctrine, for reproof, for correction, for instruction in righteousness."-2nd Timothy 3:16 And, the Word of God is true. "Your word is truth."-John 17:17b*

It is also imperative to realize that words have a specific meaning. A word cannot mean both a specific thing, and the opposite of that same thing. When God isn't speaking in symbolisms and future prophecies, His words have a specific, understandable, and consistent meaning. Most of the Bible is easy to understand simply by accepting the obvious; although the application to the Bible student's own life will vary based on his or her personal situation. Most of the difficult passages become obvious to those who are willing to read all sixty-six books for themselves. The author is determined to communicate to the reader that God has spoken clearly about every area of life.

## Come Out of Her My People: Persecution Begins

St Peter states: *"Grace and peace be multiplied to you in the knowledge of God and of Jesus our Lord, as His divine power has given to us all things that pertain to life and godliness, through the knowledge of Him who called us by glory and virtue, by which have been given to us exceedingly great and precious promises, that through these you may be partakers of the divine nature, having escaped the corruption that is in the world through lust."-2nd Peter 1:2-4*

But the interpretation of future prophecy can be difficult. Several prophetic verses contain the phrase *"let the reader understand."* Other verses indicate that God wanted certain prophecies to be "sealed up" because their application would be for future generations. These prophetic sections of scripture do not have clear meanings, nor are they to be universally understood. A good example is the prophecy found in Psalm 22. The phrases of this chapter must have appeared as a series of random visions to the Jews who recited and preserved them. It speaks of being forsaken by God, gambling over clothing, pierced hands and feet, bones pulled apart, and great thirst. Because these words were inspired, God spoke to his people through them even before the express meaning of the psalm was realized. But a mental picture of what was being described wasn't recognizable in the world around them. Death by crucifixion was not instigated by the Romans until at least five centuries after the twenty-second psalm was written! Only God could have known what His Son would endure to redeem wretched sinners like you and me. Finally, from His cross, Jesus revealed that the psalm was written about His own crucifixion.

In the same way, some End Times prophecies will not be fully understood until the time of their actual fulfillment. But this hasn't stopped fiction writers from setting their own opinions in stone (and on film). Nevertheless, as we look at various interpretations of Revelation, and finally the interpretation that God has given me; I pray that you would read the Bible on your own and attend a Bible teaching church. This is the only way to know for yourself what the Word actually says. Then the very Spirit of God can speak into your heart to tell you whether the nightly news is portraying a fulfillment of prophecy, or just another crazy day.

As previously mentioned, the four basic methods of interpreting Revelation listed in the order of their chronological popularity are: Spiritual, Historical, Futuristic, and Preteristic. Although some aspects of the Preterist method of interpretation was used during the first century, it was not known by that designation. Intertwined within the four views are two primary considerations; the timing of Christ's Millennial Reign, and the nature of the visions. (Do the visions describe actual future events, or mere illustrations of spiritual principles and moral instructions?) Before we discuss the four viewpoints, let us define the Millennial Reign. The primary Bible reference to the Millennial Reign of Christ is found in Revelation 20:1-6:

> *"Then I saw an angel coming down from heaven, having the key to the bottomless pit and a great chain in his hand. He laid hold of the dragon, that serpent of old, who is the Devil and Satan, and bound him for a thousand years; and he cast him into the bottomless pit, and shut him up, and set a seal on him, so that he should deceive the nations no more till the thousand years were finished. But after these things he must be released for a little while. And I saw thrones, and they sat on them, and judgment was committed to them. Then I saw the souls of those who had been beheaded for their witness to Jesus and for the word of God, who had not worshiped the beast or his image, and had not received his mark on their foreheads or on their hands. And they lived and reigned with Christ for a thousand years. But the rest of the dead did not live again until the thousand years were finished. This is the first resurrection. Blessed and holy is he who has part in the first resurrection. Over such the second death has no power, but they shall be priests of God and of Christ, and shall reign with Him a thousand years."*

From the time of the early church until today, there has been a controversy concerning the relation of Christ's second coming to the period of His thousand year reign upon the earth. Either Jesus returns before the 1,000 years, or after the 1,000 years. Until one thousand years had elapsed after Jesus' first coming, simple logic placed His return before the Millennial Reign. The logic goes like this: Jesus taught He could return at any moment, and, it hasn't been a thousand years. Pretty simple! This viewpoint is called "Premillennial." The opinion that Jesus would return in a physical body after the Millennial Reign, is deemed "Postmillennial."

# Come Out of Her My People: Persecution Begins

A third opinion about the Millennial Reign assumes that Jesus would return in a spiritual sense; in the form of the indwelling Holy Spirit. This Spiritual indwelling is spoken of by Jesus in the Fourteenth Chapter of John's Gospel, verses 15-20:

*"If you love Me, keep My commandments. And I will pray the Father, and He will give you another Helper, that He may abide with you forever— the Spirit of truth, whom the world cannot receive, because it neither sees Him nor knows Him; but you know Him, for He dwells with you and will be in you. I will not leave you orphans; I will come to you. A little while longer and the world will see Me no more, but you will see Me. Because I live, you will live also. At that day you will know that I am in My Father, and you in Me, and I in you."*

Pre-millennialism is conducive to the Futurist interpretation of Revelation. The Futurist pushes everything in Revelation that falls after the letters to the churches (Chapter Three) into the future. The Apostles, and other believers who lived during their time, expected the second coming of Christ before their generation passed away. So they obviously believed that the Millennial Reign of Christ on the earth would have to come after His second coming. This Pre-millennial point of view has been found in the writings of second and third century Christians and was referred to as "Chiliastic." Many early Christians were offended by the thought of returning to earth again in the future. The persecutions they were enduring and their self denial in this world, left them hungering only for heaven. They truly believed that this world had nothing for them. But the scripture clearly speaks of a time when the Messiah would reign over the earth. They weren't considering how different things would be when Jesus rules with a *"rod of iron."* (See Psalm 2:9 and Revelation 19:15.) They also suspected the Christians who wanted to return to earth had the pursuit of further worldly pleasures in mind.

Proponents of Futurism find ample evidence throughout the Bible to expect an ever-darkening world of depravity prior to Christ's return. The Futuristic viewpoint has raised objections because of its pessimistic assumptions regarding the future. Some Christian faiths and most humanists believe that civilization will culminate in a utopian state of moral and economic perfection. Well… since the last thousand years has seen violence, immorality, the respect of authority, and general social cohesiveness virtually disintegrate; most Christians would echo a hearty, "Good luck with that!"

In spite of the record, Amillennialism holds the promise of an ever-improving moral environment. (It is obvious, considering that two thousand years have already intervened that the "year" isn't taken literally in their interpretation.) The Bible does state that Jesus indwells all those who have confessed trust in Christ's vicarious sacrifice for their sins. That means Jesus inhabits the earth, embodied by those who have placed their faith in Him. The Amillennialist would conclude then, that Christ is already reigning over the earth through His people. The Amillennialist would further assert that the world will become ever more "Christianized" until Jesus returns again in bodily form. Amillennialism lends itself to the Historical method of interpreting Revelation. The Historicist looks at the apocalyptic prophecies and matches them to actual historical events. Sometimes the similarities between prophesy and reality are striking. But other times the correlations are chronologically skewed, and/or obscure in their resemblance.

If the charts on the following pages appear blurred click this link to view them at the official *"Come out of her, My people"* book site.

http://www.comeoutofhermypeople.com/endtimeschartstheories.html

# Come Out of Her My People: Persecution Begins

## The Historical View of Revelation

Initial Protestant View of the Reformation
Held from 1500 AD until 1900 AD

(Assumes a Day is as a Year)

Supports Postmillennial and Amillennial Interpretations

Details of Revelation matched with Events of **History** until the end of the Age

Crucifixion — 1260 years — 1260 years — Second Coming

Come out of her, My people by C W Steinle
Do not copy for publication without written permission

Another branch of the Historical camp holds a more chronologically precise measurement of "days" or years. By calling on several scriptural references, these Historicists estimate a day to represent a calendar year. They claim to be "Postmillennial" in their view of the Second Coming.

Some form of Preterism was most likely held by Christians of the first Century. Prior to the Romanization of Christianity, early believers would have been consoled as they were persecuted, knowing that Rome would soon be judged for its cruelty. Irenaeus (180 AD), the Bishop of Lyons and famous for his writing "Against Heresies" http://www.earlychristianwritings.com/irenaeus.html, wrote a complete commentary of the Book of Revelation. He believed the Rome Empire was Babylon, and the Roman Empire would be divided into ten kingdoms before its destruction. The Preterist view assumes the fulfillment of most of Revelation in the fall of Jerusalem. This interpretation is supported by the first verses of Jesus' Olivet Discourse. A Full Preterist believes that all of Revelation has been fulfilled, including Christ's second coming. Partial Preterism suggests that some remaining prophecies of Revelation are yet to be fulfilled; leaving the return of Christ as an imminent expectation.

Steve Gregg commends Preterism for its faithfulness to the relevance of Revelation. He states: *"This view has the advantage of immediate relevance to the original readers, a feature we would strongly expect to find in an epistle. It also is the only view that does not need an alternative to the literal sense of passages like Revelation 1:1 and 19, which affirm that the events predicted "must shortly come to pass" and "are about to take place;" and like Revelation 22:10 where John is told not to seal up the book, because "the time is at hand." When this is contrasted with Daniel's being commanded to seal up his book because it would not be immediately fulfilled (Daniel 12:9), this seems a deliberate promise that there would be no great interval between the time Revelation was written and the time of its fulfillment."*

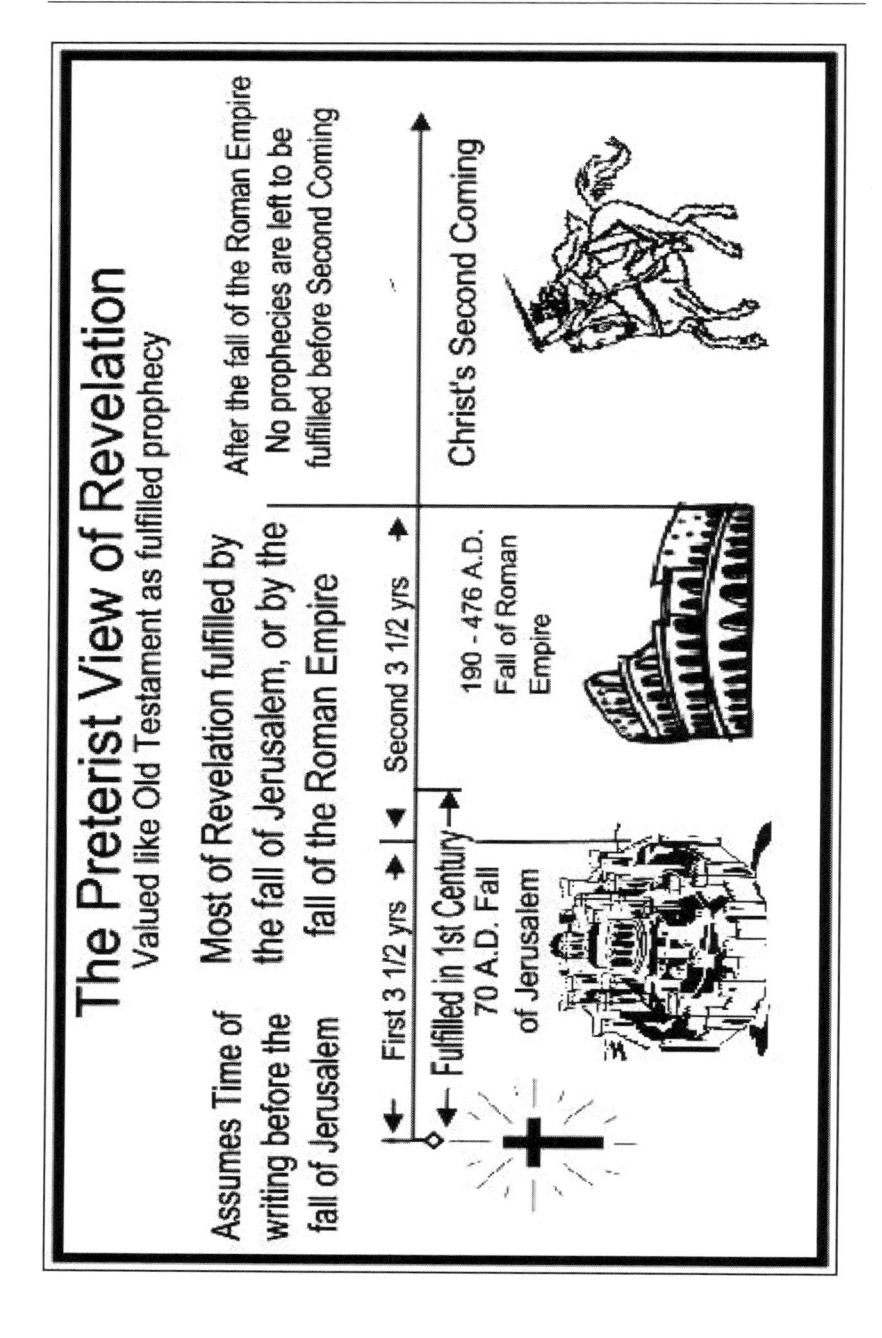

# Come Out of Her My People: Persecution Begins

## The Preterist View of Revelation
### Valued like Old Testament as fulfilled prophecy

**Assumes Time of writing before the fall of Jerusalem**

**Most of Revelation fulfilled by the fall of Jerusalem, or by the fall of the Roman Empire**

**After the fall of the Roman Empire No prophecies are left to be fulfilled before Second Coming**

First 3 1/2 yrs | Second 3 1/2 yrs

Fulfilled in 1st Century — 70 A.D. Fall of Jerusalem

190 - 476 A.D. Fall of Roman Empire

Christ's Second Coming

108

The Spiritual interpretation of Revelation could be called the Figurative View. Clement and Origen, of the Second Century, were among the first commentators to spiritualize Revelation. They didn't like the fact that Millennialism brought the End Time focus back to the Nation of Israel. Some examples of spiritual interpretation are: the assumption that the locusts' tails, from Revelation Chapter Nine, represent "false teachers;" the rider of the white horse in Chapter Nineteen represents "the light of the Word;" and the 24 elders represent the equality of non-Jews with the Jews. This Spiritual view of Revelation was the prevalent view from the fall of the Roman Empire until the time of the Reformers; nearly 1,300 years!

But when the Protestant Reformation began, the Spiritual interpretation of the Bible was rejected by reform leaders such as Martin Luther and John Calvin. Luther's commentary suggested that after the Letters to the Churches, Revelation was the actual history of the church. This Historical view became the standard Protestant interpretation and was a central difference between the Roman Catholics and themselves. Many reformers were convinced that the Roman Catholic Church was the Mystery Babylon of Revelation. So could the Roman Catholic Church really be Mystery Babylon? She most certainly has adulterated God's truth with myths about Mary, myths about Jesus, and myths about priesthood, sainthood, prayer, communion, baptism and so much more! But there is a problem today in associating Rome with either the trading capitol of the world or the world's greatest military force.

It wasn't until the time of the New England Settlement that Futurism was embraced by the Roman Catholics. It has been noted that the Roman Catholics may have contrived Futurism as a way to thwart the Protestants. A Spanish Jesuit (a branch of the Roman Catholic Church) named Francisco Ribera promulgated that John had only foreseen the immediate and the distant future, but was prevented from seeing the events in between; to-date a span of nearly 2,000 years. Francisco predicted that St. John's antichrist would reappear in the last days, and that Babylon was a future Roman state; not the Roman Catholic Church. Ribera's futuristic assumptions eliminated any possibility that their present-day Pope could be the Antichrist and foiled the Protestants' accusations.

Gradually, over the course of three hundred years, and, after the blood of the Protestant martyrs was forgotten, Futurism began to emerge in the Protestant Church. This newly proposed Futuristic view was in stark contrast to the Reformers' assumption that the majority of Revelation was <u>the history of the church</u>. Instead, the Futuristic view insisted that <u>nothing about the church</u> was mentioned after the letters to the Seven Churches. Prophecy which was to remain unsealed and pertinent was suddenly sealed until a future time or event. See a detailed analysis of Futurism's development, including some original manuscripts at:

http://www.aloha.net/~mikesch/antichrist.htm.

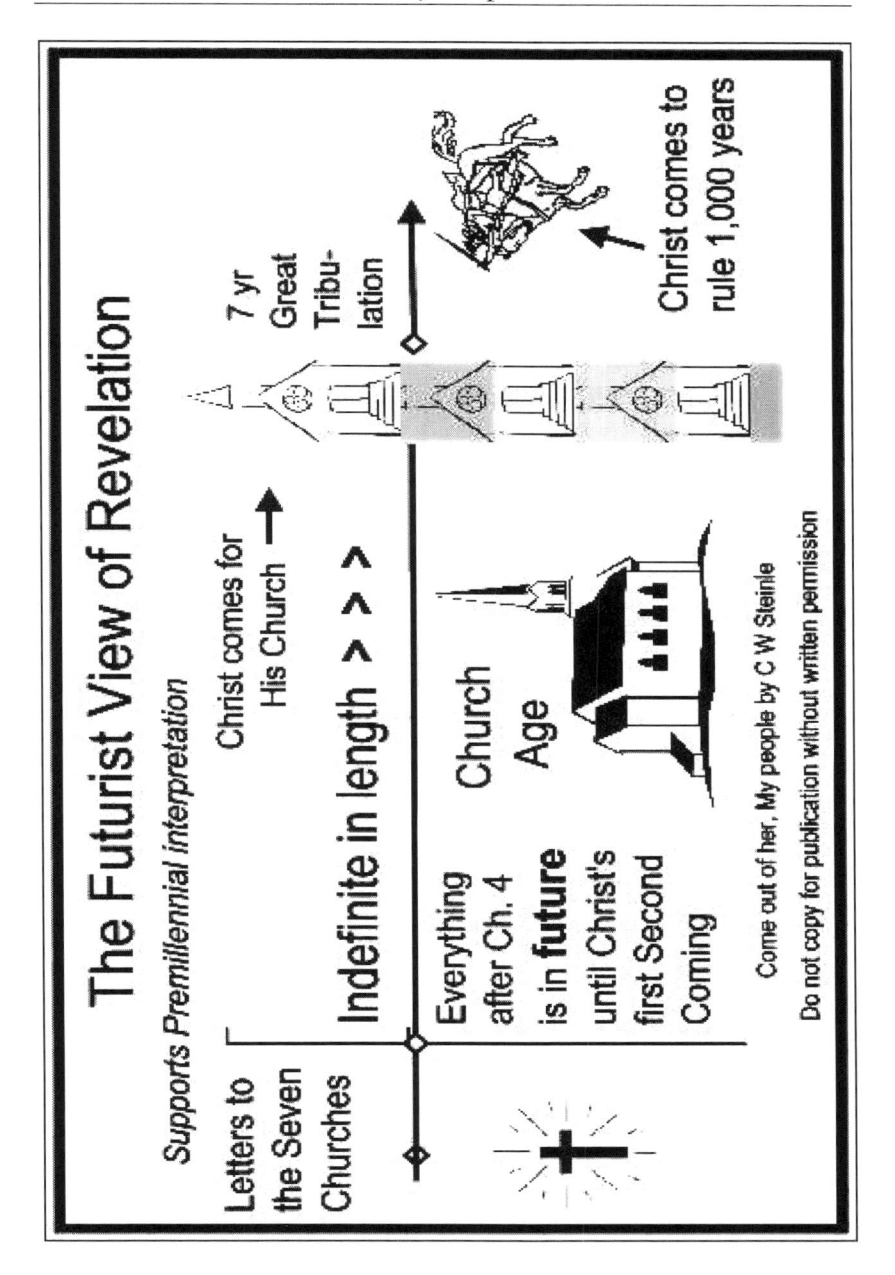

## The Futurist View of Revelation

*Supports Premillennial interpretation*

Letters to the Seven Churches

Christ comes for His Church →

Indefinite in length > > >

Church Age

Everything after Ch. 4 is in **future** until Christ's first Second Coming

7 yr Great Tribulation

Christ comes to rule 1,000 years

Come out of her, My people by C W Steinle

Do not copy for publication without written permission

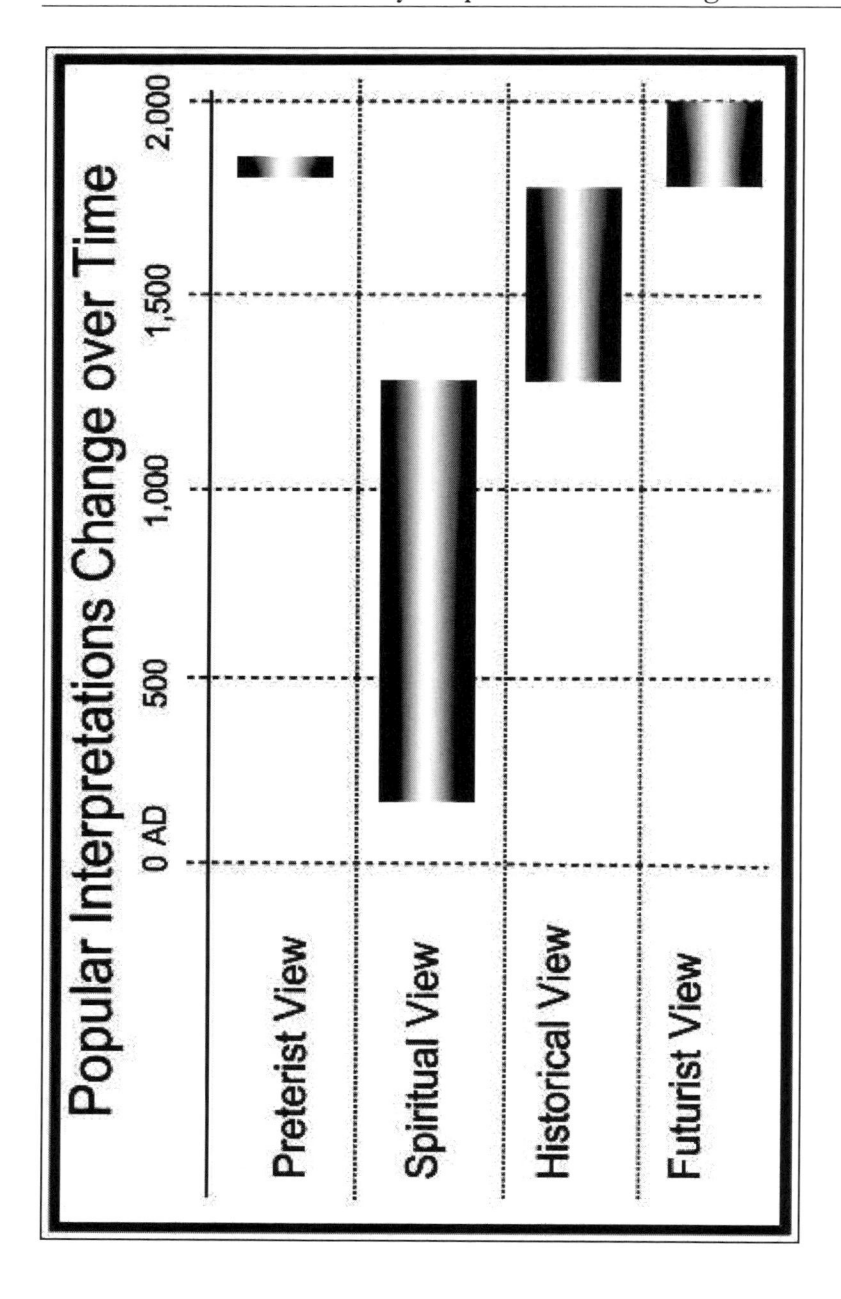

Come Out of Her My People: Persecution Begins

Popular Interpretations Change over Time

| View | Approximate time range |
|---|---|
| Preterist View | ~1800 |
| Spiritual View | ~300 – 1300 |
| Historical View | ~1300 – 1800 |
| Futurist View | ~1800 – 2000 |

112

Can both of these extreme views of Revelation be so clearly supported by scripture that there is no possibility of a moderate position somewhere in between? Or could these politically motivated assumptions be throwing the baby out with the bathwater? According to the most authoritative early church father of the Second Century, Irenaeus of Lyons, both the Historical and Futurist views have some merit. Irenaeus of Lyons lived about a hundred years after John and was instructed by Polycarp, John's disciple. John's interpretation of his own writings were most likely passed down and recorded by Irenaeus.

*"He says also: "And he will cause a mark [to be put] in the forehead and in the right hand, that no one may be able to buy or sell, unless he who has the mark of the name of the beast or the number of his name; and the number is six hundred and sixty-six," that is, six times a hundred, six times ten, and six units. [He gives this] as a summing up of the whole of that apostasy which has taken place during six thousand years."*

*"For in as many days as this world was made, in so many thousand years shall it be concluded. And for this reason the Scripture says: "Thus the heaven and the earth were finished, and all their adornment. And God brought to a conclusion upon the sixth day the works that He had made; and God rested upon the seventh day from all His works." This is an account of the things formerly created, as also it is a prophecy of what is to come. For the day of the Lord is as a thousand years; and in six days created things were completed: it is evident, therefore, that they will come to an end at the sixth thousand year."*

*"But when this Antichrist shall have devastated all things in this world, he will reign for three years and six months, and sit in the temple at Jerusalem; and then the Lord will come from heaven in the clouds, in the glory of the Father, sending this man and those who follow him into the lake of fire; but bringing in for the righteous the times of the kingdom, that is, the rest, the hallowed seventh day; and restoring to Abraham the promised inheritance, in which kingdom the Lord declared, that "many coming from the east and from the west should sit down with Abraham, Isaac, and Jacob."*

So Irenaeus agrees with the Historicists who claim that Daniel's "days" are actually a multiple defined by years. And, Irenaeus gives support to the Futurists who await a literal three and one-half years which represent the final half of Daniel's week of the covenant. (Look at the Hebrew calendar converter on the *"Come out of her, My people"* home page to see how far we might be from the six thousandth year: http://comeoutofhermypeople.com/.)

Could it be that Revelation mentions both 1,260 days, and 3½ years, because 1,260 represents years as the Historicists claim; and also points to a literal 3½ years at the end as the Futurists anticipate?

A potential problem with Ribera's Futurism deals with feasibility. Full Preterists drew criticism from Historicists, who expressed strong opposition to the Preterists' notion that the entire drama of Revelation could be acted out in just 70 years. (Full Preterists believe Revelation was fulfilled by the Fall of Jerusalem.) Now consider that many Futurists believe that it will all take place in only seven years! Another feasibility problem occurs when we try to line up a global age of commerce with a time when almost half of the planet's people are dropping out of the workforce and the purchasing base; not to mention the impact on the world's financial-insurance giants.

Have the doctors of theology who have sealed up the bulk of Revelation, moving it into the unchangeable past and the irrelevant future, altogether escaped John's warning not to remove the words of the Revelation of Jesus Christ? Is remote not akin to removed? Never underestimate the power and influence of the Roman Catholic Church. In fact, the Protestants' beliefs about Historicism yielded to Futurism about the same time as the push for councils that would bring all churches together into one peaceful group.

A final thought here. What do we do with the old adage?

*"If it's new it's not true; and, if it's true it's not new."* -- H. A. Ironside

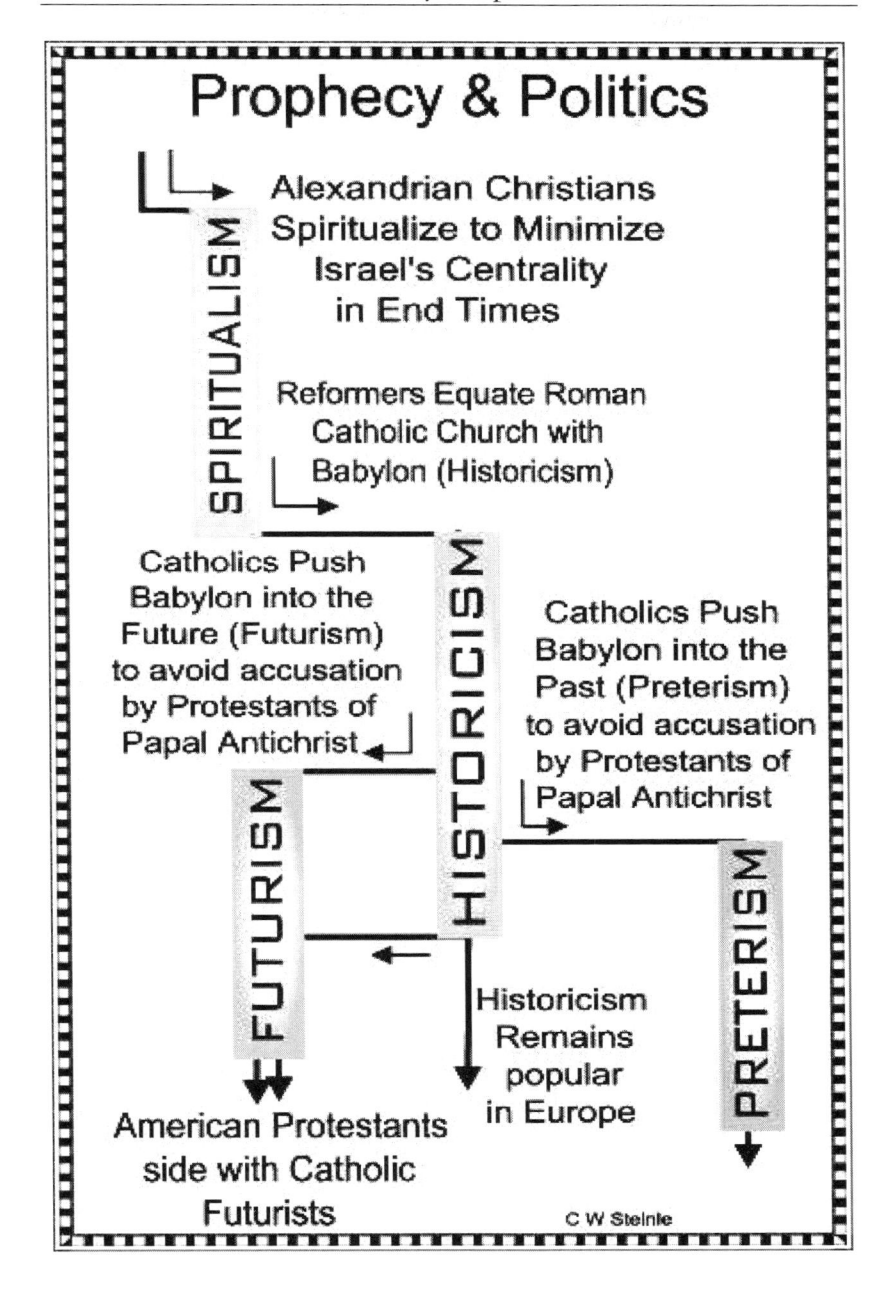

# Prophecy & Politics

**SPIRITUALISM** — Alexandrian Christians Spiritualize to Minimize Israel's Centrality in End Times

Reformers Equate Roman Catholic Church with Babylon (Historicism)

Catholics Push Babylon into the Future (Futurism) to avoid accusation by Protestants of Papal Antichrist

**HISTORICISM**

Catholics Push Babylon into the Past (Preterism) to avoid accusation by Protestants of Papal Antichrist

**FUTURISM**

**PRETERISM**

Historicism Remains popular in Europe

American Protestants side with Catholic Futurists

C W Steinle

# Come Out of Her My People: Persecution Begins

## Founders and Famous Proponents

Come out of her, My people by C W Steinle
Do not copy for publication without written permission

| Preterist | Spiritual | Historical | Futurist |
|---|---|---|---|
| Hymenaeus & Philetus (2Tim 2:17) | Clement | Rupert of Deutz | Ribera |
| Eusubius | Origen | Joachim of Floris | Walvoord |
| Luis de Alcasar | Methodius | Martin Luther | Ryrie |
| Kenneth Gentry | Victorinus | John Knox | Gaebelein |
| Jay Adams | Tyconius | John Wycliffe | Ironside |
| | Augustine | William Tyndale | John Nelson Darby |
| | Alcuin | John Calvin | C. I. Scofield |
| | Strabo | Sir Isaac Newton | Hal Lindsey |
| | William Hendriksen | John Foxe | |
| | | John Wesley | |
| | | Charles Finney | |
| | | C. H. Spurgeon | |
| | | Matthew Henry | |
| | | E. B. Elliott | |

## Chapter 2: Babylon the Great

*"MYSTERY, BABYLON THE GREAT, THE MOTHER OF ALL HARLOTS AND OF THE ABOMINATIONS OF THE EARTH,"* is the inscription found on the forehead of the Great Harlot of Revelation 17:5. People are instructed to *"Come out of her"* in Revelation 18:4, so we must determine <u>where</u> she is located. But how can we understand the meaning of these words, written almost 2,000 years ago, about this city of the future? Studying the history of Ancient Babylon and the manner in which these phrases are used in the Old Testament provides a good starting point. Much of the information about Babylon in the following paragraphs is found in *"The New Unger's Bible Dictionary."*[4]

Babylon was an ancient city-state in the plain of Shinar. The city of Babylon was located roughly 50 miles south of Baghdad. Babylon was built as a square city around the Euphrates River, whereas Baghdad was established beside the Tigris River. Babylon derived its name from the Hebrew word *"balal"* ("to confound") and refers to the confusion of tongues that took place when God put an end to their tower project (Genesis 11:9). The city began to dominate the area about 1830 B.C., when it gained success in conquering its adjoining city-states. The Kingdom of Babylon eventually covered all of Mesopotamia and the adjacent lands; an area extending from the Persian Gulf to the Red Sea, southward; including Assyria to the north, and the entire eastern coast of the Mediterranean Sea to the west. Thus, the nation of Israel was included in greater Babylon. (Because the Assyrians were closer in proximity to Israel than Babylon itself, the Jews referred to their captors as 'Assyrians'.)

The city of Babylon had a circumference of over 41 miles, according to Greek writers. The great wall was said to be 85 feet thick and eleven miles long. This wall was made of two outer walls about 24 feet thick, with an inner area filled with rubble. It was protected by a mote filled with water from the Euphrates. The Hanging Gardens, constructed by Nebuchadnezzar, were considered by the Greeks to be one of the Seven Wonders of the Ancient World. The terraces were so massive that they could support full grown trees. The city was filled with houses, three to four stories in height. A bridge connected the eastern and western sections of the city. Other prominent buildings included the king's palace and the temple of Marduk, or Bel. Babylon was magnificent in wealth, grandeur, power and size; containing around a million people within the walled city.

As we contemplate the nature of Babylon, in order to establish a 'type' of Babylon, and thereby derive our opinion about the identity of 'Mystery Babylon'; we need to understand the Jewish attitude toward Babylon at the time the Old Testament Bible prophesies were given. The Old Testament prophets had warned Israel that they could not resist the mounting strength of the Babylonian-Assyrians, unless they remained faithful to the God of Israel. God had shown the Jews time after time that their enemies would be allowed to conquer them, and rule over them, until they returned to the Lord their God. God allowed, and even commanded, the idolatrous nations around Israel to defeat the children of Israel because of their chronic waywardness. They were called adulteresses by God because they were unfaithful to Him. Finally, God allowed them to be carried away by the Assyrians, as far away as Babylon. However, God also promised to punish Babylon at a later time for her own wickedness. During the life of Daniel, and after seventy years of captivity, the Medes overthrew Babylon and the Jews were allowed to return to their own land.

The following verses from the book of Isaiah foretell the coming destruction of Babylon. Notice that *"the day of the Lord"* is said to be at hand, but the application of this chapter is *"against Babylon."* Also, note that the day of destruction has not yet come for the Medes, whom God used to destroy Babylon (verse 17). One other event needs to be mentioned, and it could be quite significant. The darkening of the sun and moon is associated with the judgment of Babylon. 'Stirring up of the dust,' so as to darken the sky, is indicative of an intense battle that razes everything standing, and also alludes to the swiftness and size of the approaching army. This description of battle was fulfilled when the Medes destroyed Babylon on October 12, 539 B.C. (After a brief attempt by Alexander the Great to restore the city, it was abandoned and quickly became a desert.) Revelation 8:12 calls for another period of darkness that will affect only part of the earth (one third).

Could it be that Chapter 8 of Revelation is also describing the judgment of a future type of Babylon?

*Isaiah 13*

*"The burden against Babylon which Isaiah the son of Amoz saw. 'Lift up a banner on the high mountain, raise your voice to them; wave your hand, that they may enter the gates of the nobles. I have commanded My sanctified ones; I have also called My mighty ones for My anger- those who rejoice in My exaltation.' The noise of a multitude in the mountains, like that of many people! A tumultuous noise of the kingdoms of nations gathered together! The LORD of hosts musters the army for battle. They come from a far country, from the end of heaven- The LORD and His weapons of indignation, to destroy the whole land. Wail, for the day of the LORD is at hand! It will come as destruction from the Almighty. Therefore all hands will be limp, every man's heart will melt, and they will be afraid. Pangs and sorrows will take hold of them; they will be amazed at one another; their faces will be like flames. Behold, the day of the LORD comes, cruel, with both wrath and fierce anger, to lay the land desolate; and He will destroy its sinners from it. For the stars of heaven and their constellations will not give their light; the sun will be darkened in its going forth, and the moon will not cause its light to shine. 'I will punish the world for its evil. And the wicked for their iniquity; I will halt the arrogance of the proud, and will lay low the haughtiness of the terrible. I will make a mortal more rare than fine gold, a man more than the golden wedge of Ophir. Therefore I will shake the heavens, and the earth will move out of her place, in the wrath of the LORD of hosts and in the day of His fierce anger. It shall be as the hunted gazelle, and as a sheep that no man takes up; every man will turn to his own people, and everyone will flee to his own land. Everyone who is found will be thrust through, and everyone who is captured will fall by the sword. Their children also will be dashed to pieces before their eyes; their houses will be plundered and their wives ravished. Behold, I will stir up the Medes against them, who will not regard silver; and as for gold, they will not delight in it. Also their bows will dash the young men to pieces, and they will have no pity on the fruit of the womb; their eye will not spare children. And Babylon, the glory of kingdoms, the beauty of the Chaldeans' pride, will be as when God overthrew Sodom and Gomorrah. It will never be inhabited, nor will it be settled from generation to generation; nor will the Arabian pitch tents there, nor will the shepherds make their sheepfolds there. But wild beasts of the desert will lie there, and their houses will be full of owls; ostriches will dwell there, and wild goats will caper there. The hyenas will howl in their citadels, and jackals in their pleasant palaces. Her time is near to come, and her days will not be prolonged.'"*

The prophecy of Joel agrees with the assumption that the time of darkening occurs <u>prior</u> to the time of God's wrath (the Day of the LORD*)*. *"The sun shall be turned into darkness, and the moon into blood, <u>before</u> the coming of the great and awesome day of the LORD." - Joel 2:31 emphasis added.* Now listen to God's repeated plea for the righteous to separate themselves from the object of His coming judgment in the following verses from Jeremiah.

> *"Move from the midst of Babylon, go out of the land of the Chaldeans; and be like the rams before the flocks."-Jeremiah 50:8*

> *"Flee from the midst of Babylon, and every one save his life! Do not be cut off in her iniquity, for this is the time of the LORD's vengeance; He shall recompense her."-Jeremiah 51:6*

> *"My people, go out of the midst of her! And let everyone deliver himself from the fierce anger of the LORD."-Jeremiah 51:45*

Now prayerfully consider that this same plea is given by God near the end of the age; *"Come out of her, My people."* It is made to the inhabitants of a mysterious type of Babylon that will exist near the time of the end. *"Mystery"* means that her identity was not yet revealed by God during John's day; and could indicate that the city did not exist at the time of his writings. Many interpreters of prophecies have concluded that Revelation's Babylon would be a spiritual or earthly system; something less than a physical entity. But the Greek word *"musterion"* simply means "hidden" or "unidentified." We should assume that the future Babylon will be another physical location in keeping with the fall of ancient Babylon. God's word is already teaming with warnings for His people to avoid the ways of the world.

Observe that Daniel did not respond to this message during the first overthrow of Babylon. Daniel stayed in Babylon, and even served the conquering Medes. This implies that <u>God may call some of His saints to stay and minister</u> to the people of Mystery Babylon, even while the masses are commanded to evacuate.

## Chapter 3: The Outline of the Age (Rev. Six)

We find a great similarity between the Book of Revelation and the Book of Daniel. The prophecies given to Daniel in Chapters 7-12 rehearse the same people, places and events as many as five times. The *"little horn"* is mentioned in Daniel 7 and 8, and is referred to as a *"vile person"* in Chapter 11. The *"daily sacrifice"* being taken away and the *"abomination of desolation"* are mentioned in Daniel Chapters 8, 9, 11, and 12. The mid-week period of 1,260 days is stated in Daniel Chapters 7, 9, and 12, and another period of 2,300 days is found in Daniel Chapter 8. The cleansing of the sanctuary and the anointing of the Holy of Holies takes place in Daniel Chapters 8 and 9, respectively. Finally, the *"time of the end"* is found in Daniel Chapters 7, 8, 9, 11, and 12.

In comparison, the Book of Revelation covers the events leading up to the *"wrath of God"* at least twice, and includes two other extraneous periods of time. In fact, most Bible scholars agree the events of Revelation are not recorded in the order of their expected realization. The author suggests that Chapter 6 covers a period from the time of the Revelation churches to the catastrophic disasters of the great earthquake, the blackened sun and moon, and the shaking of the heavens. At that time, even the kings of the earth are found taking refuge in caves. The Sixth Seal reveals that the wrath of God has come. *"For the great day of His wrath has come, and who is able to stand?"-Revelation 6:17*

The clock of time is turned back at the end of Revelation Chapter 10 when John is told, *"You must prophesy again about many peoples, nations, tongues, and kings."* During the two chapters that follow, the Book of Revelation carries us back to the beginning of the Hebrew nation, the birth and ascension of Christ Jesus (the *"male child"*), and the Diaspora of the Jews pursued by Satan. It is interesting that after these attacks on the Jews, Satan turns his attention to *"the rest of her offspring, who keep the commandments of God and have the testimony of Jesus Christ."-Revelation 12:17* After the Jews were expelled from the Promised Land by the Romans, Satan did indeed turn to the persecution of Christians. So following the Nazi Holocaust, we might also expect Satan to increase his persecution of those who believe in Jesus Christ. Certainly this has been the case, especially in socialistic and Islamic societies.

Chapter 13 begins another countdown, bringing us once again to the wrath of God; beginning with the gathering of the grapes of wrath in Revelation 14:14, and culminating with the pouring out of the bowls of God's wrath in Chapter 16:17-21. Lastly, we will discuss the focus of this book, the fall of Babylon the Great, found in Chapter 14:8. The detailed account of Babylon's fall is given in Revelation Chapters 17 and 18, where it is totally destroyed by fire. However, the fall actually occurred before God's wrath as is evidenced by John's use of the past tense in his opening words of Chapter 17. In conclusion, neither Daniel, nor Revelation, is written in chronological order. In *The Four Views of Revelation*, Steve Gregg points this out: *"There are additional indicators that the details of Revelation don't necessarily follow one another chronologically. For example, the Beast persecutes the two witnesses (11:7) before he rises to power (13:1) and Babylon is fallen in 14:8, but later not yet fallen (17:1-5; 18:21)."* These repetitions, however, may be "overlaid" to bring a deeper understanding of certain events, by examining them in greater detail than the body of text in which they were first presented. Now let's take a look at the first chain of events leading up to the time of God's wrath.

Chapter 6 records the opening of the seals of the scroll by the hand of the Lord Jesus Christ. Chapters 4 and 5 point out that He alone is worthy to take the scroll and to open its seals. To identify the point in time represented by the seals, we must go back to Chapters 2 and 3 to note that those chapters address the time period of the seven churches; located in what is now western Turkey. Chapter 4 begins with the words *"after these things."* The post-Chapter-Three-Tribulation method (Futurism) of interpreting this phrase assumes that it refers to the time after the church has been caught up to heaven (the rapture). The justification for this interpretation is that the previous verses address 'the church', and therefore *"these things"* are things that pertain to 'the church.' However the letters to the churches are directed to seven discrete churches and not to the universe of all believers in Jesus Christ. So could the rapture have occurred before any other events listed in Revelation? Of course, provided the book was to be sealed up! But if Chapter 6 is an overview, could some of the first seals be opened before the pouring out of God's wrath? Could we actually be nearing the end of John's blind spot (according to Ribera)?

Might some of Revelation be speaking about the events that fall in between John's time and the beginning of the Great Tribulation? After all, nowhere in Revelation is there an announcement that "the Tribulation" has begun. But we <u>are</u> told when the wrath of God begins. The sickle and the bowls of wrath in Revelation 14 clearly mark the time of wrath. According to Jesus, there will be a significant amount of turmoil between the beginning of sorrows and the Great Tribulation. Many have been inclined to include these afflictions as part of the first half of the Great Tribulation, giving Christians the impression that they will not be experienced during their lifetimes. When, in fact, placing them into an irrelevant future time might cause them to experience plagues which could have been avoided by responding to the command to *"Come out"*. The very words which coined the phrase "Great Tribulation" are underlined below and are found well after the *"beginning of sorrows"*. Jesus clearly included trials, death, false prophets, and lawlessness in His pre-Great Tribulation timeline.

*"For nation will rise against nation, and kingdom against kingdom. And there will be famines, pestilences, and earthquakes in various places. All <u>these are the beginning of sorrows</u>. Then they will deliver you up to tribulation and kill you, and you will be hated by all nations for My name's sake. And then many will be offended, will betray one another, and will hate one another. Then many false prophets will rise up and deceive many. And because lawlessness will abound, the love of many will grow cold. But he who endures to the end shall be saved. And this gospel of the kingdom will be preached in all the world as a witness to all the nations, and then the end will come. Therefore when you see the 'abomination of desolation spoken of by Daniel the prophet, standing in the holy place," (whoever reads, let him understand),'' then let those who are in Judea flee to the mountains. Let him who is on the housetop not go down to take anything out of his house. And let him who is in the field not go back to get his clothes. But woe to those who are pregnant and to those who are nursing babies in those days! And pray that your flight may not be in winter or on the Sabbath. For then there will be <u>great tribulation</u>, such as has not been since the beginning of the world until this time, no, nor ever shall be. And unless those days were shortened, no flesh would be saved; but for the elect's sake those days will be shortened."-Matthew 24:7-22*

## Come Out of Her My People: Persecution Begins

This excerpt from Jesus' Olivet Discourse begins and ends with "*you*" as the object of His words. He is speaking to His disciples. Although most of these events occurred during their lifetime, we continue to anticipate another wave of these troubles that will culminate in a period of catastrophic destruction. Therefore we must also assume that "you" applies to all disciples throughout this age. This is consistent with most evangelical theologians when they conclude that the pouring out of the Holy Spirit is available to all believers even though Jesus was speaking to the first century disciples when He said, "*when the Holy Spirit has come upon you.*" This observation about the second-person pronoun is made because Ribera's theory requires parsing and splicing the Olivet Discourse in order to make it fit into his scheme.

Equating Daniel's seven years to certain events in Revelation creates its own troubles when it comes to the rapture of the church. It robs the rapture of its spontaneity. Two unbending truths must be retained in any inspired prediction of the timing of the Christ's return: Jesus' return must always be anticipated as eminent; and Jesus' servants must continue to carry on their master's business until He returns. If people living at any period thought something needed to happen prior to Christ's return, they would be in violation of His teaching. How about if Israel were not a nation (prior to 1948), for instance? If we could measure from the time of the rapture to the catastrophic end of civilization as we know it, say exactly seven years, then believers might be tempted to tell themselves, "Israel must become a nation, and some Great Harlot must rise up from somewhere; and that hasn't happened yet so it's really hard for me to expect Jesus right now." (From the beginnings of Zionism until Israel gained her statehood actually took close to a hundred years.) Teaching the eminent return of Christ and tying it to some hitching post just doesn't work; unless, you're living today of course. But shouldn't the "Truth" work just as well in any generation?

It has been said when interpreting Scripture that "the obvious meaning is the obvious meaning." The most obvious interpretation of "after" would be "following the information that was previously imparted to John." This transition prepares the reader to anticipate further revelation. In his work on Revelation, Steve Gregg makes this observation. *"It should be remembered that when John says, "After these things*

*I saw ..."* (as he frequently does), *he is giving us the sequence in which he saw the visions—not necessarily implying anything about the chronological order in which the visions would find fulfillment in events."* In fact, *"after these things"* is such a common phrase to John that he uses these exact words thirteen times in his Biblical writings. When John says *"after these things"* in verse one of Chapter 7, he has just recorded the words *"For the great Day of His wrath has come, and who is able to stand?"* Would we at once conclude that Revelation has nothing more to say about the wrath of God? Certainly not! When John uses the words *"after these things"* immediately following the sealing of the 144,000 Jews in Revelation 7:9, should we conclude that the book of Revelation has nothing more to say about the Jews? No! We believe that God has reserved a precious future time to bring Israel into its glory. So why would we conclude, upon John's opening of Chapter Four of Revelation with this common phrase, that the church has just been raptured? Is that the obvious meaning? Should this same method be used to interpret the rest of Bible?

Words, by definition, possess a certain and reliable meaning. Therefore, a literal interpretation of the Bible should be the first approach used to understand Scripture. The Greek language contains words which are far more specific than the words of the English language. The first words of Chapter 4 are the Greek words Μετὰ ταῦτα. Ταῦτα[5] means "these things," so it is the first word that we need to examine. Μετὰ[6] has the primary meaning of "mid, amid, in the midst, with, or among"; and is used to depict Jesus "coming <u>with</u> the clouds of heaven" in Mark 14:62.

When used with a noun, Μετὰ has a secondary meaning of "succession either in place or time," but there are several other Greek words which have the <u>primary</u> meaning of "successively" or "consecutively." *Kathex☐s*[7] means "in order, successively, consecutively, or in connected order." *Eita*[8] is translated "then" or "after that." *Hexēs*[9] has the English meaning "to follow next in line, or, successively." Or, *metépeita*[10] could have been used, and means "after that, then, afterwards or thereafter." Other Greek words more accurately specify "after" as a succession of events.

The obvious interpretation of *"after these things"* would be; after Jesus has finished His letters to the seven churches or after the previous moments experienced by John during the Patmos revelation. One of the unfortunate results of presuming that most of Revelation will not be encountered by the church is the lack of relevance felt by the body of Christ. Ribera's dream that Protestants would bury their heads in the future and forget about the actions of the Roman Catholics and their pope has finally come true. This 'disconnect' from the foreseeable future has encouraged novelists to fantasize about end time prophecy by the volume. But rather than arguing over issues that are not specified in scripture; why not say, "If the Lord tarries, then this or that prophecy will be fulfilled." Or, "If Jesus comes immediately we can assume that some prophecies were fulfilled without being recognized by the church." In either case it might be best, and more peaceable, to be content not knowing the hour or the day of His coming; still, daily striving to be ready, and always desiring His return.

John uses the phrase *"let the reader understand"* to indicate that the meaning of certain prophecy would not become clear until it was accompanied by actual future events. The interpretation that is offered in this book for the passages that follow *"after these things"* is one that would not have been evident to a reader of Revelation prior to the middle of the second millennium. At least three events need to be identified in order to recognize the formation of a series. This is true in logic and mathematics. In studying Revelation's seven seals, two sequential events have been evident from the time of John's writings; the forth and fifth seals (taken together), and sixth seal. The forth and fifth seals represent the time of persecution and the One-Third judgments. The catastrophic destruction of the planet by the wrath of God is all but universally accepted as the end of the Tribulation, and these events correspond with the sixth seal. If we take the forth seal then, and work backwards to the time of the demise of the seven churches, do the seals overlay any recognizable periods of human history?

The answer is, "Yes!" However, we find that one time period is still in the future for us, and precedes the fifth seal. A time of persecution of God's people will accompany a time of commerce (Revelation 17:6), and we have not experienced the degree of persecution described is these verses at the time of this writing. But the magnitude of world commerce is accelerating daily. Consider the seals in the following verses and how they might be 'stretched' over time; backward and forward.

*Revelation 6*

*"Now I saw when the Lamb opened one of the seals; and I heard one of the four living creatures saying with a voice like thunder, "Come and see." And I looked, and behold, a white horse. He who sat on it had a bow; and a crown was given to him, and he went out conquering and to conquer. When He opened the second seal, I heard the second living creature saying, "Come and see." Another horse, fiery red, went out. And it was granted to the one who sat on it to take peace from the earth, and that people should kill one another; and there was given to him a great sword. When He opened the third seal, I heard the third living creature say, "Come and see." So I looked, and behold, a black horse, and he who sat on it had a pair of scales in his hand. And I heard a voice in the midst of the four living creatures saying, "A quart of wheat for a denarius, and three quarts of barley for a denarius; and do not harm the oil and the wine." When He opened the fourth seal, I heard the voice of the fourth living creature saying, "Come and see." So I looked, and behold, a pale horse. And the name of him who sat on it was Death, and Hades followed with him. And power was given to them over a fourth of the earth, to kill with sword, with hunger, with death, and by the beasts of the earth. When He opened the fifth seal, I saw under the altar the souls of those who had been slain for the word of God and for the testimony which they held. And they cried with a loud voice, saying, "How long, O Lord, holy and true, until You judge and avenge our blood on those who dwell on the earth?" Then a white robe was given to each of them; and it was said to them that they should rest a little while longer, until both the number of their fellow servants and their brethren, who would be killed as they were, was completed. I looked when He opened the sixth seal, and behold, there was a great earthquake; and the sun became black as sackcloth of hair, and the moon became like blood. And the stars of heaven fell to the earth, as a fig tree drops its late figs when it is shaken by a mighty wind. Then the sky receded as a scroll when it is rolled up, and every mountain and island was moved out of its place. And the kings of the earth, the great men, the rich men, the commanders, the mighty men, every slave and every free man, hid themselves in the caves and in the rocks of the mountains, and said to the mountains and rocks, "Fall on us and hide us from the face of Him who sits on the throne and from the wrath of the Lamb! For the great day of His wrath has come, and who is able to stand?"*

The key to understanding the meaning of multi-colored horses has been established in earlier Scripture. The following passages from Zechariah are the first, and the only verses prior to Revelation, which mention colored horses.

## Come Out of Her My People: Persecution Begins

*Zechariah 1:8-11*

*"I saw by night, and behold, a man riding on a red horse, and it stood among the myrtle trees in the hollow; and behind him were horses: red, sorrel, and white. 9 Then I said, "My lord, what are these?" So the angel who talked with me said to me, "I will show you what they are." And the man who stood among the myrtle trees answered and said, "These are the ones whom the LORD has sent to walk to and fro throughout the earth." So they answered the Angel of the LORD, who stood among the myrtle trees, and said, "We have walked to and fro throughout the earth, and behold, all the earth is resting quietly.""*

*Zechariah 6:1-8*

*"Then I turned and raised my eyes and looked, and behold, four chariots were coming from between two mountains, and the mountains were mountains of bronze. With the first chariot were red horses, with the second chariot black horses, with the third chariot white horses, and with the fourth chariot dappled horses—strong steeds. Then I answered and said to the angel who talked with me, "What are these, my lord?" And the angel answered and said to me, "These are four spirits of heaven, who go out from their station before the Lord of all the earth. The one with the black horses is going to the north country, the white are going after them, and the dappled are going toward the south country." Then the strong steeds went out, eager to go, that they might walk to and fro throughout the earth. And He said, "Go, walk to and fro throughout the earth." So they walked to and fro throughout the earth. And He called to me, and spoke to me, saying, "See, those who go toward the north country have given rest to My Spirit in the north country."*

Notice in the section from Chapter 1 of Zechariah that no individual horses are mentioned after the prophet's initial sighting. The purpose of these horses is to transport a reconnaissance team; who report, *"All the earth is resting quietly."* In Zechariah 6, the colors are correlated with the direction and the region of the earth through which the horses traverse. However, no meaning is attributed to the horses' colors. It appears that the distinction in color is made to indicate that the horses are unique in their assignment; as opposed to riding as a herd. In fact, the color of the chariots' horses is so irrelevant that the mission of the chariot led by the red horses is not even recorded.

Although the particular colors of the horses are not important, the horses do have characteristics that are important for understanding their relation to the seals of the scroll. The steeds seem to represent God's awareness of what is occurring in various areas of the earth.

They go *"to and fro"* in distinct directions. Their riders make known what the Spirit is accomplishing and report back to God the state of affairs on the earth. The most important aspect of Zechariah's horses, as they set a Biblical precedent for the colored horses of Revelation, is that they are sent to accomplish distinct, identifiable missions. There is also a noteworthy difference between the account of the apocalyptic horses and riders, from that of the of Zechariah's equines. Zechariah's vision speaks of the <u>sending</u> from heaven to earth: *"Go, walk to and fro throughout the earth."* Whereas, John's vision tells of the <u>observations</u> of distinct conditions of the world: *"Come and see."*

In an attempt to bring the false prophet into Ribera's abbreviated timeline, the Futurists' claim the white horse bears the antichrist. They claim since "anti", in the Greek, means "in place of", "counterfeit"; that the one who comes in the place of Jesus would ride a white horse like the one our Lord will return upon (Revelation 19:11). But the conclusions from Zechariah convey that "a horse is a horse. . ." The word, "antichrist" is absent from the book of Revelation. So it seems quite a stretch to conclude the false prophet enters the world at this point, simply because a white horse is mentioned. (The use of antichrist to refer to the false prophet of Revelation is a particular peeve to the author even though this lack of distinction has endured from the time of 2nd Century commentaries.)

We see that the rider of the white horse is characterized by the bow and crown, and he goes out conquering and to conquer. Several centuries after John's lifetime, the Greeks used the area of western Turkey as a battleground. The Greeks seized the Christian church buildings and the Christians themselves were victimized by the eastern Turkish warriors. In the seventh century the Muslims invaded the Turks. After 400 years of resistance, the Turks began to convert to Islam. From there, the Muslims began to conquer Europe. Once the trade routes to the Orient were blocked by the Muslims, the Western European Countries began to look for an alternate way to the East. (Christopher Columbus sailed looking for gold to fund the deliverance of the Holy Land from the Muslims.) They finally decided to try sailing around the world. The era of the conquistadors and of exploration was typified by the bow and crown. Those brave explorers were sent out with royal authority to establish their respective crowns over the Western territories. For several centuries, the thrust of

European nations was to colonize the farthest parts of the earth. They went out to conquer and were successful in conquering most of the smaller and unprepared people groups of the world.

The second seal revealed a fiery red horse, whose rider was given power to take peace from the earth and cause people to kill one another. He was armed with a great sword. When most of the world's territories had been conquered, these colonies desired to establish their own self-rule; and the era of the "world wars" began. World War I started with a small conflict, but the "peace treaties" between the world's "affiliates" quickly brought blocks of nations into deadly conflict. The world found itself killing with the sword, and being killed, for reasons most knew nothing about. World War II and subsequent wars have motivated the world's leaders to develop deterrents in order to ensure world peace. While the aggressors of the world were held in check, the golden age of global commerce began.

When the third seal was opened, a black horse was seen carrying a rider with a pair of scales. A voice was heard saying, *"A quart of wheat for a denarius (a day's wages) and three quarts of barley for a denarius, and do not harm the oil and the wine."-Revelation 6:6* The scales, monies, and commodities obviously represent commerce. So this seal represents the golden era of commerce, and will culminate in the destruction of the trading capital of the world (the Great Harlot).

When the Lord Jesus opens the fourth seal, John hears the voice of the fourth living creature beckoning him to behold a pale horse. The name of its rider was Death *"and Hades followed with him. And power was given to them over a fourth of the earth"-Revelation 6:8,* to bring destruction by means of sword, famine, plague, and the beasts of the earth. This fourth seal brings us into the era of the *"beginning of sorrows."-Matthew 24:8* The mass persecution of the saints is implied by the sword in Revelation 6:8. Death by the 'sword' is often used as a euphemism for the practice of beheading. This assumption is supported by the opening of the fifth seal that exposes *"the souls of those who had been slain for the word of God and for the testimony which they held. They cried from under the altar, 'How long, O Lord, holy and true, until You judge and avenge our blood on those who dwell on the earth?"-Revelation 6:9,10;* and, *"Then I saw the souls of those who had been beheaded for their witness to Jesus and for the word of God, who had not worshiped the beast or his image, and had not received his mark on their foreheads or on their hands. And they lived and reigned with Christ for a thousand years."-*

*Revelation 20:4* In Verse 11, a white robe is given to these martyred believers, and they are told to wait until the slaughter of God's saints reaches its fullness.

When the sixth seal is opened, we find ourselves in the midst of the catastrophic destruction of the planet, which is described in Revelation 6:16 as the *"wrath of the Lamb."* During this time period, there will be no commerce, political maneuvering, or intrigue, but only, the great and mighty men of the earth hiding in caves. This 'darkened sky' period affects the entire earth. (We will see, however, that a partial darkening occurs in Chapters 8 and 9 that affects only one-third of the earth.)

The periods of the fourth and fifth seals resemble the sword, famine, plagues, and persecution that will be a precursor to the wrath of God. To summarize, we have the **first seal era of exploration and conquest**, the **second seal era of wars**, the **third seal era of commerce**, the **fourth and fifth seals era of plagues, persecution, and famine**, and the **sixth seal era of catastrophic destruction**. Thus the time from the seven Revelation churches through the end of the age is covered by these six seals. If the time lines on the following pages appear blurred they can be viewed at the official website:

http://www.comeoutofhermypeople.com/mysterybabylontimelines.html

## Come Out of Her My People: Persecution Begins

# OUTLINE OF THE AGE

Come out of her, My people by C W Steinle
Do not copy for publication without written permission

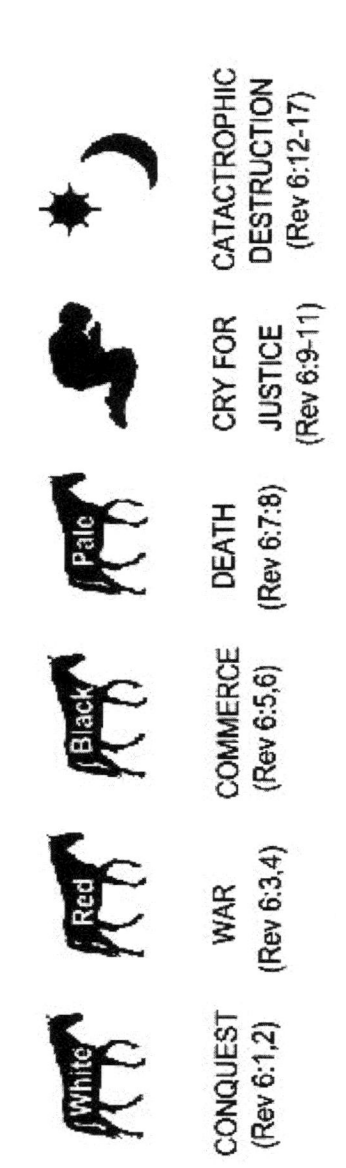

| White | Red | Black | Pale | | |
|---|---|---|---|---|---|
| CONQUEST (Rev 6:1,2) | WAR (Rev 6:3,4) | COMMERCE (Rev 6:5,6) | DEATH (Rev 6:7,8) | CRY FOR JUSTICE (Rev 6:9-11) | CATACTROPHIC DESTRUCTION (Rev 6:12-17) |

# The Olivet Discourse (Matthew 24) With The Seven Seals Timeline

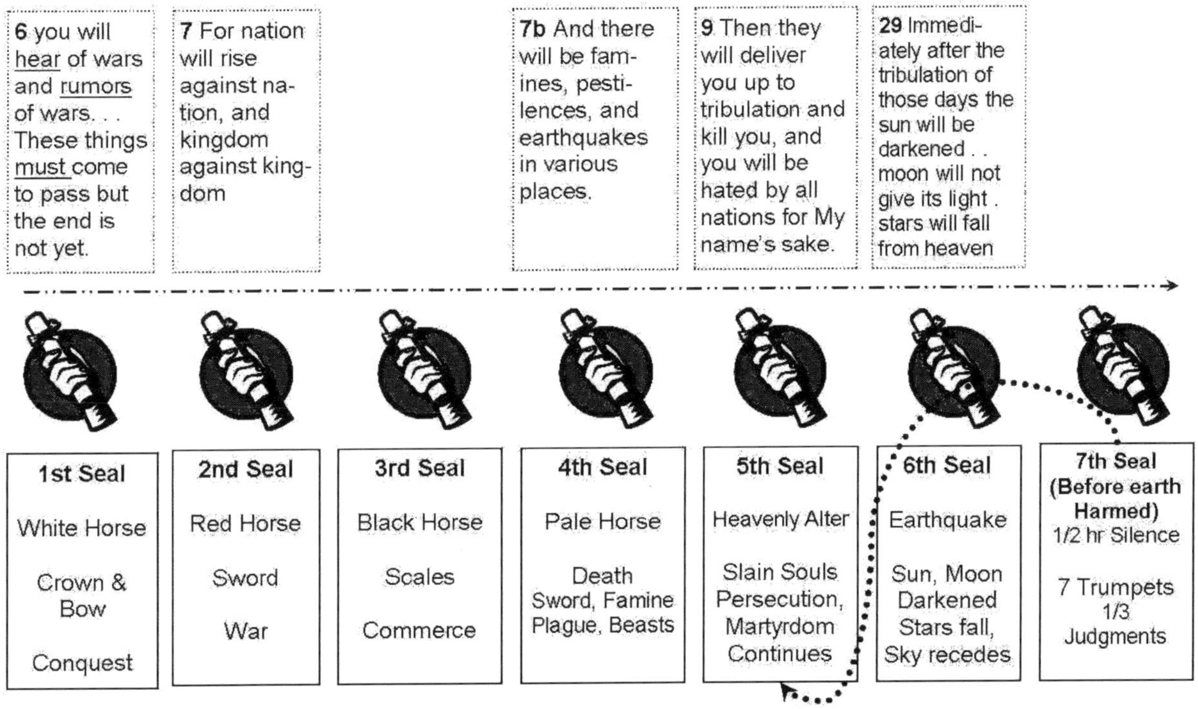

**6** you will hear of wars and rumors of wars.... These things must come to pass but the end is not yet.

**7** For nation will rise against nation, and kingdom against kingdom

**7b** And there will be famines, pestilences, and earthquakes in various places.

**9** Then they will deliver you up to tribulation and kill you, and you will be hated by all nations for My name's sake.

**29** Immediately after the tribulation of those days the sun will be darkened... moon will not give its light . stars will fall from heaven

| 1st Seal | 2nd Seal | 3rd Seal | 4th Seal | 5th Seal | 6th Seal | 7th Seal (Before earth Harmed) |
|---|---|---|---|---|---|---|
| White Horse | Red Horse | Black Horse | Pale Horse | Heavenly Alter | Earthquake | 1/2 hr Silence |
| Crown & Bow | Sword | Scales | Death | Slain Souls Persecution, Martyrdom Continues | Sun, Moon Darkened Stars fall, Sky recedes | 7 Trumpets 1/3 Judgments |
| Conquest | War | Commerce | Sword, Famine Plague, Beasts | | | |

## Chapter 4: The Heavenly Kingdom Completed

Revelation Chapter 7 takes us back to a point in time prior to the opening of the sixth seal, before the earth, sea or trees have been harmed. We are also taken to a different setting - the heavenly throne room of God.

*Revelation 7*

*"After these things I saw four angels standing at the four corners of the earth, holding the four winds of the earth, that the wind should not blow on the earth, on the sea, or on any tree. Then I saw another angel ascending from the east, having the seal of the living God. And he cried with a loud voice to the four angels to whom it was granted to harm the earth and the sea, saying, "Do not harm the earth, the sea, or the trees till we have sealed the servants of our God on their foreheads.""*

Chapter seven gives assurance that heaven will be full of both Jews and Gentiles before the end of the age. Verse three does not tell us whether the sealing of the 144,000 Jews takes place over the centuries, or if it was the campaign of a moment. The matter of importance is that there is "a completeness" to the remnant of God's chosen.

*Revelation 7 cont.*

*"And I heard the number of those who were sealed. One hundred and forty-four thousand of all the tribes of the children of Israel were sealed: of the tribe of Judah twelve thousand were sealed; of the tribe of Reuben twelve thousand were sealed; of the tribe of Gad twelve thousand were sealed; of the tribe of Asher twelve thousand were sealed; of the tribe of Naphtali twelve thousand were sealed; of the tribe of Manasseh twelve thousand were sealed; of the tribe of Simeon twelve thousand were sealed; of the tribe of Levi twelve thousand were sealed; of the tribe of Issachar twelve thousand were sealed; of the tribe of Zebulun twelve thousand were sealed; of the tribe of Joseph twelve thousand were sealed; of the tribe of Benjamin twelve thousand were sealed."*

*"After these things I looked, and behold, a great multitude which no one could number, of all nations, tribes, peoples, and tongues, standing before the throne and before the Lamb, clothed with white robes, with palm branches in their hands, and crying out with a loud voice, saying, "Salvation belongs to our God who sits on the throne, and to the Lamb!" All the angels stood around the throne and the elders*

*and the four living creatures, and fell on their faces before the throne and worshiped God, saying: "Amen! Blessing and glory and wisdom, Thanksgiving and honor and power and might, Be to our God forever and ever. Amen." Then one of the elders answered, saying to me, "Who are these arrayed in white robes, and where did they come from?" And I said to him, "Sir, you know." So he said to me, "These are the ones who come out of the great tribulation, and washed their robes and made them white in the blood of the Lamb. Therefore they are before the throne of God, and serve Him day and night in His temple. And He who sits on the throne will dwell among them. They shall neither hunger anymore nor thirst anymore; the sun shall not strike them, nor any heat; for the Lamb who is in the midst of the throne will shepherd them and lead them to living fountains of waters. And God will wipe away every tear from their eyes.""*

The impression of Chapter 7 is a heaven filled to completeness, with both Messianic Jews and Gentile believers. We are told at the beginning of Chapter seven that the earth, sea, and trees were not to be harmed until after God's servants had been sealed on their foreheads. It becomes obvious as we take a close look at this second group gathered before the throne that the Great Tribulation is underway. They are obviously Christians because their righteous covering has come to them at the expense of Jesus' shed blood. There are a great number of these believers present. By the dialog that takes place between the elder and St. John, it is obvious that God wants to draw special attention to the fact of where these Christians have come from. First we are told forthright that *"These are the ones who come out of the great tribulation."* And just to make sure we know that these have not avoided the Great Tribulation altogether, the elder recites the Lord's consolation to them that *"they shall neither hunger anymore nor thirst anymore; the sun shall not strike them, nor any heat."* There would be no need for these words of comfort if they had not just come from experiencing these very trials. But in fact they are portrayed as still smoking from the intense heat of scorching sunlight until the moment that they are shielded by their white robes. And suffering the great thirst that would logically accompany abnormally high temperatures is met with God's consolation of *"living fountains of waters."* Whatever tribulations these saints were brought out of caused such distress that uncontrollable sobbing resulted. Thus the specific consolation, *"And God will wipe away every tear from their eyes."*

Daniel 12:7 warns that the last three and one-half year period will not come until the power of the Holy People is completely shattered.

*"Then I heard the man clothed in linen, who was above the waters of the river, when he held up his right hand and his left hand to heaven, and swore by Him who lives forever, that it shall be for a time, times, and half a time; and when the power of the holy people has been completely shattered, all these things shall be finished."* When the Jews no longer had the right to enforce their own laws because of Rome's control - that's when our Savior came the first time. It shouldn't be a surprise that God's deliverance would come again at a moment that conforms to the scenario spoken to Daniel.

So what about the pre-tribulation rapture that began to be taught in the late nineteenth century? Do an internet search on "Darby" and "the rapture," or type this address into your browser:

http://christianity.about.com/od/faqhelpdesk/a/whatisrapture_3.htm

It is interesting that the Roman Catholics who developed the Futurist interpretation of Revelation would reject the rapture theory which John Nelson Darby originated about 240 years later. But most American Protestants have adopted both of these doctrines. The author desires to take a non-denominational approach to interpreting Revelation. This approach requires looking at the verses without the filter of any of the four major views. Just as God allows trials in the life of believers, God's deliverance from wrath could be fulfilled by a Christian's deliverance from hell. In other words, it might not be about this life on earth. Here is something to ponder: If all believers will be delivered from the Day of God's wrath, why did Jesus tell us to pray that we might be counted so righteous that we would receive the reward of Enoch and escape the time of tribulation?

*"But take heed to yourselves, lest your hearts be weighed down with carousing, drunkenness, and cares of this life, and that Day come on you unexpectedly. For it will come as a snare on all those who dwell on the face of the whole earth. Watch therefore, and pray always that you may be counted worthy to escape all these things that will come to pass, and to stand before the Son of Man."* - Luke 21:34-36

Have you prayed that prayer today and avoided the cares of this life and the attitude of ease? Whose theory brings about the proper fruit in your walk? You must decide for yourself. Jesus would not have asked us to pray this prayer unless it was truly possible for some to escape the Great Tribulation. And we know from Paul's writings that *"we shall not all sleep, but we will all be changed."* But we just don't know how many people will be involved, or at what time (or times) this event will take place.

## Chapter 5: The Seventh Seal and the Seven Trumpets

Most of the events in Chapters 8 and 9 concern the destruction of one-third of the earth. As we build a case for the identity of the Great Harlot (Babylon the Great), we must consider the possibility that a conspiracy of nations might inadvertently bring about the destruction of the entire Western Hemisphere (roughly one-third of the earth).

*Revelation 8, verses 1-7*

*"When He opened the seventh seal, there was silence in heaven for about half an hour. And I saw the seven angels who stand before God, and to them were given seven trumpets. Then another angel, having a golden censer, came and stood at the altar. He was given much incense, that he should offer it with the prayers of all the saints upon the golden altar which was before the throne. And the smoke of the incense, with the prayers of the saints, ascended before God from the angel's hand. Then the angel took the censer, filled it with fire from the altar, and threw it to the earth. And there were noises, thunderings, lightnings, and an earthquake. So the seven angels who had the seven trumpets prepared themselves to sound. The first angel sounded: And hail and fire followed, mingled with blood, and they were thrown to the earth. And a third of the trees were burned up, and all green grass was burned up."*

When the Lamb opens the seventh seal, we find ourselves at a point in time somewhere before the final catastrophic destructions of the sixth seal. The content of the seventh seal is the seven angelic trumpeters. As the prayers of the saints ascend before God, *"noises, thunderings, lightnings, and an earthquake"* descend from heaven. And so begins a barrage of destructive forces on one third of the globe. These agents closely resemble the chemical, biological and nuclear weapons of mass destruction of our day.

*Revelation 8 cont, verses 8,9*

*"Then the second angel sounded: And something like a great mountain burning with fire was thrown into the sea, and a third of the sea became blood. And a third of the living creatures in the sea died, and a third of the ships were destroyed."*

When we consider that in the Apostle John's day no bombs existed, the best description of multiple nuclear explosions would be a great mountain thrown into the sea, accompanied by fire. Jesus took Peter,

James and John up to an exceedingly high mountain, and that great mountain was most likely Mount Hermon on the Israeli-Lebanese-Syrian border. The base of Mount Hermon covers many miles, and its peak is most often snow capped and enshrouded in misty clouds. In the mind's eye, something like massive Mount Hermon being thrown into the sea, accompanied by flames, would be a genuine attempt on John's part to describe something beyond description 2,000 years ago. The ramifications of the explosions in Verse 8 would logically be a subsurface concussion and shock wave, agreeing with the results in Verse 9.

*Revelation 8 cont., verses 10-12*

*"Then the third angel sounded: And a great star fell from heaven, burning like a torch, and it fell on a third of the rivers and on the springs of water. The name of the star is Wormwood. A third of the waters became wormwood, and many men died from the water, because it was made bitter. Then the fourth angel sounded: And a third of the sun was struck, a third of the moon, and a third of the stars, so that a third of them were darkened. A third of the day did not shine, and likewise the night."*

Once again, these weapons of mass destruction are perceived as falling from heaven. The phrase *"burning like a torch"-Revelation 8:10* might be John's way of describing the propulsion of a guided missile. The first and second trumpets unleash an explosive and fiery destruction. The third trumpet resembles the effect of chemical warfare. The waters of a third of the rivers are tainted with a deadly poison and *"many men died from the water."-Revelation 8:11* When the fourth angel sounded, there is no mention of new weapons falling from the sky, but the smoke and earthen particles have now had a chance to become airborne so that the sun, moon and stars are darkened over the third of the earth affected. If the sealing of the 144,000 in Chapter 7 occurs quickly, then it would be necessary to hold back the wind, to prevent the contamination of the remaining two-thirds of the earth.

# Dispensation of End Times Judgements

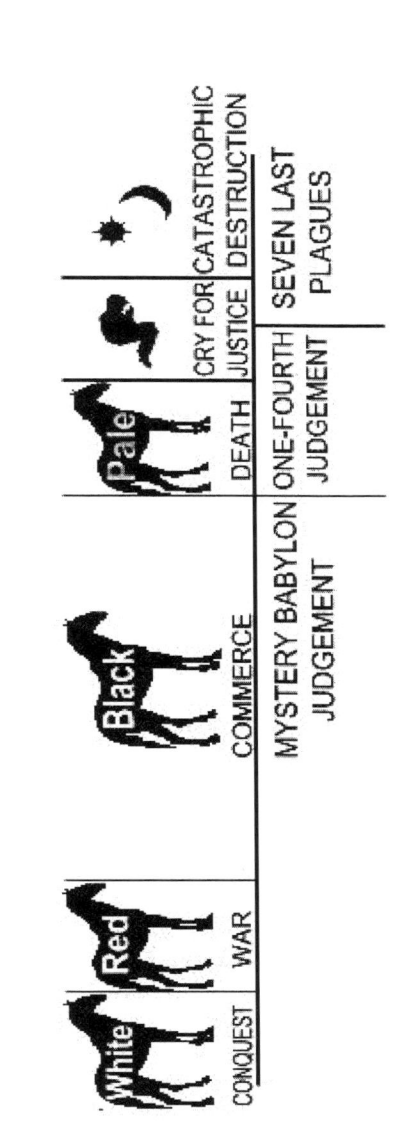

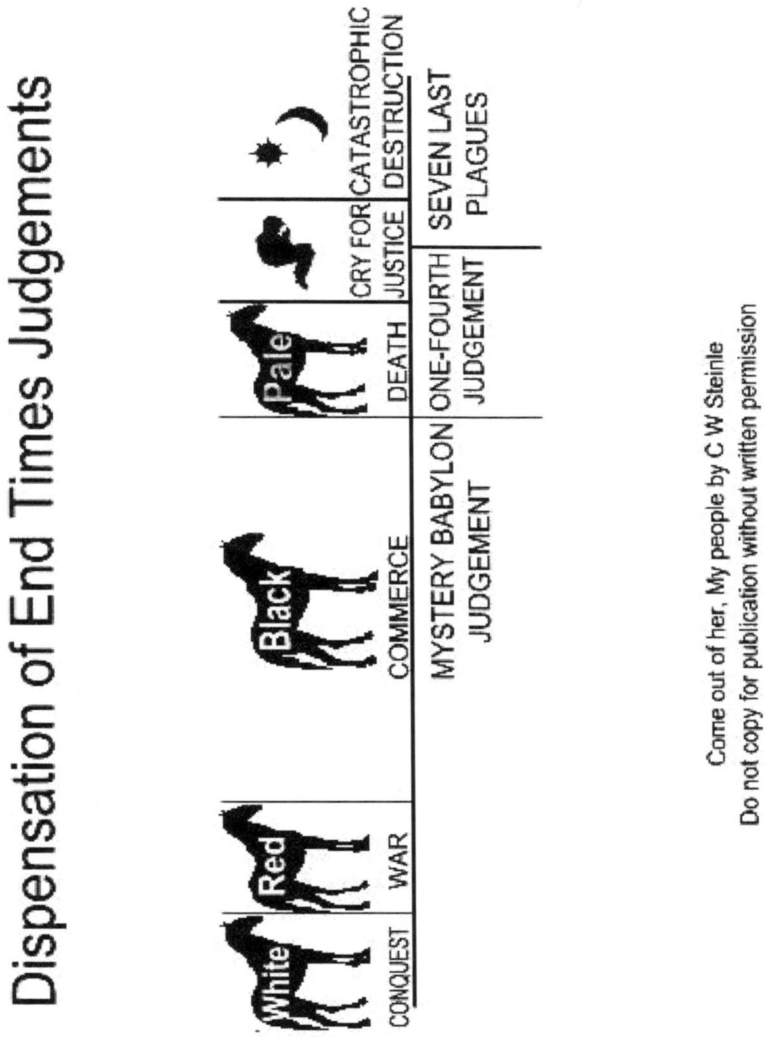

| White | Red | Black | Pale | | |
|-------|-----|-------|------|---|---|
| CONQUEST | WAR | COMMERCE | DEATH | CRY FOR JUSTICE | CATASTROPHIC DESTRUCTION |
| | | MYSTERY BABYLON JUDGEMENT | ONE-FOURTH JUDGEMENT | | SEVEN LAST PLAGUES |

Come out of her, My people by C W Steinle
Do not copy for publication without written permission

# Come Out of Her My People: Persecution Begins

*Revelation 8 cont., verse 13*

*"And I looked, and I heard an angel flying through the midst of heaven, saying with a loud voice, "Woe, woe, woe to the inhabitants of the earth, because of the remaining blasts of the trumpet of the three angels who are about to sound!"* These next three destructive forces are so potent that regions beyond the western hemisphere will be affected. Thus the warning, *"to the inhabitants of the earth."*

*Revelation 9, verses 1-12*

*"Then the fifth angel sounded: And I saw a star fallen from heaven to the earth. To him was given the key to the bottomless pit. And he opened the bottomless pit, and smoke arose out of the pit like the smoke of a great furnace. So the sun and the air were darkened because of the smoke of the pit. Then out of the smoke locusts came upon the earth. And to them was given power, as the scorpions of the earth have power. They were commanded not to harm the grass of the earth, or any green thing, or any tree, but only those men who do not have the seal of God on their foreheads. And they were not given authority to kill them, but to torment them for five months. Their torment was like the torment of a scorpion when it strikes a man. In those days men will seek death and will not find it; they will desire to die, and death will flee from them. The shape of the locusts was like horses prepared for battle. On their heads were crowns of something like gold, and their faces were like the faces of men. They had hair like women's hair, and their teeth were like lions' teeth. And they had breastplates like breastplates of iron, and the sound of their wings was like the sound of chariots with many horses running into battle. They had tails like scorpions, and there were stings in their tails. Their power was to hurt men five months. And they had as king over them the angel of the bottomless pit, whose name in Hebrew is Abaddon, but in Greek he has the name Apollyon. One woe is past. Behold, still two more woes are coming after these things."*

When the fifth angel sounded, another projectile was seen striking the earth. This device drove deep into the earth and apparently pierced the earth's crust so that a volcanic fountain was formed. John describes the scene as smoke rising out of the pit, *"like the smoke of a great furnace."* Once again, *"the sun and the air were darkened because of the smoke of the pit."*-Revelation 9:2 Verse 3 tells us that locusts came out of the smoke and power was given to them to strike people who did not have *"the seal of God on their foreheads."*-Revelation 9:4 The sting of these locusts had no effect on plant life, nor did it bring about death, but apparently acted as a type of nerve agent, and remained in the victim's system for five months. Because Satan does not have the power of a creator, these locusts must already exist; or they are the work of bio-scientists. It seems logical that these locusts might be microscopic, due to the fact that they are carried on smoke particles. Verse 7 further describes the locusts as being like horses, with golden crowns on their heads, having the faces of men, the hair of women, and the teeth of a lion. There exists a multitude of strange looking microscopic life forms; and it may be that John is conveying his description of one of these. It is also possible that John is seeing something from the spirit realm.

*Revelation 9 cont., verses 13-21*

*"Then the sixth angel sounded: And I heard a voice from the four horns of the golden altar which is before God, saying to the sixth angel who had the trumpet, "Release the four angels who are bound at the great river Euphrates." So the four angels, who had been prepared for the hour and day and month and year, were released to kill a third of mankind. Now the number of the army of the horsemen was two hundred million; I heard the number of them. And thus I saw the horses in the vision: those who sat on them had breastplates of fiery red, hyacinth blue, and sulfur yellow; and the heads of the horses were like the heads of lions; and out of their mouths came fire, smoke, and brimstone. By these three plagues a third of mankind was killed—by the fire and the smoke and the brimstone which came out of their mouths. For their power is in their mouths and in their tails; for their tails are like serpents, having heads; and with them they do harm. But the rest of mankind, who were not killed by these plagues, did not repent of the works of their hands, that they should not worship demons, and idols of gold, silver, brass, stone, and wood, which can neither see nor hear nor walk. And they did not repent of their murders or their sorceries or their sexual immorality or their thefts."*

At the sound of the sixth trumpet, four angels are released in a region of the earth where animosity toward Israel and the United States of America abounds. The weaponry brought against the condemned third of the earth is not limited to aerial weapons of mass destruction but is expanded to include enemy armies as well. Once again, creatures currently unknown are described. The word "horses" could be used to describe something larger than a man that has the ability to travel on the ground. These "horses" apparently have front and rear mounted guns or missiles. In Verse 20 we see that the other two-thirds of the earth, *"the rest of mankind,"* were not killed and continue in their idolatrous lifestyle and brazen disobedience to God.

# COMMERCE
## MYSTERY BABYLON
## JUDGEMENT

| Beasts emerge | Initial attack | Four Angels Ensure Hevean is filled: Jews & Gentiles | **Seven Trumpets 1/3 Judgements** |
|---|---|---|---|
| World trading Blocks Formed | Call to Come Out | | |

**1.** Hail, Fire, Blood 1/3 Earth, Trees, Grass, Burned

**2.** Burning Mtn Thrown to Sea. 1/3 Sea Blood Fish & Ships destroyed

**3.** Star falls on Water 1/3 of water Bitter

**4.** Sky Darkened, 1/3 Sun, Moon, Stars Struck

**5.** Star opens Bottomless Pit: Smoke & Locusts

**6.** Four Angels released 1/3 Mankind Killed

- - - - - - - - - - - - - - - - - - - - - -

The Little Book

- - - - - - - - - - - - - - - - - - - - - -

**7.** Christ's Possession of Earth Celebrated in Heaven

Come out of her, My people by C W Steinle
Do not copy for publication without
Written permission

## Chapter 6: The Secrets of the Separate Scroll

*Revelation 10, verses 1-7*

*"I saw still another mighty angel coming down from heaven, clothed with a cloud. And a rainbow was on his head, his face was like the sun, and his feet like pillars of fire. He had a little book open in his hand. And he set his right foot on the sea and his left foot on the land, and cried with a loud voice, as when a lion roars. When he cried out, seven thunders uttered their voices. Now when the seven thunders uttered their voices, I was about to write; but I heard a voice from heaven saying to me, "Seal up the things which the seven thunders uttered, and do not write them." The angel whom I saw standing on the sea and on the land raised up his hand to heaven and swore by Him who lives forever and ever, who created heaven and the things that are in it, the earth and the things that are in it, and the sea and the things that are in it, that there should be delay no longer, but in the days of the sounding of the seventh angel, when he is about to sound, the mystery of God would be finished, as He declared to His servants the prophets."*

Now that the Lamb has opened the seven seals of the first scroll, another scroll (*"little book"*) is delivered to John by a mighty angel resembling the Son of Man. The fact that this angel had *"his right foot on the sea and his left foot on the land"* might serve to indicate that he was turning John's attention to distant continents. Hebrew writings contemporaneous to Revelation use the word *"land"* when referring to the Promised Land. *"Sea"* refers to the Gentile nations. One of the secrets in this section of Scripture is the utterance of the seven thunders. We will have to wait until heaven for the words of the thunders to be revealed since John was instructed not to write them down.

The second secret is the mystery that will be finished in the days prior to the sounding of the seventh angel. We are told in Verse 7 that a *"mystery of God"* has been prophesied by the servants of God, and that it will be *"finished"* just as the seventh trumpet is about to sound.

# Come Out of Her My People: Persecution Begins

*Revelation 10 cont., verses 8-11*

*"Then the voice which I heard from heaven spoke to me again and said, "Go, take the little book which is open in the hand of the angel who stands on the sea and on the earth." So I went to the angel and said to him, "Give me the little book." And he said to me, "Take and eat it; and it will make your stomach bitter, but it will be as sweet as honey in your mouth." Then I took the little book out of the angel's hand and ate it, and it was as sweet as honey in my mouth. But when I had eaten it, my stomach became bitter. And he said to me, "You must prophesy again about many peoples, nations, tongues, and kings."*

Taking the little book and eating represents John's "digestion" of the message and of its consequences. Independent of the scroll of the Lamb, the little book just received refers to the words of God that are about to be given to John. In this separate section we find a re-telling of the Jews spiritual plight, and new prophecy to different people and other kings; *"Prophesy again about many peoples, nations, tongues, and kings."*

*Revelation 11, verses 1 and 2*

*"Then I was given a reed like a measuring rod. And the angel stood, saying, "Rise and measure the temple of God, the altar, and those who worship there. But leave out the court which is outside the temple, and do not measure it, for it has been given to the Gentiles. And they will tread the holy city underfoot for forty-two months."*

One of the first prophecies of John is that the Temple will be rebuilt in Jerusalem. It has been noted by many that the outer court has been given to the Gentiles, who *"tread the holy city underfoot for forty-two months."-Revelation 11:2* Today, the golden dome of the Shrine of the Rock is the most prominent landmark on the Holy Temple Mount. It is speculated by many that Herod's Temple (the Temple of Jesus' day) was located to the north of the Shrine. A small stone gazebo, called the Arch of the Spirits, covers an outcrop of bedrock in line with the ancient Eastern Gate to the Temple. If a temple is constructed, so as to locate the Holy of Holies over the Arch of the Spirits, there would be enough room for the temple to be dimensioned according to God's instructions. However, the space outside the Holy Place, referred to as "the outer court," cannot be re-built because it is currently occupied by the Dome of the Rock structure; thus, *"it has been given to the Gentiles."*

*Revelation 11 cont., verses 3-6*

*"And I will give power to my two witnesses, and they will prophesy one thousand two hundred and sixty days, clothed in sackcloth." These are the two olive trees and the two lampstands standing before the God of the earth. And if anyone wants to harm them, fire proceeds from their mouth and devours their enemies. And if anyone wants to harm them, he must be killed in this manner. These have power to shut heaven, so that no rain falls in the days of their prophecy; and they have power over waters to turn them to blood, and to strike the earth with all plagues, as often as they desire."*

In Verse 3 we are introduced to the two witnesses that are later martyred for their stand against evil. Power from on high is bestowed upon these prophets. And these two speak the word of God in humility (clothed in sackcloth). Just as the term *"forty-two months"* was given above, the *"1,260 days"* is given as the term of the two prophets' service. These numeric equivalents of a three and one-half year period most likely indicate that these events are part of Daniel's last week. But we don't get the impression that one-third of the earth is being destroyed during this time, or that another one-fourth of mankind is perishing. These events of the little scroll don't seem in any way bounded by, or bonded with, the Trumpet Judgments which Ribera ties to the covenant-week. However, as noted previously, the *"1,260 days"* could be referring to the years which Historicists claim the Roman Catholic Church ruled over Christendom. If this is the case, the number 42 may also have a significant prophetic application of its own. Verse 4 further identifies the prophetic duo as the two olive trees spoken of by Zechariah. Bible scholars assume that these two prophets are people, with the supernatural abilities associated with Moses and Elijah. This is the obvious interpretation of this verse. The bodies of both of these prophets were never found, according to the Bible. In fact, Jesus was seen talking to Moses and Elijah on the Mount of Transfiguration hundreds of years after these men walked the earth.

# Come Out of Her My People: Persecution Begins

*Luke 9:28-36*

*"Now it came to pass, about eight days after these sayings, that He took Peter, John, and James and went up on the mountain to pray. As He prayed, the appearance of His face was altered, and His robe became white and glistening. And behold, two men talked with Him, who were Moses and Elijah, who appeared in glory and spoke of His decease which He was about to accomplish at Jerusalem. But Peter and those with him were heavy with sleep; and when they were fully awake, they saw His glory and the two men who stood with Him. Then it happened, as they were parting from Him, that Peter said to Jesus, "Master, it is good for us to be here; and let us make three tabernacles: one for You, one for Moses, and one for Elijah"—not knowing what he said. While he was saying this, a cloud came and overshadowed them; and they were fearful as they entered the cloud. And a voice came out of the cloud, saying, "This is My beloved Son. Hear Him!" When the voice had ceased, Jesus was found alone."*

Peter makes the following certification concerning the Mount of Transfiguration experience.

*2$^{nd}$ Peter 1:16-18*

*"For we did not follow cunningly devised fables when we made known to you the power and coming of our Lord Jesus Christ, but were eyewitnesses of His majesty. For He received from God the Father honor and glory when such a voice came to Him from the Excellent Glory: "This is My beloved Son, in whom I am well pleased." And we heard this voice which came from heaven when we were with Him on the holy mountain."*

Furthermore, one of Moses' most memorable miracles was turning the waters of the Nile into blood. Likewise, Elijah's miracles include holding back the rain. So it is anticipated that the Two Witnesses will be none other than Moses and Elijah, or at least men with similar abilities.

*Revelation 11 cont., 7-13*

*"When they finish their testimony, the beast that ascends out of the bottomless pit will make war against them, overcome them, and kill them. And their dead*

*bodies will lie in the street of the great city which spiritually is called Sodom and Egypt, where also our Lord was crucified. Then those from the peoples, tribes, tongues, and nations will see their dead bodies three-and-a-half days, and not allow their dead bodies to be put into graves. And those who dwell on the earth will rejoice over them, make merry, and send gifts to one another, because these two prophets tormented those who dwell on the earth. Now after the three-and-a-half days the breath of life from God entered them, and they stood on their feet, and great fear fell on those who saw them. And they heard a loud voice from heaven saying to them, "Come up here." And they ascended to heaven in a cloud, and their enemies saw them. In the same hour there was a great earthquake, and a tenth of the city fell. In the earthquake seven thousand people were killed, and the rest were afraid and gave glory to the God of heaven."*

If we consider the possibility that these two prophets might also represent nations of our day, the United States of America and Great Britain are the best candidates for the role of the two witnesses. There would appear to be a great conflict for the United States to be both a witness of God and defender of Israel and, also, to be the Great Harlot. However, remember the reaction of John in Revelation 17:6, *"And when I saw her, I marveled with great amazement,"* and the answer of the angel to John, *"Why did you marvel? I will tell you the mystery of the woman and of the beast that carries her."-Revelation 17:7* The answer to the puzzle may lie in Verse 7 of Chapter 11, *"When they finish their testimony."* In the Old Testament, God refers to Judah and Israel as adulteresses because they were once committed to God, but yet they turned away and were disloyal to Him. Could it be, then, that the United States "finished her testimony" and that God allowed her to be judged similarly to the captivity of Judah and Israel? Perhaps the strongest indication that one of the witnesses and the Great Harlot are one-in-the-same is that the beast that comes up from the bottomless pit is responsible for the destruction of both. In Verse 7 we are introduced to the beast that ascends out of the bottomless pit. Formerly, in Chapter 9, Verse 11, we see the authority governing the demonic locusts and are told he is *"the angel of the bottomless pit,"* and he bears the name of Satan. In Chapter 11, Verse 7, *"the beast that ascends out of the bottomless pit"* must refer to the nation that he rules and that is identified with his name.

## Come Out of Her My People: Persecution Begins

*Revelation 11 cont., verses 14-19*

*"The second woe is past. Behold, the third woe is coming quickly."*

This verse tells us that Chapters 10 and 11, up until Verse 15, is a parenthetical discourse. We are reminded by Verse 14 of the trumpet sequence. The second woe is synonymous with the sixth trumpet. This trumpet releases the four angels who lead the final campaign on a third of the earth by means of two-hundred million troops.

*"Then the seventh angel sounded: And there were loud voices in heaven, saying, "The kingdoms of this world have become the kingdoms of our Lord and of His Christ, and He shall reign forever and ever!" And the twenty-four elders who sat before God on their thrones fell on their faces and worshiped God, saying: " We give You thanks, O Lord God Almighty, The One who is and who was and who is to come, Because You have taken Your great power and reigned. The nations were angry, and Your wrath has come, And the time of the dead, that they should be judged, And that You should reward Your servants the prophets and the saints, And those who fear Your name, small and great, And should destroy those who destroy the earth." Then the temple of God was opened in heaven, and the ark of His covenant was seen in His temple. And there were lightnings, noises, thunderings, an earthquake, and great hail."*

The setting for the seventh trumpet is the heavenly throne room. Just as the Lord Jesus announced that the kingdom of God was at hand, the heavenly heralds and the twenty-four elders proclaim that the day of the Lord is about to fall on the kingdom of man. As a poem of thanks for God's omnipotence, and the announcement that the day of God's judgment upon nations is recited, a heavenly percussion section gives its accompaniment with *"lightnings, and noises, thunderings, an earthquake, and great hail."*

Chapter 12 takes us outside of time with a heavenly vision (sign) in which we zoom out in our perspective. Just as we were taken back to the end of the seven churches of Asia Minor, and covered the ages up until the end of the earth as we know it; Chapter 12 covers a time period from before the birth of Christ through the era of persecution, represented by the fifth seal of the scroll opened in Revelation 6:9.

*Revelation 12, verses 1-6*

*"Now a great sign appeared in heaven: a woman clothed with the sun, with the moon under her feet, and on her head a garland of twelve stars. Then being with child, she cried out in labor and in pain to give birth. And another sign appeared in heaven: behold, a great, fiery red dragon having seven heads and ten horns, and seven diadems on his heads. His tail drew a third of the stars of heaven and threw them to the earth. And the dragon stood before the woman who was ready to give birth, to devour her Child as soon as it was born. She bore a male Child who was to rule all nations with a rod of iron. And her Child was caught up to God and His throne. Then the woman fled into the wilderness, where she has a place prepared by God, that they should feed her there one thousand two hundred and sixty days."*

The entirety of Chapter 12 is a stand-alone allegory in which the key representations are the *"woman,"* the *"dragon,"* the *"Child,"* and *"the rest of her offspring."* The *"woman"* in Verse 1, clad with the sun, moon, and twelve stars, is easily identified as the nation of Israel when we recall the interpretation of Joseph's dream in Genesis 37:9; *"Then he dreamed still another dream and told it to his brothers, and said, 'Look, I have dreamed another dream. And this time, the sun, the moon, and the eleven stars bowed down to me.'"* This interpretation is further validated in Verse 5, in which the life of Christ on earth is encapsulated. The *"dragon"* is a sign representing Satan. Verse 4 tells us that his full following of demonic angels had been deployed on the earth.

We learn from the account of Christ's birth in the gospels that Herod did make attempts to *"devour her Child,"* which caused Joseph to take his family to Egypt for a time. Herod was so overcome by Satan's influence that he murdered countless infant males who were born around the time of Jesus' birth. Once the long-awaited Messiah had come and completed His ministry, *"the woman fled into the wilderness."* Verse 6 describes the expulsion of the Jews from Israel (the Diaspora) and the absorption of Jews into the surrounding nations. The reference to *"1,260 days"* in Verse 6 indicates that a flight of the Jews will also occur during the *"last week."*

## Come Out of Her My People: Persecution Begins

*Revelation 12 cont., verses 7-12*

*"And war broke out in heaven: Michael and his angels fought with the dragon; and the dragon and his angels fought, but they did not prevail, nor was a place found for them in heaven any longer. So the great dragon was cast out, that serpent of old, called the Devil and Satan, who deceives the whole world; he was cast to the earth, and his angels were cast out with him. Then I heard a loud voice saying in heaven, "Now salvation, and strength, and the kingdom of our God, and the power of His Christ have come, for the accuser of our brethren, who accused them before our God day and night, has been cast down. And they overcame him by the blood of the Lamb and by the word of their testimony, and they did not love their lives to the death. Therefore rejoice, O heavens, and you who dwell in them! Woe to the inhabitants of the earth and the sea! For the devil has come down to you, having great wrath, because he knows that he has a short time."*

Jesus, as the second person of the Trinity, has always had authority over all creation, including the most powerful of angels. It would appear that when the Jews were chased into the wilderness, Satan and his angels were also ejected from heaven. But the earth has not yet experienced the full force of Satan's fury. Likewise, believers still have an advocate in heaven Who is defending us against the accusations of Satan.

*1st John 2:1 "My little children, these things I write to you, so that you may not sin. And if anyone sins, we have an Advocate with the Father, Jesus Christ the righteous."*

Although these events were foreshadowed in the first century, and then again in WWII, they must be pointing to a future fall of Satan. The spiritual battles faced by today's Christians continue to be wrought with temptations of condemnation over past sins. The knowledge that Jesus is there in heaven defending us against Satan's accusations is essential for our victory over guilt.

Satan's banishment brings a bittersweet effect for believers. The accuser of the brethren is no longer heard in the heavenlies, but the faithful on the earth suffer persecution unto death. Verse 12 echoes this bittersweet blessing; *"Therefore rejoice, O heavens, and you who dwell in them! Woe to the inhabitants of the earth and the sea!"* So not only do the believers suffer because of Satan's predicament, but the inhabitants of the earth suffer as well.

*Revelation 12 cont., verses 13-17*

*"Now when the dragon saw that he had been cast to the earth, he persecuted the woman who gave birth to the male Child. But the woman was given two wings of a great eagle, that she might fly into the wilderness to her place, where she is nourished for a time and times and half a time, from the presence of the serpent. So the serpent spewed water out of his mouth like a flood after the woman, that he might cause her to be carried away by the flood. But the earth helped the woman, and the earth opened its mouth and swallowed up the flood which the dragon had spewed out of his mouth. And the dragon was enraged with the woman, and he went to make war with the rest of her offspring, who keep the commandments of God and have the testimony of Jesus Christ."*

Because Chapter 12 takes us back to the time of Christ, it seems reasonable to consider that the rest of the chapter covers the years from the time of Christ to the end. The *"woman,"* who is the nation of Israel, was persecuted by Rome and fled into the wilderness during the time that the New Testament was written. But the use of the phrase *"for a time and times and half a time"* in Verse 14 indicates further persecution during the End Times.

It is interesting how well the description of the *"flood"* in Verses 15 and 16 relate to the persecution of the Jews by the Nazis. The Jews had been dispersed into the *"wilderness"* by being scattered throughout the world. The *"flood"* that was sent forth by Satan may be describing the armies of Hitler. In the Book of Daniel, we read in Chapter 9, Verse 26; *"And the people of the prince who is to come shall destroy the city and the sanctuary. The end of it shall be with a flood, and till the end of the war desolations are determined."* And in Daniel 11:22 we read; *"With the force of a flood they shall be swept away from before him and be broken, and also the prince of the covenant."* In both of these verses the *"flood"* represents an unstoppable military force. Revelation 12:15 states the serpent's intentions; *"that he might cause her to be carried away by the flood."* Here, *"to be carried away"* implies being annihilated. Satan's efforts were thwarted when the world defeated

Hitler's armies, and in Verse 16 we read; *"But the earth helped the woman, and the earth opened its mouth and swallowed up the flood which the dragon had spewed out of his mouth."* These Scriptures could be describing the Holocaust of the Second World War. Or perhaps both; the Diaspora, and the Holocaust of the Second World War, are foreshadowing a persecution yet to come. Verse 17 describes Satan as intensely frustrated because of the survival of the Jews. His final attack comes upon the believers in Jesus Christ.

## Chapter 7: The Beasts of Power and Deception

Here we must pause and consider whether the beast we have been introduced to is actually some monstrous creature, or whether we are still discussing a nation. God has already established the correct interpretation of these beasts and horns, if we use the Biblical interpretation rule of "first mention," as was previously discussed. We conclude that none of the beasts in Daniel were literal creatures, just as the horns were not literal horns. It is true that John's visions in Revelation have been romantically interpreted in the past. For instance, the word "antichrist" is not found in the Book of Daniel nor in the Book of Revelation. This term is used in 1st John to define a spiritual principality. *"Beloved, do not believe every spirit, but test the spirits, whether they are of God; because many false prophets have gone out into the world. By this you know the Spirit of God: Every spirit that confesses that Jesus Christ has come in the flesh is of God, and every spirit that does not confess that Jesus Christ has come in the flesh is not of God. And this is the spirit of the Antichrist, which you have heard was coming, and is now already in the world."-1st John 4:1-3* This *"spirit of the Antichrist"* is responsible for false gospels and cult religions that deny the incarnation of God as Jesus Christ. This Scripture points out that, *"many false prophets have gone out into the world."* Jesus made a distinction between false christs and false prophets, and John, although familiar with the term *"Antichrist,"* is led by the Holy Spirit to call the leader of the beast from the earth the *"false prophet."*

A complete reading of the Book of Revelation reveals that the beast is called a *"beast"* throughout the text. Thus, we must consider the strict interpretation, which consistently renders this beast as a people or nation, not a person or supernatural gargoyle. This beast is ultimately judged and sent into the *"lake of fire,"* or perdition. It is difficult for us, who are believers in the Lord Jesus Christ, to grasp such a universal judgment until we remember that Jesus spoke of the judgment of the nations in Matthew 25:31-41.

*"When the Son of Man comes in His glory, and all the holy angels with Him, then He will sit on the throne of His glory. All the nations will be gathered before Him, and He will separate them one from another, as a shepherd divides his sheep from the goats. And He will set the sheep on His right hand, but the goats on the left.*

*Then the King will say to those on His right hand, 'Come, you blessed of My Father, inherit the kingdom prepared for you from the foundation of the world: for I was hungry and you gave Me food; I was thirsty and you have Me drink; I was a stranger and you took Me in; I was naked and you clothed Me; I was sick and you visited Me; I was in prison and you came to Me.' Then the righteous will answer Him, saying, 'Lord, when did we see You hungry and feed You, or thirsty and give You drink? When did we see You a stranger and take You in, or naked and clothe You? Or when did we see You sick, or in prison, and come to You?' And the King will answer and say to them, 'Assuredly, I say to you, inasmuch as you did it to one of the least of these My brethren, you did it to Me.' Then He will also say to those on the left hand, 'Depart from Me, you cursed, into the everlasting fire prepared for the devil and his angels'."*

Here Jesus used the analogy of sheep and goats to represent a distinction between the nations that would be saved, and the nations that would face eternal judgment. This is not the only time in Scripture that nations are judged. When Abraham and his descendants were given the Promised Land, they were not allowed to conquer it immediately. The Bible tells us that the Canaanites were to bring God's wrath to its fullness through ever increasing wickedness. God told the Israelites to completely destroy the Canaanites and inhabit their land. The Canaanites were on the brink of extinction anyway because they had begun to kill their own babies. God considered the sacrifice of their children to the heathen gods of the surrounding nations to be the final sin that brought His wrath to its fullness. In the days of Noah, God brought judgment upon the entire earth except for Noah and seven of his relatives. So we must consider that this nation, or federated world union, represented by the beast in John's vision, might be judged by God as a whole. Even so, we know from Revelation 20:11-15 that all Christ-rejecting souls will be judged individually at the Great White Throne Judgment.

*Revelation 20, verses 11-15*

*"Then I saw a great white throne and Him who sat on it, from whose face the earth and the heaven fled away. And there was found no place for them. And I saw the dead, small and great, standing before God, and books were opened. And another book was opened, which is the Book of Life. And the dead were judged according to their works, by the things which were written in the books. The sea gave up the dead who were in it, and Death and Hades delivered up the dead who were in them. And they were judged, each one according to his works. Then Death and Hades*

were cast into the lake of fire. This is the second death. And anyone not found written in the Book of Life was cast into the lake of fire."

Before we study Chapter 13, it is necessary once again to review the Biblical interpretation of beasts, horns, and heads. Daniel 7:23 expressly refers to the fourth beast as a fourth kingdom. *"Thus he said: 'The fourth beast shall be a fourth kingdom on earth, which shall be different from all other kingdoms, and shall devour the whole earth, trample it and break it in pieces.'"* Horns are interpreted as kings, as in Daniel 8:20, which reads, *"The ram which you saw, having the two horns – they are the kings of Media and Persia;"* and in Revelation 17:12, which reads, *"The ten horns which you saw are ten kings."* Heads are interpreted as mountains, as in Revelation 17:9, *"Here is the mind which has wisdom: The seven heads are seven mountains on which the woman sits."* Because most walled cities were built on hills in Bible times, the heads could also be synonymous with cities.

*Revelation 13, verses 1 and 2*

*"Then I stood on the sand of the sea. And I saw a beast rising up out of the sea, having seven heads and ten horns, and on his horns ten crowns, and on his heads a blasphemous name. Now the beast which I saw was like a leopard, his feet were like the feet of a bear, and his mouth like the mouth of a lion. The dragon gave him his power, his throne, and great authority."*

As we begin to study the beast rising up from the sea, it is important to understand that this is the same beast upon which the Great Harlot resides. Chapters 17 and 18 fill out the details of the identity, and fall, of the *"woman"* and *"the beast that carries her."* Because Chapters 13, 17 and 18 discuss the same beasts and events, we will also study these chapters in a parallel fashion.

In the Books of Daniel and Revelation, we find examples of nations, *"beasts,"* that are later referenced by their leaders. These transitions are easy to follow because these leaders have previously been referred to as *"horns."* As we began Chapter 13, the beast is obviously a kingdom or nation. We are able to locate the beast by taking note that John stood on the edge of the sea and he was obviously gazing toward the sea in order to see the beast rising up out of the sea. In Chapter 17, Verse 1, the Great Harlot is said to sit *"on many waters."*

In Revelation 17:3, John must be carried away *"into the wilderness"* to see *"a woman,"* who is the Great Harlot, *"sitting on a scarlet beast which was full of names of blasphemy, having seven heads and ten horns."* The word *"wilderness"* in this verse means a remote place, or a place that sits alone. This implies that the beast is located far away from the places known during John's day. Chapter 17, Verse 15, states, *"The waters which you saw, where the harlot sits, are peoples, multitudes, nations, and tongues."* The beast is clearly a melting pot for the peoples of the world. One last hint is given which describes the beast, and it is found in Revelation 16:18-20.

*"And there were noises and thunderings and lightnings; and there was a great earthquake, such a mighty and great earthquake as had not occurred since men were on the earth. Now the great city was divided into three parts, and the cities of the nations fell. And great Babylon was remembered before God, to give her the cup of the wine of the fierceness of His wrath. Then every island fled away, and the mountains were not found. And great hail from heaven fell upon men, each hailstone about the weight of a talent. Men blasphemed God because of the plague of the hail, since that plague was exceeding great."*

As a result of the greatest earthquake known to man, Babylon the Great was *"remembered before God"* as the islands flee and the mountains are removed. This verse implies that Babylon the Great is an island, and is sunk as a result of the great earthquake. Note that this <u>removal by water</u> takes place during the time of God's wrath; and that the previous destruction of Babylon the Great, which occurred before the time of God's wrath in Revelation 14:8, was the <u>result of fire;</u> *"And she will be utterly burned with fire, for strong is the Lord God who judges her."* Therefore, in summary, this beast is a nation surrounded by water, in a place far away from the civilization that John knew, and was a melting pot of peoples from all over the world.

The beast from the sea is continually referred to as having *"seven heads and ten horns."* We find the first occurrence of such a beast in Daniel 7:7. Here we find the beast with ten horns is *"dreadful and terrible, exceedingly strong."* Throughout the Bible, horns are used as a symbol of power. As we have already quoted from Daniel 7:24, *"the ten horns are ten kings."* The seven heads of the beast from the sea are seven hills or cities. Several cities are known to be built on seven hills. The one most commonly identified is Rome, but Jerusalem and Shiloh were also built on seven hills.

The animal characteristics found in Revelation 13:2 are a conglomeration of separate beasts from the sea, also found in Daniel 7:3-6.

*"And four great beasts came up from the sea, each different from the other. The first was like a lion, and had eagle's wings. I watched till its wings were plucked off; and it was lifted up from the earth and made to stand on two feet like a man, and a man's heart was given to it. And suddenly another beast, a second, like a bear. It was raised up on one side, and had three ribs in its mouth between its teeth. And they said thus to it: 'Arise, devour much flesh!' After this I looked, and there was another, like a leopard, which had on its back four wings of a bird. The beast also had four heads, and dominion was given to it."*

One was like a lion, one was like a bear, and another like a leopard. Then Daniel sees the fourth beast with the ten horns which was different and greater than the former three. *"After this I saw in the night visions, and behold, a fourth beast, dreadful and terrible, exceedingly strong. It had huge iron teeth; it was devouring, breaking in pieces, and trampling the residue with its feet. It was different from all the beasts that were before it, and it had ten horns."-Daniel 7:7* The beast from the sea in Revelation has the characteristics of all four of the beasts in Daniel's vision.

We understand from the fulfillment of Daniel's vision concerning the Roman Empire and its conquest over the other "beasts," that John's beast is probably a type of the Roman Empire. Rome was a different type of empire. This beast, like no other, was ruled from Rome, a city which sits on seven hills. The beast rising up out of the sea had similar characteristics to the Roman Empire. These characteristics included having partially sovereign city-states, with a federal command center and a republican senate. We find a mystery in how this beast is connected with the other nations. Because it is represented by the leopard, the bear, and the lion, it would appear that the multi-state nation of the beast from the sea is part of a larger and similar world federation.

*Revelation 13 cont., verse 3*

*"And I saw one of his heads as if it had been mortally wounded, and his deadly wound was healed. And all the world marveled and followed the beast."*

Revelation 13:3 describes an event that may be the same as the first attack on Babylon the Great, which occurs in Revelation 14:8 and is described in Revelation 18:2. We know that the destruction of Babylon the Great takes place in two phases. The warning to *"Come out of her, my people"* comes between a preliminary attack, and the total destruction in one hour; where *"the great city Babylon shall be thrown down, and shall not be found anymore."-Revelation 18:21* There would be no reason for the warning to *"Come out"* to be given with only minutes left to respond before the destruction. And, there would be no reason for the warning to *"Come out"* to be given after the destruction had already occurred. Here in Revelation 13:3 we see that one of his heads had been wounded in such a manner that the victim would usually have died. Just as the beast was described by various animals, it is also described with a personal pronoun. But if we are faithful to the definitions of beasts, horns and heads, then Verse 3 may mean that a hill or city was struck with a nearly fatal blow.

Could this be describing the attack on the twin towers, which resulted in the world questioning the survival of the world's trading capital? Some of Wall Street's operations were damaged, and the market was closed for several days. It must have appeared to the rest of the world that the United States of America's survival was in jeopardy. The United States stock market had just reached a crescendo, and it looked like she was destined for another Great Depression, at the least. But at the writing of this book, the Dow Jones Industrial Average has regained its all-time high. The Pentagon, in Washington D.C., was also struck. The Pentagon was presumed to be impenetrable. For several hours the citizens of the United States, as well as the rest of the world, were left to wonder if the command post of the United States military had been disabled. More than one hundred Pentagon workers were killed, but the ability to control the armed forces was not diminished. *"And his deadly wound was healed. And all the world marveled and followed the beast."-Revelation 13:3*

*Revelation 13 cont., verses 4-7*

*"So they worshiped the dragon who gave authority to the beast; and they worshiped the beast, saying, 'Who is like the beast? Who is able to make war with him?' And he was given a mouth speaking great things and blasphemies, and he was given authority to continue for forty-two months. Then he opened his mouth in blasphemy against God, to blaspheme His name, His tabernacle, and those who dwell in heaven. It was granted to him to make war with the saints and to overcome them. And authority was given him over every tribe, tongue, and nation."*

When the United States of America was humbled by civil and world wars, the nation submitted to the authority of our Creator. Today the United States has rejected the authority of God and submitted to the authority of Satan, not entirely, but in the majority. Although Christians 'join' their religion by placing personal trust in Jesus and His sacrificial death on the cross, other religions around the world believe they are members of their faith from birth. Based upon the picture of American life presented by global media, the world views Christians as decadent and libertarian. The United States has become the predominant source of pornography, sexual immorality, and capitalistic greed. The world *"gave authority* (yielded) *to the beast."* The worship of the beast was the acknowledgement that this nation was like no other nation; thus the statement, *"Who is like the beast?"* The acknowledgement that no one was able to wage war with this nation confirms the fact that the wound was not inflicted upon a person, but upon a nation. Nations wage war, but individuals are killed.

Verse 5 once again confirms the assertion that the beast from the sea is a kingdom and not a king. First of all, people do not come up out of the sea, do not resemble various animals, do not have mountains or cities or kings, and do not need to be given a mouth. The ability to communicate with the rest of the world was perfected first in the United States of America. In only a few years, communications advanced from the telegraph to mass media; and even the internet. Unfortunately, the media has begun to promote ungodly philosophies and lifestyles. The blasphemy currently spoken by radio and video images goes beyond the ridicule of God, "His *name, His tabernacle, and those who dwell in heaven."-Revelation 13:6*

The next verse reveals a time to come, inevitably a very short time. Soon, persecution against Christians could become a reality in the United States of America as the majority of its citizens may be convinced that the way to peace is the rejection of all "radical" religions. Or, the leadership of the United States could actually embrace a religion that already violently opposes Christianity. The worldwide persecution of the saints is one of two remaining prophecies to be fulfilled before the destruction of Babylon the Great. The authority of the United States over all the rest of mankind has already become a reality. America acknowledges herself as the world's peacekeeper. But other nations perceive her strength as domination.

# Come Out of Her My People: Persecution Begins

*Revelation 13 cont., verses 8-10*

*"All who dwell on the earth will worship him, whose names have not been written in the Book of Life of the Lamb slain from the foundation of the world. If anyone has an ear, let him hear. He who leads into captivity shall go into captivity; he who kills with the sword must be killed with the sword. Here is the patience and the faith of the saints."*

Once the earth sees the beast persecuting believers all over the world, and being helpless to wage war, a situation will exist similar to the regime of Hitler. The worship of the beast will be a fear void of respect. (The saints themselves will always, and only, worship the Lord God of Israel; Father, Son, and Holy Spirit.)

*"If anyone has an ear, let him hear."* The verse that follows this command would seem to be some sort of riddle if these words had not already been given application in a previous Scripture. We find in Verse 10 a paraphrasing of verses found in Chapter 15 of Jeremiah. Authentic Bible study suggests that we look at the "first mention" of any word, phrase, type or symbol. The context of Jeremiah 15 is the warning of God's people to leave the Promised Land, and to cooperatively be led into captivity by the Assyrians. God was bringing chastening upon the land of His people because they had turned away from Him to follow after loathsome idols and customs that God deemed detestable. In the following verses from Jeremiah, God clearly casts His people out.

*"Then the LORD said to me, 'Even if Moses and Samuel stood before Me, My mind would not be favorable toward this people. Cast them out of My sight, and let them go forth. And it shall be, if they say to you, 'Where should we go?' then you shall tell them, 'Thus says the LORD: Such as are for death, to death; and such as are for the sword, to the sword; and such as are for the famine, to the famine; and such as are for the captivity, to the captivity.' 'And I will appoint over them four forms of destruction,' says the LORD: 'the sword to slay, and the dogs to drag, the birds of the heavens and the beasts of the earth to devour and destroy.'"-Jeremiah 15:1-3*

God's answer to their question, *"Where should we go?"* was to offer three undesirable choices, along with the choice to obey God's plan; which was captivity. It is also noteworthy, when considering the Bible study principle of "first mention," that under the symbol of the pale horse in Revelation 6:8 the plagues taking place at this point in time are the killing *"with sword, with hunger, with death, and by the beasts of the earth."*

It follows then, due to the placement of the warning to go into captivity, along with the plagues that God would bring on those who chose to remain; that these situations could both occur at the same time in the End Times.

The direct translation of Revelation 13:10a in the Greek is, *"if anyone has captivity, he will go away; if anyone is with the sword, it is necessary for him to be killed."*[1] This instruction to *"go away"* once again echoes the call of Revelation 18:4 to *"Come out of her, my people."* The authorities during the years of Jeremiah's warnings accused him of being a traitor and a discourager of the people of Israel. Revelation 13:10b offers further instruction and consolation. The decision to respond by those who have an *"ear to hear"* will require great patience and great faith. Just as in the day of Israel's captivity, the choice to move one's family and belongings to a foreign country will indeed require much faith. Patience (endurance) will also be necessary to discern the timing of God's command.

*Revelation 13 cont., verses 11-13*

*"Then I saw another beast coming up out of the earth, and he had two horns like a lamb and spoke like a dragon. And he exercises all the authority of the first beast in his presence, and causes the earth and those who dwell in it to worship the first beast, whose deadly wound was healed. He performs great signs, so that he even makes fire come down from heaven on the earth in the sight of men."*

John now sees a second *"beast coming up out of the earth."* We are expressly instructed that the two horns of this beast do not represent two kings. Instead these small horns cause this beast to resemble a lamb. A lamb has little horns and in Daniel 7:8 *"a little one"* was raised to power, and this horn had *"the eyes of a man, and a mouth speaking pompous words."* Unlike the beast from the sea, the beast from the earth could refer to a person. And this would agree with the former prophecy of Daniel. It will be revealed later in Revelation that this person is the *"false prophet."* Even though the beast from the earth is said to have the same authority as the first beast, it must operate under the oversight (*"in the sight"*) of the first beast. Somehow, the second beast causes all of the other nations to *"worship the first beast."* The word *"worship"* means to "give worth" or "acknowledge worthiness." Apparently, the beast from the sea is lauded because of its recovery from a would-be deadly wound. Once again, in Verse 13 we find a nation with the ability to make *"fire come down from heaven on the earth."*

Because the second beast is exercising the same authority as the first beast, we must assume that the beast from the sea is also able to make fire come down from heaven.

*Revelation 13 cont., verses 14 and 15*

*"And he deceives those who dwell on the earth by those signs which he was granted to do in the sight of the beast, telling those who dwell on the earth to make an image to the beast who was wounded by the sword and lived. He was granted power to give breath to the image of the beast, that the image of the beast should both speak and cause as many as would not worship the image of the beast to be killed."*

The beast from the earth tells all *"who dwell on the earth to make an image to* (or in the likeness of) *the beast."* Here we know that we are talking about the first beast because it is the one that had been wounded. Since we have already established that the beast is a kingdom or government, we must investigate the possibility that the image is an intangible replication. The most significant feature of the beast from the sea is its Roman-like form of government. We remember from the book of Daniel that the ten-horned Roman beast was different from all the other beasts. The other beasts were kingdoms, and Rome was a republic. Rome had representatives, or senators, and the other beasts/kingdoms were ruled by royal sovereigns.

The representational type of government, or democracy, was resurrected after the French Revolution and was fully developed and incorporated in the United States of America. The premise that this form of government was the beast's distinguishing trait is supported by the statement, *"the beast that was, and is not, and yet is."-Revelation 17:8* In this verse, the literal Greek translation of *"and yet is"* is actually *"shall be present."*[2] This Roman form of government prevailed during the life of John but was not an acceptable form of government for over a thousand years, and yet is present at the time of the end in John's vision.

Let us take a critical look at these two forms of government: kingdom vs. democracy. It will be difficult, or impossible, for the reader who has not submitted to our Lord and Savior, Jesus Christ, to receive the truth of the following statements. Submission to authority carries the connotation of oppression to those who have not studied the many verses on submission found in the New Testament. This submission begins with obedience to the gospel. Jesus said, *"All should honor the Son just as they honor the Father. He who does not honor the Son does not honor the*

*Father who sent Him."-John 5:23* Just as God the Son submitted to God the Father, we must submit to Jesus, the Son of God. This requirement is an integral part of obeying the gospel. The Bible not only commands us to submit to Jesus, but also tells us we must submit to one another. There are at least seven sections of Scripture in six books of the New Testament that discuss submission. God's Word also tells us that we must be subject to kings and their agents.

It is more palatable to consider the act of submission when we realize the truth regarding authority and submission. In reality, we are all under authority. The Bible teaches that children are to honor and obey their parents, wives are to submit to their husbands, servants (employees) are to obey their masters (employers), and everyone is to obey the king and his officials. The king and his officials are responsible to God, and all the rest obey God by submitting to the authorities that He has placed over them. Consider Romans 13:1-5:

*"Let every soul be subject to the governing authorities. For there is no authority except from God, and the authorities that exist are appointed by God. Therefore whoever resists the authority resists the ordinance of God, and those who resist will bring judgment on themselves. For rulers are not a terror to good works, but to evil. Do you want to be unafraid of the authority? Do what is good, and you will have praise from the same. For he is God's minister to you for good. But if you do evil, be afraid; for he does not bear the sword in vain; for he is God's minister, an avenger to execute wrath on him who practices evil. Therefore you must be subject, not only because of wrath but also for conscience' sake."*

So we see that God claims responsibility for the authorities that He allows to rule over us. We see this again in 1st Peter 2:13-24:

*"Therefore submit yourselves to every ordinance of man for the Lord's sake, whether to the king as supreme, or to governors, as to those who are sent by him for the punishment of evildoers and for the praise of those who do good. For this is the will of God, that by doing good you may put to silence the ignorance of foolish men- as free, yet not using liberty as a cloak for vice, but as bondservants of God. Honor all people. Love the brotherhood. Fear God. Honor the king. Servants, be submissive to your masters with all fear, not only to good and gentle, but also to the harsh. For this is commendable, if because of conscience toward God one endures grief, suffering wrongfully. For what credit is it if, when you are beaten for your faults, you take it patiently? But when you do good and suffer, if you take it patiently, this is commendable before God. For to this you were called, because Christ also suffered for us, leaving us an example, that you should follow in His steps: 'Who committed*

*no sin, nor was deceit found in His mouth'; who, when He was reviled, did not revile in return; when He suffered, He did not threaten, but committed Himself to Him who judges righteously; who Himself bore our sins in His own body on the tree, that we, having died to sins, might live for righteousness-by whose stripes you were healed."*

One might ask, "What about suffering under an unjust government?" 1st Peter 2:21 told us that some are called to suffer. As Christians we are to trust God, and wait for heaven. This is not to say that the world should stand aside and let a wicked king slaughter his citizens. In fact, it is the duty of the other kingdoms of the world to take action, and put an end to his unrighteous reign. Indeed, we see from history that such corrective actions have been taken. We must conclude, then, that the Christian should be satisfied with the kingdom form of government.

Now let us look at the democratic form of government in light of the Scriptures. Jeremiah, the prophet, said in Jeremiah 17:9; *"The heart is deceitful above all things, and desperately wicked; who can know it?"* Romans Chapters 3-5 teach us that all men have inherited a sinful heart, which includes the propensity for sin, and a certainty that sin will be performed. Romans 3:23 concludes by saying, *"For all have sinned and fall short of the glory of God."* Only faith in Jesus can redeem the heart of a man from its fallen state. However, Jesus taught us that few would be the ones who would pass through the narrow gate and believe in His vicarious sacrifice for their own sins. Simple logic tells us that the majority of any given population will have hearts ruled by their sin-nature. In a democracy, the sinful majority will seek to, and will be successful in, undermining the authority established on God's moral standards. In the end, it is better for society to be ruled by a righteous king, than by a majority of fallen men.

The deception to be perpetrated, referred to in Revelation 13:14, might be to convince the world that the entire earth should be cast after the image of the Roman (democratic) type of government. It will be easy for the beast from the earth to convince the world that a democracy would always be better than kingdom-rule. In these last days, kingdoms might be prohibited. The unbelieving world might ignore the fact that a kingdom-government is "the image" of the Heavenly Kingdom. Fallen man would rather sin than submit. He prefers lawlessness rather than deliverance from sin. Only the cross of Christ can draw a man to forsake his own fallen sin-nature.

*"Jesus answered them, "Most assuredly, I say to you, whoever commits sin is a slave of sin. And a slave does not abide in the house forever, but a son abides forever. Therefore if the Son makes you free, you shall be free indeed."-John 8:34-36*

So if the United States of America is the beginning of the beast, we need to consider if an equally powerful world-wide organization has been created in its likeness. Could it be the United Nations; or some yet-to-be-created form of government by-the-people of the world? Proverbs 14:12 reads, *"There is a way that seems right to a man, but its end is the way of death."* It does seem right that mankind should govern itself; however the outcome will be total lawlessness - just what fallen man has always wanted. The truism, "Absolute power corrupts absolutely," is just as true for the masses as for the potentate. The False Prophet will cause the whole world to copy, and replicate, the model of self-rule exemplified by the beast from the sea. Just as a mouth was given to the beast from the sea, the image of the beast is also given the ability to communicate on the same grand scale.

At some point, the image of the beast will either be represented by some tangible form; or else the chief characteristics of the beast will be memorialized. This is necessary in order to fulfill the words of Jesus in Matthew 24:15, *"Therefore when you see the 'abomination of desolation' spoken of by Daniel the prophet, standing in the holy place."* With today's technology it would be a simple thing to make a multi-media tribute to this end-time Roman Empire. Walking, talking, robotic presenters are already in use in places like hi-tech amusement parks and museums.

There are yet other applications of "setting up" the image in a place of governmental authority. Israel's survival as a Jewish state is just as precarious as a Christian democracy in the United States. The only way that Israel can demand that all of her citizens be Jews or proselytes is to have an authoritarian form of government. The ultimate government of Israel will take the form of the Son of God ruling from Mount Zion. It could be, that in a last attempt to purify the nation of Israel, that she would attempt to appoint a king. If the image of the beast (democracy) is the only form of government considered worthy in the last days, the beast may require his image to be set up in Mount Zion; denying Israel the right to adopt a kingdom form of government.

Another grim prospect should be faced by Christians and Jews alike. What if Muslims, observing that the key to control is through majority rule, decided to take over by sheer reproduction and recruitment? Countries that are already predominantly Islamic oppress, punish, and even kill Christians and Jews within their borders. Because Revelation was written about the Kingdom of the Holy One of Israel, a democratic Islamic nation or league of nations might behave very much like the Beast of John's prophecy.

*Revelation 13 cont., verses 16-18*

*"He causes all, both small and great, rich and poor, free and slave, to receive a mark on their right hand or on their foreheads, and that no one may buy or sell except one who has the mark or the name of the beast, or the number of his name. Here is wisdom. Let him who has understanding calculate the number of the beast, for it is the number of a man: His number is 666."*

The practice of marking, or sealing, someone is not new. On the night of Passover, the doorposts were marked with lamb's blood to protect the Jewish residents from the angel of death. Ezekiel was told to mark those who wept over Jerusalem so they would not be killed by God's judgment on those who had turned away from Him. And the Letter to the Ephesians tells Christians that they are sealed with the Holy Spirit of promise, for the day of redemption. The mark of the beast will be a qualification to do business on earth, but a disqualification from sharing in God's eternal inheritance.

We are familiar with the requirements of giving our bank card number, and other forms identification, to make a purchase. It would almost appear that the financial engineers are following the script of the Scriptures. In an attempt to eliminate identity theft, to eradicate illegal immigration, to inhibit tax evasion, and for national security purposes, it may soon be necessary to identify people with some type of implanted device. The requirement of wearing some type of identification will be an acknowledgement of citizenship in the beast's domain. Also, it is not difficult to imagine that the mouth, and the image, given to the beast are merely computerized audio and video images.

At this point in time, taking the *"mark"* identifier might seem to be logical and even innocent. The following verses show that God's warning, stating the mark will bring His wrath, isn't announced until after the fall of Babylon the Great.

*"And another angel followed, saying, 'Babylon is fallen, is fallen, that great city, because she has made all nations drink of the wine of the wrath of her fornication. Then a third angel followed them, saying with a loud voice, 'If anyone worships the beast and his image, and receives his mark on his forehead or on his hand, he himself shall also drink of the wine of the wrath of God, which is poured out full strength into the cup of His indignation. He shall be tormented with fire and brimstone in the presence of the holy angels and in the presence of the Lamb.'"-Revelation 14:8-10*

We previously observed that the United States of America must first enter into the persecution of believers in order to be positively identified as Babylon the Great. The second, and final, act that will positively identify the United States will be the standardized implementation of some type of personal identifier that also signifies allegiance to the Beast or the False Prophet.

Verse 18 begins by stating that wisdom will be required to determine the meaning of the beast's number. The one who has understanding will use some sort of calculation to arrive at its significance. If Chapters 8 and 9 of Revelation are describing the destruction of the Great Harlot, then her number would be one-third because of the continual reference to the destruction of one-third of: the population, the sky concealing the sun and moon, and the waters. The calculation of dividing three into two (two-thirds), yields .666. Therefore, the number, or portion, of the beast remaining after the destruction of the Great Harlot would be two-thirds, or .666. This is a decimal rather than an integer. It is not a natural number, but a man-made number, (the number of a man).

The following verses from the book of Zechariah provide significant support for the conclusion that 666 is the fraction .666. A case might also be made that one-third of mankind will experience the trouble in this world that many people call the first half of the Tribulation.

## Come Out of Her My People: Persecution Begins

*Zechariah 13:7-9*

*"Awake, O sword, against My Shepherd, Against the Man who is My Companion', Says the LORD of hosts. Strike the Shepherd, And the sheep will be scattered; Then I will turn My hand against the little ones. And it shall come to pass in all the land," Says the LORD, "That two-thirds in it shall be cut off and die, But one-third shall be left in it: I will bring the one-third through the fire, Will refine them as silver is refined, And test them as gold is tested. They will call on My name, And I will answer them. I will say, 'This is My people'; And each one will say, 'The LORD is my God.'"*

In Old Testament writings, the phrase *"the land"* refers to the Promised Land. We don't see in Scripture, or in the fulfillment of prophecy, an instance when two-thirds of the Jews "in the land" are struck. But God has made a distinction between the Nation of Israel and the people of God. Paul, the redeemed rabbi, says the Elect of God now includes all who are saved through the election of grace: *"Even so then, at this present time there is a remnant according to the <u>election of grace</u>. 6 And if by grace, then it is no longer of works; otherwise grace is no longer grace. But if it is of works, it is no longer grace; otherwise work is no longer work. 7 What then? Israel has not obtained what it seeks; but <u>the elect</u> have obtained it and the rest were blinded."-Romans 11:5* This is not "replacement theology" (a teaching wherein all prophetic references to God's people are said to point to the Christian church.) But it is unification theology where there is no difference between Jews and Gentiles. Israel, as a nation, and particularly Jerusalem, is the object of its own prophecies; that is, the government and geography of Israel. As far as the election of people is concerned, the church is one body made up of believing Jews and Gentiles.

*"But now in Christ Jesus you who once were far off have been brought near by the blood of Christ. For He Himself is our peace, <u>who has made both one</u>, and has broken down the middle wall of separation, having abolished in His flesh the enmity, that is, the law of commandments contained in ordinances, so as to create in Himself <u>one new man</u> from the two, thus making peace, and that He might reconcile them both to God in <u>one body</u> through the cross, thereby putting to death the enmity."-Ephesians 2:14-16* What God has joined together, let man not separate.

The prophet Malachi states that the time of refining foretold by Zechariah above would occur on <u>the Day</u> when the Lord returns; obviously indicating the End Times.

*Malachi 3:2.3*

*"But who can endure the day of His coming? And who can stand when He appears? For He is like a refiner's fire And like launderers' soap. He will sit as a refiner and a purifier of silver; He will purify the sons of Levi, And purge them as gold and silver, That they may offer to the LORD An offering in righteousness."*

The two-thirds, however, will be *"cut off, and die."* By the words "cut off" we conclude that these will be rejected by God. In the words of Jesus; *"Enter by the narrow gate; for wide is the gate and broad is the way that leads to destruction, and there are many who go in by it. 14 Because narrow is the gate and difficult is the way which leads to life, and there are few who find it."- Matthew 7:13* So we see that the majority will rebel and the minority will experience refinement, but live. As Satan attempts to copy God's Kingdom of Heaven in which two-thirds of the angels remain faithful to Him; the kingdom of earth will be comprised of two-thirds of the world's population; although another one-forth will die shortly thereafter.

Irenaeus, the second century Bishop of Lyons, stated that the three sixes represent a period of six thousand years. He also relates two of the sixes to the image which Nebuchadnezzar set up in Babylon. An in-depth article explaining Irenaeus' eschatology can be viewed at:

http://www.biblicalstudies.org.uk/pdf/eq/1969-1_030.pdf

Another fascinating interpretation of the mark has been revealed by Wallid Shoebat, a converted Arab Christian. The last three letters of Rev. 13:18 are three Greek symbols Χ ξ ζ. They are three different symbols and therefore cannot be "www" as some have posited. Wallid insists that God was showing John three Arabic symbols.

Χ س ع

John was given the symbols only, without interpretation; therefore the need to ask for interpretation from someone in the future who would know what these symbols meant. These symbols would need to be rotated somewhat, but from right to left they read, "In the name of, Allah and Islam." He also suggests that "mark" means "badge of servitude," such as an arm band. How about a headband or ball cap? Search the web and watch the video! Currently, a video clip can be seen at:

http://www.youtube.com/watch?v=GtquNNEO7Fw

## Come Out of Her My People: Persecution Begins

The ramifications of Wallid's theory are that the Muslims might gain such control that they could require allegiance to Allah in order for anyone to buy and sell goods! However, Wallid is in error when he states that numerology was considered to be sorcery by early Christians. Irenaeus gives several names as possible candidates for the name of the Beast in his *"Against Heresies,"* Book V, Chapter XXX.

*"Such, then, being the state of the case, and this number being found in all the most approved and ancient copies [of the Apocalypse], and those men who saw John face to face bearing their testimony [to it]; while reason also leads us to conclude that the number of the name of the beast, [if reckoned] according to the Greek mode of calculation by the [value of] the letters contained in it, will amount to six hundred and sixty and six; that is, the number of tens shall be equal to that of the hundreds, and the number of hundreds equal to that of the units (for that number which [expresses] the digit six being adhered to throughout, indicates the recapitulations of that apostasy, taken in its full extent, which occurred at the beginning, during the intermediate periods, and which shall take place at the end). . . It is therefore more certain, and less hazardous, to await the fulfillment of the prophecy, than to be making surmises, and casting about for any names that may present themselves, inasmuch as many names can be found possessing the number mentioned; and the same question will, after all, remain unsolved. For if there are many names found possessing this number, it will be asked which among them shall the coming man bear. It is not through a want of names containing the number of that name that I say this, but on account of the fear of God, and zeal for the truth: for the name Evanthas (Euanqas) contains the required number, but I make no allegation regarding it. Then also Lateinos (Lateinos) has the number six hundred and sixty-six; and it is a very probable [solution], this being the name of the last kingdom [of the four seen by Daniel]. For the Latins are they who at present bear rule; I will not, however, make any boast over this [coincidence]. Teitan too, (Teitan, the first syllable being written with the two Greek vowels e and i), among all the names which are found among us, is rather worthy of credit. For it has in itself the predicted number, and is composed of six letters, each syllable containing three letters; and [the word itself] is ancient, and removed from ordinary use; for among our kings we find none bearing this name Titan, nor have any of the idols which are worshipped in public among the Greeks and barbarians this appellation. Among many persons, too, this name is accounted divine, so that even the sun is termed "Titan" by those who do now possess [the rule]. This word, too, contains a certain outward appearance of vengeance, and of one inflicting merited punishment because he (Antichrist) pretends that he vindicates the oppressed. And besides this, it is an ancient name, one worthy of credit, of royal dignity, and still further, a name*

*belonging to a tyrant. Inasmuch, then, as this name "Titan" has so much to recommend it, there is a strong degree of probability, that from among the many [names suggested], we infer, that perchance he who is to come shall be called "Titan." We will not, however, incur the risk of pronouncing positively as to the name of Antichrist; for if it were necessary that his name should be distinctly revealed in this present time, it would have been announced by him who beheld the apocalyptic vision. For that was seen no very long time since, but almost in our day, towards the end of Domitian's reign."*

## Chapter 8: Approaching the Time of God's Wrath

*Revelation 14, verses 1-5*

*"Then I looked, and behold, a Lamb standing on Mount Zion, and with Him one hundred and forty-four thousand, having His Father's name written on their foreheads. And I heard a voice from heaven, like the voice of many waters, and like the voice of loud thunder. And I heard the sound of harpists playing their harps. They sang as it were a new song before the throne, before the four living creatures, and the elders; and no one could learn that song except the hundred and forty-four thousand who were redeemed from the earth. These are the ones who were not defiled with women, for they are virgins. These are the ones who follow the Lamb wherever He goes. These were redeemed from among men, being firstfruits to God and to the Lamb. And in their mouth was found no deceit, for they are without fault before the throne of God."*

Although Chapter 14 begins with the picture of a Lamb standing on Mount Zion, we learn from the verses that follow that we are seeing another heavenly sign. The 144,000 who are sealed with His father's name are singing *"before the throne, before the four living creatures, and the elders"* that abide in the throne room of heaven. Just as we saw the multitudes from the nations in heaven in Chapter 7 of Revelation, so now we find the 144,000 who were sealed in Chapter 7 joining the others who have come out of the great tribulation.

*Revelation 14 cont., verses 6 and 7*

*"Then I saw another angel flying in the midst of heaven, having the everlasting gospel to preach to those who dwell on the earth—to every nation, tribe, tongue, and people— saying with a loud voice, 'Fear God and give glory to Him, for the hour of His judgment has come; and worship Him who made heaven and earth, the sea and springs of water.'"*

Jesus foretold that the preaching of the gospel to the whole earth would be the final event before the end. *"And this gospel of the kingdom will be preached in all the world as a witness to all the nations, and then the end will come."*-Matthew 24:14 Proverbs 1:7 states, *"The fear of the Lord is the beginning of knowledge,"* so the evangelical angel begins to explain the gospel with the command *"Fear God and give glory to Him."*-Revelation 14:7 Because of God's great love for each and every soul, He sends His angel to give a final opportunity for anyone who might choose to repent and be reconciled to Him. It is one thing to be told that God will judge the acts of those who have been given a free will, but the reality that the *"hour of His judgment has come"-Revelation 14:7* will instill an urgency to secure peace with God.

Paul, the apostle, stated the gospel most succinctly in I Corinthians 15:1-4 where he wrote:

*"Moreover, brethren, I declare to you the gospel which I preached to you, which also you received and in which you stand, by which also you are saved, if you hold fast that word which I preached to you – unless you believed in vain. For I delivered to you first of all that which I also received: that Christ died for our sins according to the Scriptures, and that He was buried, and that He rose again the third day according to the Scriptures."*

The way to peace with God comes only through the knowledge that Jesus died as a sacrifice for our sins, making a substitutionary atonement for the death sentence that fallen man deserves. It is necessary for each and every soul to acknowledge that a portion of the sin placed upon the Lamb of God, was that soul's own personal sin. Isaiah 53:6 says, *"And the Lord has laid on Him the iniquity of us all."* 2$^{nd}$ Corinthians 5:21 says, *"For He made Him who knew no sin to be sin for us, that we might become the righteousness of God in Him."* Although the Bible tells us that Jesus died for the sins of the whole world, a conscious and deliberate commitment is required for an individual to respond to God's covenant of grace.

Think of it as personally taking the sacrifice of Jesus and presenting it to the Father as your own offering to take away your sins. God has freely given His Son for this very purpose. This salvation is not earned or even deserved but is available to everyone who will come, just as they are, and receive the gift of God. The resurrection of Jesus from the dead is God's proof to us that Jesus' sacrificial offering has been accepted as payment in full for our sin. Those who inhabit the earth in the final hours before God's judgment will have the opportunity to choose their eternal destiny. It only takes a moment to speak a humble prayer of repentance and reliance on the cross to assure our acceptance into God's kingdom. A basic example of such a prayer is given in

Romans 10:9, *"if you confess with your mouth the Lord Jesus and believe in your heart that God has raised Him from the dead, you will be saved."* Believing *"in your heart"* is knowing that Jesus took your personal sins, and understanding that you now have a place in heaven, where you are blameless in Christ. Romans 10:13 promises us, *"Whoever calls on the name of the Lord shall be saved."*

*Revelation 14 cont., verses 8-11*

*"And another angel followed, saying, "Babylon is fallen, is fallen, that great city, because she has made all nations drink of the wine of the wrath of her fornication." Then a third angel followed them, saying with a loud voice, "If anyone worships the beast and his image, and receives his mark on his forehead or on his hand, he himself shall also drink of the wine of the wrath of God, which is poured out full strength into the cup of His indignation. He shall be tormented with fire and brimstone in the presence of the holy angels and in the presence of the Lamb. And the smoke of their torment ascends forever and ever; and they have no rest day or night, who worship the beast and his image, and whoever receives the mark of his name."*

In Verse 8 an angelic messenger announces that Babylon the Great has *"fallen,"* literally *"fell"*[3] in the Greek. The timing of the fall of Babylon the Great is crucial in understanding the application of the command to *"Come out of her, my people"* found in Revelation 18:4. In Revelation Chapters 17 and 18, John is carried away to a remote place and shown in detail the fall of this Mystery Babylon. Verse 8 of Chapter 14 also brings to our attention that she involved all other nations in her adulteress behavior. The adultery of a nation, in Biblical terms, occurs when people who belong to God turn their hearts away from Him.

The angelic voice in Verse 8 spoke the words *"Babylon is fallen,"* but the angel with the message of the gospel in Verse 6 spoke with a loud voice, obviously to the peoples of the world. The message of the third angel in Verse 9 once again heralds his message with a loud voice, speaking his message to the inhabitants of the earth. We are given an example of God speaking by angels to the children of Israel in Judges 2:1-4:

## Come Out of Her My People: Persecution Begins

*"Then the Angel of the Lord came up from Gilgal to Bochim, and said: 'I led you up from Egypt and brought you to the land of which I swore to your fathers; and I said, 'I will never break My covenant with you. And you shall make no covenant with the inhabitants of this land; you shall tear down their altars. But you have not obeyed My voice. Why have you done this?' Therefore I also said, 'I will not drive them out before you; but they shall be thorns in your side, and their gods shall be a snare to you.' So it was, when the Angel of the Lord spoke these words to all the children of Israel, that the people lifted up their voices and wept."*

By the tearful repentance of the people of Israel, we know that they heard the voice of God loud and clear. We don't know if the people saw the Angel of the Lord in the form of a man, and we don't know if the people heard an audible voice, but somehow the message was communicated to all the people of Israel. Here in Verses 9-11, specific instructions are given to all mankind. The angel uses the punishment of Babylon the Great as an example to those who would become citizens of the world-nation of the beast. Anyone who *"worships the beast and his image, and receives his mark on his forehead or on his hand"-Revelation 14:9* shall also receive the <u>same</u> punishment as Babylon, which has now fallen. We can conclude from this statement that the citizens of this city-state had already worshiped the beast and his image, and received his mark. Therefore, the third angel is warning the <u>rest</u> of the world that they <u>also</u> will receive the wrath of God in full strength if they submit to the beast, as Babylon the Great had done.

*Revelation 14 cont., verses 12 and 13*

*"Here is the patience of the saints; here are those who keep the commandments of God and the faith of Jesus. Then I heard a voice from heaven saying to me, "Write: 'Blessed are the dead who die in the Lord from now on.'" "Yes," says the Spirit, "that they may rest from their labors, and their works follow them."*

The *"patience of the saints"* refers to their steadfastness and perseverance in the face of impossible circumstances. God has now spoken that receiving the mark will bring His wrath. Yet without the mark, no one will be able to obtain the necessities of life. As of the writing of this Fourth Edition, more than three million

American consumers have agreed to be identified by using biometrics. Biometrics uses the unique dimensions of a person's fingerprints or eyes and then compares them to a computerized file. These places on the body could be considered the hands and the forehead. This method of identification does not require a mark. It is, however, an indication that this kind of identification is already becoming a reality. But Verse 13 contains consolation for those who keep the faith and obey God in the face of death. It is interesting that rather than having an angel speak these words of consolation, these words are written at the instruction of God here in Verse 13. Those saints who must endure this time on the earth will read these words, written centuries before, *"Blessed are the dead who die in the Lord from now on.' 'Yes', says the Spirit, 'that they may rest from their labors, and their works follow them."* Because the warning against taking the mark, and this consolation to accept death, are not given before the destruction of Babylon the Great, it is possible that grace may be given to those who take the mark in ignorance before Babylon's destruction. The safe course of action will be to obey God's Word to *"Come out!"* Isaiah 48:20-22 assures us He will care for our needs if we will separate ourselves from the wicked, who are soon to be punished:

*"Go forth from Babylon! Flee from the Chaldeans! With a voice of singing, declare, proclaim this, utter it to the end of the earth; say, "The LORD has redeemed His servant Jacob!" And they did not thirst when He led them through the deserts; He caused the waters to flow from the rock for them; He also split the rock, and the waters gushed out. "There is no peace," says the LORD, "for the wicked."*

# Come Out of Her My People: Persecution Begins

## Chapter 9: The Wrath of God

In case the reader is unfamiliar with God's Word, and perceives a contradiction between the love of God and the wrath of God; let us review some Scriptures that explain God's righteous indignation. *"Do you not know that the unrighteous will not inherit the kingdom of God? Do not be deceived. Neither fornicators, nor idolaters, nor adulterers, nor homosexuals, nor sodomites, nor thieves, nor covetous, nor drunkards, nor revilers, nor extortioners will inherit the kingdom of God."- 1st Corinthians 6:9-10* Ephesians 5:5-6 reads, *"For this you know, that no fornicator, unclean person, nor covetous man, who is an idolater, has any inheritance in the kingdom of Christ and God. Let no one deceive you with empty words, for because of these things the wrath of God comes upon the sons of disobedience."* *"Disobedience"* refers to disobedience to God's new covenant. Romans 3:23 assures us that *"all have sinned and fall short of the glory of God."* God's covenant of grace extends forgiveness of sin, and reconciliation to Himself, through the substitutionary sacrifice of Jesus on the cross. God's wrath will be poured out on those who have chosen to remain alienated and unreconciled to God. In the Old Testament, the coming of God's kingdom is referred to as *"the day of the LORD."* Malachi 3:2 asks the question, *"But who can endure the day of His coming? And who can stand when He appears? For He is like a refiner's fire and like launderers' soap."* Those who would scoff at God's plan, and His love for every soul, need to hear the words of Peter in 2nd Peter 3:3-10:

*"Knowing this first: that scoffers will come in the last days, walking according to their own lusts, and saying, 'Where is the promise of His coming? For since the fathers fell asleep, all things continue as they were from the beginning of creation.' For this they willfully forget: that by the word of God the heavens were of old, and the earth standing out of water and in the water, by which the world that then existed perished, being flooded with water. But the heavens and the earth which are now preserved by the same word, are reserved for fire until the day of judgment and perdition of ungodly men. But, beloved, do not forget this one thing, that with the Lord one day is as a thousand years, and a thousand years as one day. The Lord is not slack concerning His promise, as some count slackness, but is longsuffering toward us, not*

## Come Out of Her My People: Persecution Begins

*willing that any should perish but that all should come to repentance. But the day of the Lord will come as a thief in the night, in which the heavens will pass away with a great noise, and the elements will melt with fervent heat; both the earth and the works that are in it will be burned up."*

So let us rejoice in the words of Jesus, *"For God so loved the world that He gave His only begotten Son, that whoever believes in Him should not perish but have everlasting life."-John 3:16*

Now begins the time of God's wrath. (See figure four.) The account of God's wrath being poured out on the earth begins in Revelation 14:14, and continues through the end of Chapter 16. These verses follow.

*Revelation 14 cont., verses 14-20*

*"Then I looked, and behold, a white cloud, and on the cloud sat One like the Son of Man, having on His head a golden crown, and in His hand a sharp sickle. And another angel came out of the temple, crying with a loud voice to Him who sat on the cloud, "Thrust in Your sickle and reap, for the time has come for You to reap, for the harvest of the earth is ripe." So He who sat on the cloud thrust in His sickle on the earth, and the earth was reaped. Then another angel came out of the temple which is in heaven, he also having a sharp sickle. And another angel came out from the altar, who had power over fire, and he cried with a loud cry to him who had the sharp sickle, saying, "Thrust in your sharp sickle and gather the clusters of the vine of the earth, for her grapes are fully ripe." So the angel thrust his sickle into the earth and gathered the vine of the earth, and threw it into the great winepress of the wrath of God. And the winepress was trampled outside the city, and blood came out of the winepress, up to the horses' bridles, for one thousand six hundred furlongs."*

*Revelation 15, verses 1-8*

*"Then I saw another sign in heaven, great and marvelous: seven angels having the seven last plagues, for in them the wrath of God is complete. And I saw something like a sea of glass mingled with fire, and those who have the victory over the beast, over his image and over his mark and over the number of his name, standing on the sea of glass, having harps of God. They sing the song*

*of Moses, the servant of God, and the song of the Lamb, saying: "Great and marvelous are Your works, Lord God Almighty! Just and true are Your ways, O King of the saints! Who shall not fear You, O Lord, and glorify Your name? For You alone are holy. For all nations shall come and worship before You, For Your judgments have been manifested." After these things I looked, and behold, the temple of the tabernacle of the testimony in heaven was opened. And out of the temple came the seven angels having the seven plagues, clothed in pure bright linen, and having their chests girded with golden bands. Then one of the four living creatures gave to the seven angels seven golden bowls full of the wrath of God who lives forever and ever. The temple was filled with smoke from the glory of God and from His power, and no one was able to enter the temple till the seven plagues of the seven angels were completed."*

## Come Out of Her My People: Persecution Begins

| DEATH | CRY FOR JUSTICE | CATASTROPHIC DESTRUCTION | CHRIST'S RETURN |
|---|---|---|---|
| 1/4 EARTH KILLED;<br>• SWORD<br>• PESTILENCE<br>• WILD BEASTS<br><br>PROBABLY THE RAMAFICATIONS OF BABYLON'S JUDGEMENT: LAWLESSNESS, PILLAGING, DESEASE, AND THE WILDERNESS; CREATED UPON, AND SURROUNDING, THE DEVASTATED PORTION OF THE EARTH | SEVEN LAST PLAUGES<br><br>BOWLS OF THE WRATH OF GOD:<br><br>1. SORES<br>2. SEA BECOMES BLOOD ALL MARINE LIFE DIES<br>3. ALL OTHER WATER NOW BLOOD<br>4. SUN SCORCHES MEN<br>5. DARKNESS & PAIN<br>6. EUPHRATES DRIES UP KINGS GATHER FOR ARMEGEDDON<br>7. PLATES SHIFT 100 LB. HAIL STONES | | MARRIAGE SUPPER OF THE LAMB<br><br>BATTLE OF ARMAGEDDON<br><br>DEFEAT OF BEAST, FALSE PROPHET<br><br>SATAN BOUND FOR 1,000 YRS.<br><br>MILLENNIUM REIGN OF JESUS & SAINTS<br><br>SATAN DECEIVES AND GATHERS FOR WAR<br><br>SATAN CAST INTO LAKE OF FIRE<br><br>EARTH & HEAVEN FLEE AWAY AND MELT<br><br>WHITE THRONE JUDGEMENT<br><br>DEATH/HADES IN LAKE OF FIRE<br><br>NEW; HEAVEN, EARTH, JERUSALEN, & TEMPLE |

Figure 4

*Revelation 16*
*"Then I heard a loud voice from the temple saying to the seven angels, "Go and pour out the bowls of the wrath of God on the earth." So the first went and poured out his bowl upon the earth, and a foul and loathsome sore came upon the men who had the mark of the beast and those who worshiped his image. Then the second angel poured out his bowl on the sea, and it became blood as of a dead man; and every living creature in the sea died. Then the third angel poured out his bowl on the rivers and springs of water, and they became blood. And I heard the angel of the waters saying: "You are righteous, O Lord, The One who is and who was and who is to be, because You have judged these things. For they have shed the blood of saints and prophets, and You have given them blood to drink. For it is their just due." And I heard another from the altar saying, "Even so, Lord God Almighty, true and righteous are Your judgments." Then the fourth angel poured out his bowl on the sun, and power was given to him to scorch men with fire. And men were scorched with great heat, and they blasphemed the name of God who has power over these plagues; and they did not repent and give Him glory. Then the fifth angel poured out his bowl on the throne of the beast, and his kingdom became full of darkness; and they gnawed their tongues because of the pain. They blasphemed the God of heaven because of their pains and their sores, and did not repent of their deeds. Then the sixth angel poured out his bowl on the great river Euphrates, and its water was dried up, so that the way of the kings from the east might be prepared. And I saw three unclean spirits like frogs coming out of the mouth of the dragon, out of the mouth of the beast, and out of the mouth of the false prophet. For they are spirits of demons, performing signs, which go out to the kings of the earth and of the whole world, to gather them to the battle of that great day of God Almighty. "Behold, I am coming as a thief. Blessed is he who watches, and keeps his garments, lest he walk naked and they see his shame." And they gathered them together to the place called in Hebrew, Armageddon. Then the seventh angel poured out his bowl into the air, and a loud voice came out of the temple of heaven, from the throne, saying, "It is done!" And there were noises and thunderings and lightnings; and there was a great earthquake, such a mighty and great earthquake as had not occurred since men were on the earth. Now the great city was divided into three parts, and the cities of the nations fell. And great Babylon was remembered before God, to give her the cup of the wine of the fierceness of His wrath. Then every island fled away, and the mountains were not found. And great hail from heaven fell upon men, each hailstone about the weight of a talent. Men blasphemed God because of the plague of the hail, since that plague was exceedingly great."*

## Come Out of Her My People: Persecution Begins

Notice in Verse 13 that the unclean spirits come out of the mouth of the dragon, which is Satan, and out of the mouth of the beast, which is most likely a world government, and out of the mouth of the false prophet. The beast of the sea continues to be referred to as a beast. When the Lord Jesus comes to reign on the earth, the people left on earth will gather to make war against Him. Revelation 19:17-21 describes this battle.

*"Then I saw an angel standing in the sun; and he cried with a loud voice, saying to all the birds that fly in the midst of heaven, 'Come and gather together for the supper of the great God, that you may eat the flesh of kings, the flesh of captains, the flesh of mighty men, the flesh of horses and of those who sit on them, and the flesh of all people, free and slave, both small and great.' And I saw the beast, the kings of the earth, and their armies, gathered together to make war against Him who sat on the horse and against His army. Then the beast was captured, and with him the false prophet who worked signs in his presence, by which he deceived those who received the mark of the beast and those who worshiped his image. These two were cast alive into the lake of fire burning with brimstone. And the rest were killed with the sword which proceeded from the mouth of Him who sat on the horse. And all the birds were filled with their flesh."*

Revelation 19:19 specifically mentions *"the beast, the kings of the earth, and their armies."* We know that this beast is described as having ten horns (or ten kings). So, most likely, the beast still describes a union of nations. Revelation 19:20 tells us the beast and the false prophet were cast into the lake of fire. The dragon (Satan) is cast into the lake of fire later in Revelation 20:10. Because we have already been told that the citizens of the beast, who have received the mark, will experience the wrath of God, and be tormented with fire and brimstone; we must conclude that these people, that gathered for war, were considered to be part of the beast, because there is no separate mention of the masses being thrown into the fire. Once again, we find support for the assumption that the beast is a world-nation, of which, every citizen is condemned.

## Chapter 10: Mystery Babylon

Revelation 17 and 18 take us back to a time before the wrath of God. Revelation 17:2 is written in past tense, even though John is seeing a vision of times that have not yet come to pass; even today. We have already discussed many of the events in Chapter 17, so we will save our commentary for the end of this chapter.

*Revelation 17*

*"Then one of the seven angels who had the seven bowls came and talked with me, saying to me, "Come, I will show you the judgment of the great harlot who sits on many waters, with whom the kings of the earth committed fornication, and the inhabitants of the earth were made drunk with the wine of her fornication." So he carried me away in the Spirit into the wilderness. And I saw a woman sitting on a scarlet beast which was full of names of blasphemy, having seven heads and ten horns. The woman was arrayed in purple and scarlet, and adorned with gold and precious stones and pearls, having in her hand a golden cup full of abominations and the filthiness of her fornication. And on her forehead a name was written: MYSTERY, BABYLON THE GREAT, THE MOTHER OF HARLOTS AND OF THE ABOMINATIONS OF THE EARTH. I saw the woman, drunk with the blood of the saints and with the blood of the martyrs of Jesus. And when I saw her, I marveled with great amazement. But the angel said to me, "Why did you marvel? I will tell you the mystery of the woman and of the beast that carries her, which has the seven heads and the ten horns. The beast that you saw was, and is not, and will ascend out of the bottomless pit and go to perdition. And those who dwell on the earth will marvel, whose names are not written in the Book of Life from the foundation of the world, when they see the beast that was, and is not, and yet is. "Here is the mind which has wisdom: The seven heads are seven mountains on which the woman sits. There are also seven kings. Five have fallen, one is, and the other has not yet come. And when he comes, he must continue a short time. The beast that was, and is not, is himself also the eighth, and is of the seven, and is going to perdition. "The ten horns which you saw are ten kings who have received no kingdom as yet, but they receive authority for one hour as kings with the beast. These are of one mind, and they will give their power and authority to the beast. These will make war with the Lamb, and the Lamb will overcome them, for He is Lord of lords and King of kings; and those who are with Him are called, chosen, and faithful." Then he said to me, "The waters which you saw, where the harlot sits, are peoples, multitudes,*

## Come Out of Her My People: Persecution Begins

*nations, and tongues. And the ten horns which you saw on the beast, these will hate the harlot, make her desolate and naked, eat her flesh and burn her with fire. For God has put it into their hearts to fulfill His purpose, to be of one mind, and to give their kingdom to the beast, until the words of God are fulfilled. And the woman whom you saw is that great city which reigns over the kings of the earth."*

We have already discussed the likelihood that the Roman Empire is the beast which *"was, and then is not, and yet will be."* Because the Bible does not teach the annihilation of the soul, the fact that it *"is not,"* for some period of time, rules out the possibility that this beast is a person. The fact that seven mountains, mentioned in Verse 9, have seven kings supports the theory that these seven *"heads"* are actually city-states. The five that have fallen may refer to five of the members of the old Roman Empire that are no longer in existence. *"One is, and the other has not yet come."* One of these city-states exists at the time of John's writing. *"And the other has not yet come."* This one who had not yet come could very well be speaking of the United States of America because it was unknown to John. The fact that Babylon the Great is titled a *"mystery"* in Verse 5 indicates that the city-state's identity was not yet revealed at the time of John's vision. *"And when he comes, he must continue a short time."* If the judgment of the Great Harlot occurs soon, the United States will have continued *"a short time"* in comparison to the old world nations. Verse 16 states that even though the Great Harlot is part of the beast, the ten-horned majority will hate the Harlot. The reason for the world's hatred of the Great Harlot is given in Verse 18. Because this great city-state is so powerful that no single nation can *"make war with her,"* the rest of the world must join together to overpower her.

*Revelation 18*

*"After these things I saw another angel coming down from heaven, having great authority, and the earth was illuminated with his glory. And he cried mightily with a loud voice, saying, "Babylon the great is fallen, is fallen, and has become a dwelling place of demons, a prison for every foul spirit, and a cage for every unclean and hated bird! For all the nations have drunk of the wine of the wrath of her fornication, the kings of the earth have committed*

*fornication with her, and the merchants of the earth have become rich through the abundance of her luxury."* And I heard another voice from heaven saying, *"Come out of her, my people, lest you share in her sins, and lest you receive of her plagues. For her sins have reached to heaven, and God has remembered her iniquities. Render to her just as she rendered to you, and repay her double according to her works; in the cup which she has mixed, mix double for her. In the measure that she glorified herself and lived luxuriously, in the same measure give her torment and sorrow; for she says in her heart, 'I sit as queen, and am no widow, and will not see sorrow.' Therefore her plagues will come in one day—death and mourning and famine. And she will be utterly burned with fire, for strong is the Lord God who judges her.* "The kings of the earth who committed fornication and lived luxuriously with her will weep and lament for her, when they see the smoke of her burning, standing at a distance for fear of her torment, saying, 'Alas, alas, that great city Babylon, that mighty city! For in one hour your judgment has come.' "And the merchants of the earth will weep and mourn over her, for no one buys their merchandise anymore: merchandise of gold and silver, precious stones and pearls, fine linen and purple, silk and scarlet, every kind of citron wood, every kind of object of ivory, every kind of object of most precious wood, bronze, iron, and marble; and cinnamon and incense, fragrant oil and frankincense, wine and oil, fine flour and wheat, cattle and sheep, horses and chariots, and bodies and souls of men. The fruit that your soul longed for has gone from you, and all the things which are rich and splendid have gone from you, and you shall find them no more at all. The merchants of these things, who became rich by her, will stand at a distance for fear of her torment, weeping and wailing, and saying, 'Alas, alas, that great city that was clothed in fine linen, purple, and scarlet, and adorned with gold and precious stones and pearls! For in one hour such great riches came to nothing.' Every shipmaster, all who travel by ship, sailors, and as many as trade on the sea, stood at a distance and cried out when they saw the smoke of her burning, saying, 'What is like this great city?' "They threw dust on their heads and cried out, weeping and wailing, and saying, 'Alas, alas, that great city, in which all who had ships on the sea became rich by her wealth! For in one hour she is made desolate.' "Rejoice over her, O heaven, and you holy apostles and prophets, for God has avenged you on her!" Then a mighty angel took up a stone like a great millstone and threw it into the sea, saying, "Thus with violence the great city Babylon shall be thrown down, and shall not be found anymore. The sound of harpists, musicians, flutists, and trumpeters shall not be heard in you anymore. No craftsman of any craft*

## Come Out of Her My People: Persecution Begins

*shall be found in you anymore, and the sound of a millstone shall not be heard in you anymore. The light of a lamp shall not shine in you anymore, and the voice of bridegroom and bride shall not be heard in you anymore. For your merchants were the great men of the earth, for by your sorcery all the nations were deceived. And in her was found the blood of prophets and saints, and of all who were slain on the earth."*

Not only does the phrase *"is fallen, is fallen"* bring to mind the fall of the twin towers, but it also alludes to a two phase destruction of the Great Harlot. Phase one takes place in Verse 2 where Babylon the Great is described as *"fallen."* The first mention of *"Babylon is fallen, is fallen!"* is found in Isaiah 21:9, and is a prophetic warning. The subsequent fall of Ancient Babylon did not occur until a generation had passed from the time of the warning. Jeremiah again echoes this warning, *"Babylon has suddenly fallen and been destroyed."*- Jeremiah 51:8   But, the actual fall of Babylon did not occur until the lifetime of Daniel. So it stands to reason that the first reference to the fall, found in the detailed account in Revelation 18:2, would also be an advanced warning of a <u>future</u> sudden destruction.

John writes that Babylon *"has become a dwelling place"* of demonic agents, indicating they didn't always dwell there.   As was previously stated, Biblical harlotry depicts turning away from God and turning to idolatry. Verse 3 records that the other nations were not only oppressed and intimidated by Babylon the Great, but they were also polluted and enriched by her. Two reasons are given in Verse 4 to *"Come out of her."*

The first reason is so that God's people would not be involved in her sins. 1st John 3:8b proclaims, *"For this purpose the Son of God was manifested, that He might destroy the works of the devil."* Instead of turning to Jesus for deliverance from sin, the people of this nation are bounding headlong into sin. Jesus declared the Holy Spirit would have a tri-fold mission.  *"And when He has come, He will convict the world of sin, and of righteousness, and of judgment: of sin, because they do not believe in Me; of righteousness, because I go to My Father and you see Me no more; of judgment, because the ruler of this world is judged."*- John 15:8-11

The conviction of sin is essential in both; causing a discomfort with sin that makes us run to Christ; and invoking an appreciation of Christ, who is our effective sacrifice for sin. The Holy Spirit magnifies the depravity of our sin; and He uses the law to make sin "exceedingly sinful." (See Romans 7:13.) When the laws of a nation contradict the laws of God, that nation is fighting against the work of the Holy Spirit, Who is God Himself. Even a casual review of the Bible reveals that God is against: premarital sex, adultery, homosexuality, and the killing of babies. If these are all legalized, the conscience is dulled to actions that should bring about deep guilt and shame. God calls His people to come out in order to separate themselves from the sins of *THE MOTHER OF HARLOTS AND OF THE ABOMINATIONS OF THE EARTH*.

The second reason given to *"Come out of her"* is to avoid the plagues that are about to come upon the Great Harlot. From our earlier discussion, these plagues could very well be the trumpet plagues of Chapters 8 and 9 that destroy one-third of the earth. It is logical for a Christian to consider that it might be better to die with the Great Harlot because of the turmoil that will rule the earth until the End Times are completed. However, we ought to obey our Lord. Jesus said, *"And you will be hated by all for My name's sake. But he who endures to the end will be saved."-Matthew 10:22* So then, we should preserve our life until the time that the mark of the beast is required. Only at that time will the words *"Blessed are the dead who die in the Lord from now on"-Revelation 14:13* be applicable.

The final attack of Mystery Babylon will come suddenly, and the window of escape will be shut. *"And she will be utterly burned with fire, for strong is the Lord God who judges her."-Revelation 18:8* If the fall of the twin towers is, indeed, the beginning of the fall of the great city-state that currently rules over the kings of the earth, then we are living in the time before the destruction of the United States of America.

**Yet, there are two prophecies that remain unfulfilled at the writing of this book.**

## Come Out of Her My People: Persecution Begins

The first unfulfilled prophecy is the persecution of Christians - to the shedding of blood. Sinners hate to be confronted by the ones who are able to live righteously by the power of the Holy Spirit (ignoring a few hypocrites), and they also despise the Word of God that exposes and convicts them of their lawlessness. All that is needed for their anger to turn to bloodshed is for a violent generation to arise. Or could the blood of countless abortions already have fulfilled this prophecy? Another possibility has now emerged. What if a majority of United States citizens embraced a religion that already openly persecutes God's people, both Christians and Jews? (This seemed impossible five years ago at this book's first writing.)

The second unfulfilled prophecy is the marking, or embedding, of some identifier that would enable the citizens of the United States to buy and sell; although the mark could be an insignia worn on the arm or as a headband. (The latter of course could never be done in innocence.)

In conclusion, the Christians of the United States of America should be watchful, and unless they are called by God to stay and minister, they should prepare to *"Come out"* at the first sign that these final prophecies are being fulfilled.

Please read the entire Book of Revelation. See the Appendix for Chapters 1-5 and 19-22.

# Appendix: The Book of Revelation 1 - 5; 9 - 21

Revelation 1

**1** The Revelation of Jesus Christ, which God gave Him to show His servants—things which must shortly take place. And He sent and signified it by His angel to His servant John, **2** who bore witness to the word of God, and to the testimony of Jesus Christ, to all things that he saw. **3** Blessed is he who reads and those who hear the words of this prophecy, and keep those things which are written in it; for the time is near. **4** John, to the seven churches which are in Asia: Grace to you and peace from Him who is and who was and who is to come, and from the seven Spirits who are before His throne, **5** and from Jesus Christ, the faithful witness, the firstborn from the dead, and the ruler over the kings of the earth. To Him who loved us and washed us from our sins in His own blood, **6** and has made us kings and priests to His God and Father, to Him be glory and dominion forever and ever. Amen. **7** Behold, He is coming with clouds, and every eye will see Him, even they who pierced Him. And all the tribes of the earth will mourn because of Him. Even so, Amen. **8** "I am the Alpha and the Omega, the Beginning and the End," says the Lord, "who is and who was and who is to come, the Almighty." **9** I, John, both your brother and companion in the tribulation and kingdom and patience of Jesus Christ, was on the island that is called Patmos for the word of God and for the testimony of Jesus Christ. **10** I was in the Spirit on the Lord's Day, and I heard behind me a loud voice, as of a trumpet, **11** saying, "I am the Alpha and the Omega, the First and the Last," and, "What you see, write in a book and send it to the seven churches which are in Asia: to Ephesus, to Smyrna, to Pergamos, to Thyatira, to Sardis, to Philadelphia, and to Laodicea." **12** Then I turned to see the voice that spoke with me. And having turned I saw seven golden lampstands, **13** and in the midst of the seven lampstands One like the Son of Man, clothed with a garment down to the feet and girded about the chest with a golden band. **14** His head and hair were white like wool, as white as snow, and His eyes like a flame of fire; **15** His feet were like fine brass, as if refined in a furnace, and His voice as the sound of

## Come Out of Her My People: Persecution Begins

many waters; **16** He had in His right hand seven stars, out of His mouth went a sharp two-edged sword, and His countenance was like the sun shining in its strength. **17** And when I saw Him, I fell at His feet as dead. But He laid His right hand on me, saying to me, "Do not be afraid; I am the First and the Last. **18** I am He who lives, and was dead, and behold, I am alive forevermore. Amen. And I have the keys of Hades and of Death. **19** Write the things which you have seen, and the things which are, and the things which will take place after this. **20** The mystery of the seven stars which you saw in My right hand, and the seven golden lampstands: The seven stars are the angels of the seven churches, and the seven lampstands which you saw are the seven churches.

Revelation 2

**1** "To the angel of the church of Ephesus write, 'These things says He who holds the seven stars in His right hand, who walks in the midst of the seven golden lampstands: **2** "I know your works, your labor, your patience, and that you cannot bear those who are evil. And you have tested those who say they are apostles and are not, and have found them liars; **3** and you have persevered and have patience, and have labored for My name's sake and have not become weary. **4** Nevertheless I have this against you, that you have left your first love. **5** Remember therefore from where you have fallen; repent and do the first works, or else I will come to you quickly and remove your lampstand from its place—unless you repent. **6** But this you have, that you hate the deeds of the Nicolaitans, which I also hate. **7** "He who has an ear, let him hear what the Spirit says to the churches. To him who overcomes I will give to eat from the tree of life, which is in the midst of the Paradise of God.'" **8** "And to the angel of the church in Smyrna write, 'These things says the First and the Last, who was dead, and came to life: **9** "I know your works, tribulation, and poverty (but you are rich); and I know the blasphemy of those who say they are Jews and are not, but are a synagogue of Satan. **10** Do not fear any of those things which you are about to suffer. Indeed, the devil is about to throw some of you into prison, that you may be tested, and you will have tribulation ten days. Be faithful until death, and I will give you the crown of life. **11** "He who has an ear, let him hear what the Spirit says to the churches. He who overcomes shall not be hurt by the second death.'" **12** "And to the angel of the church in Pergamos write, 'These things says He who has the sharp two-edged sword: **13** "I know your works, and where you dwell, where Satan's throne is. And you hold fast to My name, and did not deny My faith even in the days in which Antipas was My faithful martyr, who was killed among you, where Satan dwells. **14** But I have a few things against you, because you have there those who hold the doctrine of Balaam, who taught Balak to put a stumbling block before the children of Israel, to eat things sacrificed to idols, and to commit sexual immorality. **15** Thus you also have those who hold the doctrine of the Nicolaitans, which thing I hate. **16** Repent, or else I will come to you quickly and will fight against them with the sword of My mouth. **17** "He who has an ear, let him hear what the Spirit says to the churches. To him who overcomes I will give some of the hidden manna to eat. And I will give him a white stone, and on the stone a new name written which no one knows except him who receives it.'" **18** "And to the angel of the church in Thyatira write, 'These things says the Son of God, who has eyes like a flame of fire, and His feet like fine brass: **19** "I know your works, love, service, faith, and your patience; and as for your works, the last are more than the first. **20** Nevertheless I have a few things against you, because you allow that woman Jezebel, who calls herself a prophetess, to teach and seduce My servants to commit sexual immorality and eat things sacrificed to idols. **21** And I gave her time to repent of her sexual immorality, and she did not repent. **22** Indeed I will cast her into a sickbed, and those who commit adultery with her into great tribulation, unless they repent of their deeds. **23** I will kill her children with death, and all the churches shall know that I am He who searches the minds and hearts. And I will give to each one of you according to your works. **24** "Now to you I say, and to the rest in Thyatira, as many as do not have this doctrine, who have not known the depths of Satan, as they say, I will put on you no other burden. **25** But hold fast what you have till I come. **26** And he who overcomes, and keeps My works until the end, to him I will give power over the nations— **27** ' He shall rule them with a rod of iron; They shall be dashed to pieces like the potter's vessels'— as I also have received from My Father; **28** and I will give him the morning star. **29** "He who has an ear, let him hear what the Spirit says to the churches.'"

# Come Out of Her My People: Persecution Begins

Revelation 3

**1** "And to the angel of the church in Sardis write, 'These things says He who has the seven Spirits of God and the seven stars: "I know your works, that you have a name that you are alive, but you are dead. **2** Be watchful, and strengthen the things which remain, that are ready to die, for I have not found your works perfect before God. **3** Remember therefore how you have received and heard; hold fast and repent. Therefore if you will not watch, I will come upon you as a thief, and you will not know what hour I will come upon you. **4** You have a few names even in Sardis who have not defiled their garments; and they shall walk with Me in white, for they are worthy. **5** He who overcomes shall be clothed in white garments, and I will not blot out his name from the Book of Life; but I will confess his name before My Father and before His angels. **6** "He who has an ear, let him hear what the Spirit says to the churches.'" **7** "And to the angel of the church in Philadelphia write, 'These things says He who is holy, He who is true, "He who has the key of David, He who opens and no one shuts, and shuts and no one opens": **8** "I know your works. See, I have set before you an open door, and no one can shut it; for you have a little strength, have kept My word, and have not denied My name. **9** Indeed I will make those of the synagogue of Satan, who say they are Jews and are not, but lie—indeed I will make them come and worship before your feet, and to know that I have loved you. **10** Because you have kept My command to persevere, I also will keep you from the hour of trial which shall come upon the whole world, to test those who dwell on the earth. **11** Behold, I am coming quickly! Hold fast what you have, that no one may take your crown. **12** He who overcomes, I will make him a pillar in the temple of My God, and he shall go out no more. I will write on him the name of My God and the name of the city of My God, the New Jerusalem, which comes down out of heaven from My God. And I will write on him My new name. **13** "He who has an ear, let him hear what the Spirit says to the churches.'" **14** "And to the angel of the church of the Laodiceans write, 'These things says the Amen, the Faithful and True Witness, the Beginning of the creation of God: **15** "I know your works, that you are neither cold nor hot. I could wish you were cold or hot. **16** So then, because you are lukewarm, and neither cold nor hot, I will vomit you out of My mouth.

**17** Because you say, 'I am rich, have become wealthy, and have need of nothing'—and do not know that you are wretched, miserable, poor, blind, and naked— **18** I counsel you to buy from Me gold refined in the fire, that you may be rich; and white garments, that you may be clothed, that the shame of your nakedness may not be revealed; and anoint your eyes with eye salve, that you may see. **19** As many as I love, I rebuke and chasten. Therefore be zealous and repent. **20** Behold, I stand at the door and knock. If anyone hears My voice and opens the door, I will come in to him and dine with him, and he with Me. **21** To him who overcomes I will grant to sit with Me on My throne, as I also overcame and sat down with My Father on His throne. **22** "He who has an ear, let him hear what the Spirit says to the churches."'"

Revelation 4

**1** After these things I looked, and behold, a door standing open in heaven. And the first voice which I heard was like a trumpet speaking with me, saying, "Come up here, and I will show you things which must take place after this." **2** Immediately I was in the Spirit; and behold, a throne set in heaven, and One sat on the throne. **3** And He who sat there was like a jasper and a sardius stone in appearance; and there was a rainbow around the throne, in appearance like an emerald. **4** Around the throne were twenty-four thrones, and on the thrones I saw twenty-four elders sitting, clothed in white robes; and they had crowns of gold on their heads. **5** And from the throne proceeded lightnings, thunderings, and voices. Seven lamps of fire were burning before the throne, which are the seven Spirits of God. **6** Before the throne there was a sea of glass, like crystal. And in the midst of the throne, and around the throne, were four living creatures full of eyes in front and in back. **7** The first living creature was like a lion, the second living creature like a calf, the third living creature had a face like a man, and the fourth living creature was like a flying eagle. **8** The four living creatures, each having six wings, were full of eyes around and within. And they do not rest day or night, saying: "Holy, holy, holy, Lord God Almighty, Who was and is and is to come!" **9** Whenever the living creatures give glory and honor and thanks to Him who sits on the throne, who lives forever and ever, **10** the twenty-four elders fall down before Him who sits on the throne and worship Him who lives forever and ever, and cast their crowns before the throne, saying: **11** "You are worthy, O Lord, To receive glory and honor and power; For You created all things, And by Your will they exist and were created."

Revelation 5

**1** And I saw in the right hand of Him who sat on the throne a scroll written inside and on the back, sealed with seven seals. **2** Then I saw a strong angel proclaiming with a loud voice, "Who is worthy to open the scroll and to loose its seals?" **3** And no one in heaven or on the earth or under the earth was able to open the scroll, or to look at it. **4** So I wept much, because no one was found worthy to open and read the scroll, or to look at it. **5** But one of the elders said to me, "Do not weep. Behold, the Lion of the tribe of Judah, the Root of David, has prevailed to open the scroll and to loose its seven seals."**6** And I looked, and behold, in the midst of the throne and of the four living creatures, and in the midst of the elders, stood a Lamb as though it had been slain, having seven horns and seven eyes, which are the seven Spirits of God sent out into all the earth. **7** Then He came and took the scroll out of the right hand of Him who sat on the throne. **8** Now when He had taken the scroll, the four living creatures and the twenty-four elders fell down before the Lamb, each having a harp, and golden bowls full of incense, which are the prayers of the saints. **9** And they sang a new song, saying: " You are worthy to take the scroll, And to open its seals; For You were slain, And have redeemed us to God by Your blood Out of every tribe and tongue and people and nation, **10** And have made us kings and priests to our God; And we shall reign on the earth." **11** Then I looked, and I heard the voice of many angels around the throne, the living creatures, and the elders; and the number of them was ten thousand times ten thousand, and thousands of thousands, **12** saying with a loud voice: " Worthy is the Lamb who was slain To receive power and riches and wisdom, And strength and honor and glory and blessing!" **13** And every creature which is in heaven and on the earth and under the earth and such as are in the sea, and all that are in them, I heard saying: " Blessing and honor and glory and power Be to Him who sits on the throne, And to the Lamb, forever and ever!" **14** Then the four living creatures said, "Amen!" And the twenty-four elders fell down and worshiped Him who lives forever and ever.

Revelation 19

**1** After these things I heard a loud voice of a great multitude in heaven, saying, "Alleluia! Salvation and glory and honor and power belong to the Lord our God! **2** For true and righteous are His judgments, because He has judged the great harlot who corrupted the earth with her fornication; and He has avenged on her the blood of His servants shed by her." **3** Again they said, "Alleluia! Her smoke rises up forever and ever!" **4** And the twenty-four elders and the four living creatures fell down and worshiped God who sat on the throne, saying, "Amen! Alleluia!" **5** Then a voice came from the throne, saying, "Praise our God, all you His servants and those who fear Him, both small and great!" **6** And I heard, as it were, the voice of a great multitude, as the sound of many waters and as the sound of mighty thunderings, saying, "Alleluia! For the Lord God Omnipotent reigns! **7** Let us be glad and rejoice and give Him glory, for the marriage of the Lamb has come, and His wife has made herself ready." **8** And to her it was granted to be arrayed in fine linen, clean and bright, for the fine linen is the righteous acts of the saints. **9** Then he said to me, "Write: 'Blessed are those who are called to the marriage supper of the Lamb!'" And he said to me, "These are the true sayings of God." **10** And I fell at his feet to worship him. But he said to me, "See that you do not do that! I am your fellow servant, and of your brethren who have the testimony of Jesus. Worship God! For the testimony of Jesus is the spirit of prophecy." **11** Now I saw heaven opened, and behold, a white horse. And He who sat on him was called Faithful and True, and in righteousness He judges and makes war. **12** His eyes were like a flame of fire, and on His head were many crowns. He had a name written that no one knew except Himself. **13** He was clothed with a robe dipped in blood, and His name is called The Word of God. **14** And the armies in heaven, clothed in fine linen, white and clean, followed Him on white horses. **15** Now out of His mouth goes a sharp sword, that with it He should strike the nations. And He Himself will rule them with a rod of iron. He Himself treads the winepress of the fierceness and wrath of Almighty God. **16** And He has on His robe and on His thigh a name written: KING OF KINGS AND LORD OF LORDS. **17** Then I saw an angel standing in the sun; and he cried with a loud voice, saying to all the birds that fly in the midst of heaven, "Come and

# Come Out of Her My People: Persecution Begins

gather together for the supper of the great God, **18** that you may eat the flesh of kings, the flesh of captains, the flesh of mighty men, the flesh of horses and of those who sit on them, and the flesh of all people, free and slave, both small and great." **19** And I saw the beast, the kings of the earth, and their armies, gathered together to make war against Him who sat on the horse and against His army. **20** Then the beast was captured, and with him the false prophet who worked signs in his presence, by which he deceived those who received the mark of the beast and those who worshiped his image. These two were cast alive into the lake of fire burning with brimstone. **21** And the rest were killed with the sword which proceeded from the mouth of Him who sat on the horse. And all the birds were filled with their flesh.

Revelation 20

**1** Then I saw an angel coming down from heaven, having the key to the bottomless pit and a great chain in his hand. **2** He laid hold of the dragon, that serpent of old, who is the Devil and Satan, and bound him for a thousand years; **3** and he cast him into the bottomless pit, and shut him up, and set a seal on him, so that he should deceive the nations no more till the thousand years were finished. But after these things he must be released for a little while. **4** And I saw thrones, and they sat on them, and judgment was committed to them. Then I saw the souls of those who had been beheaded for their witness to Jesus and for the word of God, who had not worshiped the beast or his image, and had not received his mark on their foreheads or on their hands. And they lived and reigned with Christ for a thousand years. **5** But the rest of the dead did not live again until the thousand years were finished. This is the first resurrection. **6** Blessed and holy is he who has part in the first resurrection. Over such the second death has no power, but they shall be priests of God and of Christ, and shall reign with Him a thousand years. **7** Now when the thousand years have expired, Satan will be released from his prison **8** and will go out to deceive the nations which are in the four corners of the earth, Gog and Magog, to gather them together to battle, whose number is as the sand of the sea. **9** They went up on the breadth of the earth and surrounded the camp of the saints and the beloved city. And fire came down from God out of heaven and devoured them. **10** The devil, who deceived them, was cast into the lake of fire and brimstone where the beast and the false prophet are. And they will be tormented day and night forever and ever. **11** Then I saw a great white throne and Him who sat on it, from whose face the earth and the heaven fled away. And there was found no place for them. **12** And I saw the dead, small and great, standing before God, and books were opened. And another book was opened, which is the Book of Life. And the dead were judged according to their works, by the things which were written in the books. **13** The sea gave up the dead who were in it, and Death and Hades delivered up the dead who were in them. And they were judged, each one according to his works. **14** Then Death and Hades were cast into the lake of fire. This is the second death. **15** And anyone not found written in the Book of Life was cast into the lake of fire.

Revelation 21

**1** Now I saw a new heaven and a new earth, for the first heaven and the first earth had passed away. Also there was no more sea. **2** Then I, John, saw the holy city, New Jerusalem, coming down out of heaven from God, prepared as a bride adorned for her husband. **3** And I heard a loud voice from heaven saying, "Behold, the tabernacle of God is with men, and He will dwell with them, and they shall be His people. God Himself will be with them and be their God. **4** And God will wipe away every tear from their eyes; there shall be no more death, nor sorrow, nor crying. There shall be no more pain, for the former things have passed away." **5** Then He who sat on the throne said, "Behold, I make all things new." And He said to me, "Write, for these words are true and faithful." **6** And He said to me, "It is done! I am the Alpha and the Omega, the Beginning and the End. I will give of the fountain of the water of life freely to him who thirsts. **7** He who overcomes shall inherit all things, and I will be his God and he shall be My son. **8** But the cowardly, unbelieving, abominable, murderers, sexually immoral, sorcerers, idolaters, and all liars shall have their part in the lake which burns with fire and brimstone, which is the second death." **9** Then one of the seven angels who had the seven bowls filled with the seven last plagues came to me and talked with me, saying, "Come, I will show you the bride, the Lamb's wife." **10** And he carried me away in the Spirit to a great and high mountain, and showed me the great city, the holy Jerusalem, descending out of heaven from God, **11** having the glory of God. Her light was like a most precious stone, like a jasper stone, clear as crystal. **12** Also she had a great and high wall with twelve gates, and twelve angels at the gates, and names written on them, which are the names of the twelve tribes of the children of Israel: **13** three gates on the east, three gates on the north, three gates on the south, and three gates on the west. **14** Now the wall of the city had twelve foundations, and on them were the names of the twelve apostles of the Lamb. **15** And he who talked with me had a gold reed to measure the city, its gates, and its wall. **16** The city is laid out as a square; its length is as great as its breadth. And he measured the city with the reed: twelve thousand furlongs. Its length, breadth, and height are equal. **17** Then he measured its wall: one hundred and forty-four cubits, according to the measure of a man, that is, of an angel. **18** The construction of its wall was of jasper; and the city was pure gold, like clear glass. **19** The foundations of the wall of the city were adorned with all kinds of precious stones: the first foundation was jasper, the second sapphire, the third chalcedony, the fourth emerald, **20** the fifth sardonyx, the sixth sardius, the seventh chrysolite, the eighth beryl, the ninth topaz, the tenth chrysoprase, the eleventh jacinth, and the twelfth amethyst. **21** The twelve gates were twelve pearls: each individual gate was of one pearl. And the street of the city was pure gold, like transparent glass. **22** But I saw no temple in it, for the Lord God Almighty and the Lamb are its temple. **23** The city had no need of the sun or of the moon to shine in it, for the glory of God illuminated it. The Lamb is its light. **24** And the nations of those who are saved shall walk in its light, and the kings of the earth bring their glory and honor into it. **25** Its gates shall not be shut at all by day (there shall be no night there). **26** And they shall bring the glory and the honor of the nations into it. **27** But there shall by no means enter it anything that defiles, or causes an abomination or a lie, but only those who are written in the Lamb's Book of Life.

Revelation 22

**1** And he showed me a pure river of water of life, clear as crystal, proceeding from the throne of God and of the Lamb. **2** In the middle of its street, and on either side of the river, was the tree of life, which bore twelve fruits, each tree yielding its fruit every month. The leaves of the tree were for the healing of the nations. **3** And there shall be no more curse, but the throne of God and of the Lamb shall be in it, and

His servants shall serve Him. **4** They shall see His face, and His name shall be on their foreheads. **5** There shall be no night there: They need no lamp nor light of the sun, for the Lord God gives them light. And they shall reign forever and ever. **6** Then he said to me, "These words are faithful and true." And the Lord God of the holy prophets sent His angel to show His servants the things which must shortly take place. **7** "Behold, I am coming quickly! Blessed is he who keeps the words of the prophecy of this book." **8** Now I, John, saw and heard these things. And when I heard and saw, I fell down to worship before the feet of the angel who showed me these things. **9** Then he said to me, "See that you do not do that. For I am your fellow servant, and of your brethren the prophets, and of those who keep the words of this book. Worship God." **10** And he said to me, "Do not seal the words of the prophecy of this book, for the time is at hand. **11** He who is unjust, let him be unjust still; he who is filthy, let him be filthy still; he who is righteous, let him be righteous still; he who is holy, let him be holy still." **12** "And behold, I am coming quickly, and My reward is with Me, to give to every one according to his work. **13** I am the Alpha and the Omega, the Beginning and the End, the First and the Last." **14** Blessed are those who do His commandments, that they may have the right to the tree of life, and may enter through the gates into the city. **15** But outside are dogs and sorcerers and sexually immoral and murderers and idolaters, and whoever loves and practices a lie. **16** "I, Jesus, have sent My angel to testify to you these things in the churches. I am the Root and the Offspring of David, the Bright and Morning Star." **17** And the Spirit and the bride say, "Come!" And let him who hears say, "Come!" And let him who thirsts come. Whoever desires, let him take the water of life freely. **18** For I testify to everyone who hears the words of the prophecy of this book: If anyone adds to these things, God will add to him the plagues that are written in this book; **19** and if anyone takes away from the words of the book of this prophecy, God shall take away his part from the Book of Life, from the holy city, and from the things which are written in this book. **20** He who testifies to these things says, "Surely I am coming quickly." Amen. Even so, come, Lord Jesus! **21** The grace of our Lord Jesus Christ be with you all. Amen.

###

Made in the USA
San Bernardino, CA
10 December 2013